FANATICUS

Praise for *Fanaticus*

"In *Fanaticus*, Justine Gubar takes the reader on an unforgettable exploration of the least understood, least appreciated and—occasionally—least defensible facet of our sports-soaked culture: the fans. Gubar skillfully peels back layer after layer of our fandom to explain why we care so much, and what happens when we do. Along the way, Gubar expels myths, digs up surprising truths, and explains a lot about human nature itself. The ride is equal parts fun and frightening, but always fascinating. After *Fanaticus*, you will never be able to look at your games, and the people who love them, the same way."—**John U. Bacon, best-selling author of** *Fourth and Long: The Fight for the Soul of College Football*

"*Fanaticus* is a riveting, well-researched look at one of the most interesting topics in sports today: the behavior—and misbehavior—of the modern sports fan. Justine Gubar expertly leads us to an important national conversation about fans in the 21st century. Her timing is perfect. As sports become an even bigger part of our culture, the story of obsessed sports fans grows in importance by the day."—**Christine Brennan, sports columnist,** *USA TODAY*; **commentator, ABC News and CNN; and author of** *Best Seat in the House*

"*Fanaticus* explores a place too-often ignored in sports reporting—the seamy world of miscreant fans. Justine Gubar's powers of observation, combined with her reporting skills, make her the perfect tour guide."—**Tim Keown,** *ESPN the Magazine*, **and coauthor of three** *New York Times* **best-selling books**

"Justine Gubar's fearless brand of investigative journalism at ESPN has placed her in the cross-hairs of many angry mobs who didn't want to know the truth about their favorite teams and players. From her startling and disturbing firsthand experiences to an overview of fan behavior, she captures the essence of a fascinating societal niche in *Fanaticus: Mischief and Madness in the Modern Sports Fan*. For anyone who has ever gone to a game and wondered why the person next to them is behaving like a lunatic, this book helps provide the answer."—**Pat Forde, national columnist, Yahoo Sports**

"Combining the curiosity of a hard-charging investigator with the heart of a superb story-teller, Justine Gubar has written a fantastic book about fandom that will surprise and delight you. By tracing the roots of fans' extreme behavior, from the mobs at the Roman Colosseum to the mobs now bellowing on social media platforms, *Fanaticus* will change how you view the way we cheer, boo, root, and fight over our beloved teams. I love this book."—**Don Van Natta Jr., investigative reporter, ESPN; Pulitzer Prize winner; and** *New York Times* **best-selling author of** *First Off the Tee, Her Way*, **and** *Wonder Girl*

"Sports is the great tent where society gathers—it's where we cheer, it's where we hope, it's where we find common ground, and unfortunately, it's also where some choose to get angry or even violent. Justine Gubar does a remarkable job unmasking the breadth and depth of sports fanaticism and explaining how devotion can turn into obsession, and even into danger. Fascinating read—plus, how do you not love a book which has a first chapter called 'And Then We Burn a Couch'?"—**Rachel Nichols, anchor, CNN**

"Compelling. Powerful. Definitive. A must-read for anyone seeking a broader understanding of the nucleus of sports culture—the fan—against the larger backdrop of society. Thoroughly researched through a wide lens, this enlightening treatise starts strong and finishes strong . . . with so much thought-provoking material in between."—**Jarrett Bell, NFL columnist, *USA TODAY* Sports**

"With *Fanaticus*, Justine Gubar offers a fascinating glimpse into the psyche and history of sport's lunatic fringe. Part personal exploration and part case study, *Fanaticus* transports readers deep into the world of sports fandom."—**Mark Fainaru-Wada, investigative reporter, ESPN, and coauthor of *New York Times* best-selling book *League of Denial***

"This is an important and engaging work. In *Fanaticus*, Justine Gubar takes us inside the phenomenon of emotionally overheated fan misbehavior. It's a trip you will not forget."—**Bob Ley, anchor, ESPN**

"The life of a sports fan is an evolving one. One that has roots in overzealous passion. And one that has seen its passion take a dark turn into violence and crime. Justine Gubar does a phenomenal job of traveling the globe and shedding light on these fanatics, so that we can read about them safely from our couches."—**Michelle Beadle, host, ESPN**

"This book starts as a journey into the strange world of sports fandom and quickly becomes a journey into the myth of civilization, unwinding and uncovering the purest essence of ourselves and leading, ultimately, to a few simple truths: love and hate are the same thing, and we are all merely animals living on a rock."—**Wright Thompson, senior writer, *ESPN the Magazine*, and coeditor of *Best American Sports Writing 2015***

"Justine Gubar was a splendid ESPN producer who went to Ohio, did some investigating, and got some vile voicemails and emails. Now she's a splendid ESPN producer who has been from Antwerp to Albuquerque and back to antiquity for this vital tour of our human lunacy."—**Chuck Culpepper, sportswriter, *Washington Post*, and author of William Hill award finalist *Bloody Confused: A Clueless American Sportswriter Seeks Solace in English Soccer***

FANATICUS

Mischief and Madness in the Modern Sports Fan

Justine Gubar

ROWMAN & LITTLEFIELD
Lanham • Boulder • New York • London

Published by Rowman & Littlefield
A wholly owned subsidiary of The Rowman & Littlefield Publishing Group, Inc.
4501 Forbes Boulevard, Suite 200, Lanham, Maryland 20706
www.rowman.com

Unit A, Whitacre Mews, 26-34 Stannary Street, London SE11 4AB

British Library Cataloguing in Publication Information Available

Library of Congress Cataloging-in-Publication Data

Gubar, Justine.
Fanaticus : mischief and madness in the modern sports fan / Justine Gubar.
pages cm
Includes bibliographical references and index.
ISBN 978-1-4422-2892-4 (hardback : alk. paper) — ISBN 978-1-4422-2893-1 (ebook) 1. Sports
spectators—Psychology. 2. Sports spectators—Social conditions. 3. Sports—Sociological aspects. I.
Title.
GV715.G83 2015
306.4'83—dc23
2014048892

Printed in the United States of America

To L. G., who started a family tradition when he took me to my first baseball game at age three

To S. G., who checked the score on TV only to see when we were coming home

CONTENTS

INTRODUCTION

Nasty sentiments flashed across my computer screen: "Just another OSU fan telling you to f@#$ off, bitch." Then came more: "You're not even on a same level as a prostitute. People like you are a disgrace to the practice of journalism." The messages kept coming: "I simply advise you to do what's right and if you don't, realize that Buckeye Nation will not show you mercy." Messages from enraged Ohio State football fans—known in the sports world as some of the most zealous in the country—were showing up on Twitter and Facebook. Angry fans even found my home phone number and posted it online. They went after me anywhere I had a profile. I took down my pictures, changed my numbers, and wondered if I was in real danger.

I'm a television producer for ESPN, the top sports network in the United States. I investigate such off-the-field issues in sports as recruiting violations, player misbehavior, and doping. I research and write scripts, supervise camera crews at events and interviews, and collaborate with on-air correspondents. Think *All the President's Men* meets *Broadcast News*, with some of *The Blind Side* thrown in. The public knows the names of the on-air personalities I work with, but usually not mine. When a story hits hard, people can get angry. We go after difficult stories to hold those in charge accountable. We feel a sense of obligation to the fans, who invest an inordinate amount of money and loyalty in their favorite teams and athletes. But sometimes fan behavior really turns out to be indefensible.

How did this anger come to boil over? In the spring and summer of 2011, one of the biggest sports news stories was the resignation of Jim Tressel, head football coach at The Ohio State University, who lied to his bosses about his players breaking rules. What started with a few star football players trading in on their fame to get cheap tattoos turned into allegations of widespread corruption, illegal benefits, and cover-ups. The scandal wasn't about skirting the rules of play, cheating on tests, or breaking the law. It involved breaking the amateurism rules of the organization that governs college football, the National Collegiate Athletic Association. The NCAA ultimately handed out punishments designed to hamper the competitive future of the Ohio State football team. Investigative reporting by media outlets, including ESPN, had set the stage for the forced resignation of Tressel, as well as the abrupt departure of Ohio State's star quarterback, Terrelle Pryor. Despite these stunning exits, the scandal festered. After all, this was one of the most successful college football teams in the United States, with a huge fan base spread throughout the country. When Ohio State was involved, just about everyone in the sports world paid attention.

Ohio State football fans were distraught that their program was under fire and complained about the media scrutiny. Since I was a card-carrying member of that group, the chatter about me started during my fifth week in Columbus, Ohio, as I was digging for information. One afternoon, a local sports talk radio show host somehow got my name and announced that I was spending too much time in "their city," talking to former players, local car dealers, tattoo artists, and memorabilia dealers about how players could leverage their celebrity status to obtain items like cars and tattoos at a discount.

According to a friend who was listening, the radio host tried calling me on my hotel phone to talk to me about my visit. When I didn't pick up, he joked that he was going to send me flowers and chocolates if I'd just go home. This conversation riled up the Columbus faithful, and that's when the nastiness started, with irate fans filling up the Twitterverse and my inbox with their rants.

Even when I departed Ohio, without any chocolate or flowers, the rage followed me to my hometown of San Francisco. Someone had posted my home number on the Internet, and my voice mail was laced with angry messages. The comments about my physical appearance were some of the most searing. After listening to these messages, I contacted ESPN corporate security, which recommended I file a complaint with the police. I got a new number (which I still haven't memorized) and removed my picture from Facebook, where I could see pictures of the people who were saying these things. It was clear that some of these guys were exacting revenge for not having a prom date. They were in no position to be talking about *my* looks.

I knew that it was unlikely that any of these fans would physically come after me in my Victorian condo in San Francisco's Castro neighborhood; however, I was shaken by what had happened and couldn't stop thinking about it.

Printed on the flip side of my business card is our corporate mission: "To serve sports fans. Anytime. Anywhere." But here's the paradox: While we exalt the passion of sports fans, we must also face the dangerous and dark side of their behavior.

Fans launch tirades that blast the media all the time. I'm certainly not the only journalist to feel the intensity of angry fans. One colleague of mine, a quarterback-turned-football commentator, moved his family to another state after he was incessantly harassed for criticizing his former team's on-field performance.

I knew that my experience was just a drop in the bucket: In my job, I regularly came across stories of unruly spectators at stadiums rioting after a game, harassing opposing fans and players in boozy anonymity and lighting up the Internet with hateful speech. After a combustible cocktail of competition, alcohol, and testosterone, you never know what might happen: Fights, fires, destruction. Sometimes even murder.

This kind of craziness made me wonder: Why can fans be so hateful? What is inside people that leads to this behavior? And what is it about sports that sets the stage for these actions? Does fandom have to boil over like this? I wondered about the trajectory: Are sports fans really getting more violent? If so, why is this happening?

This book answers these questions. I've called upon my 20 years of experience as an investigative journalist, documentarian, and sports enthusiast to explore the roots of extreme fanaticism, from organized thuggery to digital hate speech. I've spoken with athletes, fans, journalists, security professionals, sociologists, and psychologists. Drawing on diverse fields of study, personal experience, interviews, and anecdotes, *Fanaticus* catalogs shocking and outrageous incidents from throughout the world, firsthand accounts from transgressors and victims, and analyzes the behavioral forces at work. I take a critical lens to professional sports leagues, college athletics, law enforcement, the beverage industry, and the media to explain what may seem like an upsurge in fan misbehavior and dispel common myths that are often invoked to understand the madness.

While focused on sports, it's my belief that *Fanaticus* transcends the sports world—it's for anyone who is interested in what drives human behavior and answers the universal question: What causes seemingly unremarkable people to abandon societal norms and act out in unimaginable ways?

A UNIVERSAL LANGUAGE

Sports is an activity that syncs with the human psyche, gives rise to billion-dollar industries, and leaves an indelible mark on culture. A great athletic endeavor can inspire such virtues as teamwork, courage, and fortitude. Many children dream of growing up to be professional athletes more than any other occupation. Adults get transported back to their youth, remembering a special sports event that was a rite of passage. A New York Jets fan in his mid-50s sums up a common feeling about attending a sporting event: "I love the idea of still feeling like a little kid."

Functioning as connective tissue, sports can draw people together with its universality. Even the Vatican understands this power. According to the late John Paul II, "Sport can promote the building of a more fraternal and united world, thus helping to overcome situations of reciprocal misunderstanding between individuals and peoples." That's a mouthful, but I think the pontiff is simply saying that sports bring together people who don't have a hell of a lot of other things in common. I've seen this firsthand in foreign countries where it was hard to explain my destination to a cab driver but easy to converse about the Yankees' superstars. The United Nations embraces athletes as ambassadors, calling its involvement with sports a natural partnership: "Sport has been increasingly recognized and used as a low-cost and high-impact tool in humanitarian, development, and peace-building efforts."

Few other endeavors are simultaneously embraced institutionally and at a grassroots level. More than half of Americans tell pollsters they consider themselves sports fans. That's more than 200 million people, often showing their allegiance to a team in spectacular ways. At Major League Baseball games, marriage proposals flash across the scoreboard between innings. Parents name their children after their favorite sports network: ESPN's public relations department keeps a running tally of kids named ESPN; it hit 30 in 2013. Lifelong fans ask to be buried in team jerseys. Stadiums, ballparks, and arenas are besieged with requests to sprinkle ashes of loved ones onto the field or ice. In Philadelphia, a man was arrested trying to spread the ashes of his mother, a die-hard Eagles fan, during a game. As a way to honor this desire, stadiums in Argentina and Germany have opened adjoining cemeteries because so many people wanted to spread their relatives' remains on these sacred grounds.

Sport is unique in its psychic grasp. British author Nick Hornby writes about his obsession with the Arsenal Football Club in the best-selling book *Fever Pitch*. Several years later, a movie Americanized the story and made Jimmy Fallon, the protagonist, a Boston Red Sox fan. The team and country may have changed but not the emotion behind it. Both treatments try to explain the metaphysical hold of fandom. Writes Hornby, "Please, be tolerant of those who describe a sporting moment as their best ever. We do not lack imagination, nor have we had sad and barren lives; it is just that real life is paler, duller, and contains less potential for unexpected delirium." Hornby concludes that loving a sports team is better than sex.

In researching my book, I personally observed how proud many people feel about their obsession. I had lunch in Chicago with Cubs fan Grant DePorter, who runs Harry Caray's restaurant chain. With memorabilia lining the interior, the eateries are a shrine to the Cubs, as well as to Caray, the late Cubs announcer. DePorter called his fandom his religion and said the memorabilia are his holy relics. Desperate to see the Cubs win a championship in his lifetime, he thought he had a solution to break the curse. He decided to purchase the ball that infamous fan Steve Bartman had tried to catch from his seat in 2003, an action that was blamed for the Cubs' heartbreaking playoff loss. The ball somehow wound up on the Internet, for sale in an auction. Said DePorter, "My wife is screaming at me, 'What are you doing?' and I said, 'Well I kind of feel like I need to do this.' But she said absolutely not and made me go to bed." But DePorter snuck out of bed and went back to bidding. A mere $114,000 later, the ball was his. What did he do with his pricey acquisition? He blew it up in a public spectacle on live television with the hope that destroying the ball would bring closure to a sad chapter in Cubs history, deliver a change of fortune to the team, and ultimately get them to the World Series for the first time since 1945.

In Seattle, I attended the final game of the 2013 regular season for the Major League Soccer team the Seattle Sounders with Steve Collins. Collins is one of the officers of the Emerald City Supporters, a fan group for the Sounders. In charge of the huge banners called *tifos*, he designs them and then oversees the fans who spend weeks painting them in support of the team. They unfurl the *tifo* at the beginning of a game, and the art gets displayed for a few precious seconds. All that hard work literally lasts for an instant. Collins tells me that if I sit in their section, I have to sing with them, so I do. We sing, jump, and sway. Most of the time, we watch the game on the Jumbotron behind us because the undulating flags obstruct the view in our section. At halftime, Collins leaves. Apparently, he's too superstitious to sit through the entire game. He believes the team does better when he is not there.

THE MADNESS OF WINNING AND LOSING

If you break down the word *fan*, the origins are revealing. In English, the word comes from the Latin term *fanaticus*. In Latin, fanaticus indicated a religious devotee, one who would partake in orgiastic rites at a temple or sacred place. Italians call fans *tifosi*, which originates from the Greek word for the disease typhoid and its associated states of contagion and confusion. According to a Chinese speaker and Stanford football fan I know, in Chinese the word for fan is *quimi*, and the literal translation of its two characters is "a person bewitched or charmed by a ball." These word origins show that fandom stems from an emotional state that is not as simple as supporting your local sports team. There's something deeper and more endemic, a tie to collective madness, religious frenzy, or even magical spells.

The magical spell of my childhood was baseball's New York Mets, a way of life in my family. More than 50 years ago, my father suggested the use of the team's theme song, "Meet the Mets," as his wedding song, but my mother nixed it in favor of "Moon River." It was not hard for me to live up to my chromosomal destiny. My father started taking me to games when I was about three. At the ballpark, he would ask strangers in line for the women's restroom to escort me in and keep an eye on me. I loved the atmosphere at the ballpark and tried to be a fan just like my dad, reading the sports pages and memorizing statistics. There were times when he practically foamed at the mouth when a game did not go our way. The obsession overtook him and transformed my straight-laced professional father into a rabid, but never profane, man, one who was known to sneak out of family events to find a television and tune out everything else but his sports teams.

Rooting for our teams became my ritual, too. The little girl who needed a female bathroom escort grew up to be a fan in her own right and wound up with a job in television sports.

These days, however, I am troubled about fandom and its violent and hostile extremes. The violence takes many forms. Sometimes this means rioting in the streets. After the Red Sox beat their archrivals, the New York Yankees, at Yankee Stadium in 2004, to reach the World Series for the first time in almost two decades, the scene on the streets of Boston turned dangerous. Raucous fans climbed trees and traffic lights. Rioters overturned trash cans and newspaper boxes right in front of police officers and lit cars on fire. The police eventually fired a crowd control weapon at the revelers that struck and killed Victoria Snelgrove, a 21-year-old student at Emerson College.

We see violence at the hands of the mentally ill. In 1993, Gunter Parche ran onto a tennis court and stabbed star player Monica Seles in the back with a boning knife as she rested in a chair between games. Parche was not jailed, sentenced only to psychological treatment. Welsh rugby fan Geoffrey Huish hacked off his own testicles to celebrate when Wales beat world champion England in 2005. Afterward, Huish spent several months in a psych ward.

We see the extreme scapegoating of an individual in the face of an upsetting loss. Look at the hundreds of people who stood outside Wrigley Field and chanted "asshole" at the aforementioned Steve Bartman, the fan who interfered with a foul ball and was blamed for the Chicago Cubs' playoff loss. A lifelong Cubs fan, Bartman had a dream seat in the first row of the stands near left field in foul territory for the sixth game of the 2003 National League Championship Series against the Florida Marlins. With one out in the eighth inning and the Cubs up by three, Bartman reached for a foul ball and disrupted a potential catch by Cubs outfielder

Moises Alou. If Alou had caught the ball, it would have been the second out in the inning, leaving the Cubs just four outs away from advancing to the World Series. But Alou didn't come away with the ball—and neither did Bartman. Alou turned to the fans in the stands and started screaming about their interference. The Cubs ended up surrendering eight runs in the inning, thanks to poor relief pitching and a crucial error by their shortstop. They went on to lose the game.

That night, Bartman was escorted from the stadium by security. After his name and address were made public, he needed police protection. He never spoke publicly about that game except for a brief apology issued the next day. Bartman was a scapegoat, perhaps the biggest of all time. When he reached for that ball, he was doing what any fan in those seats would have done and, in fact, what neighboring fans were doing at the exact same time. His interference wasn't intentional. Bartman wasn't the pitcher who couldn't prevent the Marlins from scoring and taking the lead in Game Six, and he didn't play in Game Seven. Yet, other fans laid the responsibility for the Cubs' massive unraveling at his feet and turned Bartman into a symbol for fan frustration. When the Cubs were eliminated in the seventh game the next day, the "Steve Bartman incident" was seen as the team's undoing. Bartman was actually lucky in one sense. No one was able to physically attack him.

Some of the most vicious violence takes place in the game of soccer (the American term), or football, as the rest of the world refers to it. This is the sport where we learn of the most documented aberrant behavior thanks to a global obsession with rowdy gang-like fans—most famously known as hooligans in the United Kingdom. These mobs create so much trouble that teams have literally had to lock them out. In March 2012, the German football team, Dynamo Dresden, sold out its 32,000-seat stadium for a match where no spectators were admitted. The ban was imposed because at a match several months earlier, fans threw firecrackers and flares onto the field. Police arrested 15 people after they caused more than $200,000 worth of damage. Fans bought tickets to support their team despite the fact that they wouldn't be let in to what became known as the "ghost game." Throughout the world, closing down sections of a stadium to fans and/or banning their attendance altogether is considered an effective deterrent to bad behavior.

In football, fan violence often mirrors political realities. During the late winter of 2012, in the Egyptian city of Port Said, 79 people were killed in a brawl between rival groups of football fans at a match between Al Masry of Port Said and Al Ahly of Cairo. Fans died of knife wounds and blows to the head. Some were thrown from the stands. Others were trampled as they tried to escape. Many blamed the military-led government for provoking the violence by providing inadequate security at the match. Die-hard Egyptian football fans had played a vital role in Egypt's Arab Spring and the 18-day popular uprising that, a year earlier, had toppled longtime dictator Hosni Mubarak by prominently defending Tahrir Square, the movement's epicenter. This match was believed to be the deadliest soccer match anywhere since 1996, when 84 people died in a stampede during a World Cup qualifier in Guatemala City.

Fan violence is often rooted in religious conflicts. For more than a century, two Scottish football clubs, the Celtics and Rangers, both in Glasgow, have been bitter enemies. This rivalry is known as the "Old Firm" and is steeped in religious schism. Historically, the Celts are Irish Catholic and call for Scottish independence. The Rangers fans are Protestant and support the Union Jack. From 1996 to 2003, it is estimated that eight deaths were directly linked to matches between the Celtics and Rangers, along with thousands of assaults and arrests.

While fans of opposing teams are subject to harassment and violence, so are the players. In 2011, a Romanian fan charged onto the field and attacked a player, breaking his cheekbone with a hard object. Mayhem ensued as players attacked the fan, and the match was called off. In many parts of the world, fans try to provoke dark-skinned players by calling them "monkeys" during the heat of play.

A CLOSER EXAMINATION

The reasons for the hostility are myriad; analysis of fan behavior keeps psychologists and sociologists busy. In a certain type of social setting, normal people can forsake self-restraint and accountability and do abnormal things that they claim not to understand after the fact. Sports may be the perfect storm for these circumstances. Research says that fans with a belief that they will remain anonymous would consider injuring a fan, player, or coach. When a team wins or loses, a fan's passion often leads them to get carried away. Losing hurts and fans act out in frustration. Winning feels great and fans act out in the midst of celebration.

Alcohol plays a huge role in fueling these fires, buoyed by the teams, leagues, concession companies, and brewers poised to make lots of money from sales and sponsorships. But there is more to mayhem than just liquid courage. Rudeness converges from different angles. The product on the field, television, and the Internet can glorify violence and outlandish behavior. Mobs of student fans galvanize to get under the skin of opposing teams and be immortalized as an in-game cutaway. Cyber mobs troll the Internet ready to pounce. The nastier they are, the more attention they usually get. Meanwhile, fans continue to pay more and more money to cheer on the athletes and may come to expect they are "entitled to" or "owed" a certain experience, a kind of investor entitlement.

People make good money in the business of mayhem. There's a limit to monitoring alcohol and behavior so as not to detract from the popularity and sanctity of the product. With billions of dollars at stake, the sports industry needs fans to keep opening their wallets.

Once I started paying special attention to the misdeeds of sports fans, I noticed that almost every time an incident gets propelled into the headlines, people decry an epidemic of fan misbehavior. I couldn't help but wonder if this indignation was justified or just a reactionary moral panic based on sensational media reports that focus on the worst deviant and outrageous behavior. It became clear rather quickly that there's no reliable way to draw accurate conclusions unless one is looking at a focused population like American football or Canadian hockey—and even then empirical data can be a challenge. If you are interested in a broad approach—different sports in different parts of the world—it's impossible to know if fan violence is getting better or worse.

Even if the cries that fan mayhem is growing are reactionary, they are still based on something significant, because fan misbehavior hasn't ceased throughout time. Incidents happen frequently enough that it's important to examine them, anecdote by anecdote, to figure out what it all means.

I wrote this book to appeal to sports fans and nonsports fans alike, which I am sure will annoy factions in both categories. I want to make my observations accessible to as many readers as possible as an examination of not only sports, but human nature. Why? Because there is no shortage of shocking anecdotes, and there are too many to include in these pages. If enough people feel they are experiencing an "epidemic," then it is a problem and an aspect of human nature that needs attention before it gets even worse. If the word *fanaticus* sounds monstrous to you, it probably should.

I

AND THEN WE BURN A COUCH

Your right to celebrate ends where the rights of others and the law begin.—University of Massachusetts Office of Student Affairs on responsible fan behavior

It was the kind of game sports fans dream about. Super Bowl XLVI, the ultimate game of the 2011 season, pitted the New York Giants against the New England Patriots. The rivalry was established, the stakes enormous, the hype genuine. Four years earlier, the Patriots, led by superstar quarterback Tom Brady, had seen their perfect season spoiled at the hands of Eli Manning and the Giants in Super Bowl XLII. They were once again facing off in the Super Bowl, each striving to prove that it was the top team in the game.

Lucas Oil Stadium, in downtown Indianapolis, was packed with almost 70,000 spectators. More than 110 million people were watching on television. American idol winner Kelly Clarkson belted out the national anthem. New England won the coin toss, the first time an AFC team had done so in 15 years. The game was on—and the action did not disappoint. The Giants jumped to a 9–0 lead before the Patriots scored 17 unanswered points in the second and third quarters. Midway through the third, the Giants climbed their way back into the game with two field goals.

With four minutes and six seconds remaining in the game, the Patriots were clinging to a two-point lead, on top by a score of 17–15. New England had driven 48 yards in nine plays after taking over possession at its own 8. When Tom Brady dropped back to pass to Wes Welker, his receiver was wide open 23 yards downfield toward the left. Brady fired and while Welker got both hands on the ball, he wasn't able to hold onto it. After failing to pad their lead, the Patriots couldn't stave off the Giants' offense. Back on offense, Manning nailed receiver Mario Manningham with a 38-yard sideline strike. Manning-to-Manningham worked again for 16 yards, and suddenly New York had a first down at New England's 34-yard line with two minutes and 52 seconds to play. Ahmad Bradshaw ran it in for the go-ahead touchdown.

But this left time on the clock for the New England Patriots to put the ball in the hands of the comeback specialist Brady. With one last possession and 57 seconds left on the clock, his Hail Mary heave on the final play fell incomplete. The Giants won Super Bowl XLVI, 21–17. Fans began to either celebrate or commiserate, depending on their allegiance.

THE POWER OF A CROWD

Cullen Roe, a sophomore at the University of Massachusetts (UMass) at Amherst and a lifelong New England Patriots fan, watched the tense game with his buddies at his dorm. When the contest ended, about ten of them headed toward a cafeteria in the part of campus known as the Southwest Residential Area. He was angry, "pissed off," he said, about the loss. He had expected the Patriots to win. He wanted them to win, badly.

Roe and his friends had been drinking beer during the game and were hungry. The cafeteria usually served late-night fare, even breakfast at that hour. But a crowd of students was blocking the cafeteria and milling around in an outdoor courtyard. Roe and his crew were curious to see what was going on. It didn't matter that it was a chilly February night in New England with snow on the ground.

Roe looked around and realized that he wasn't the only upset fan. They had entered into pandemonium in the courtyard. "Everyone was in the moment," said Roe. And that moment was becoming more and more unpredictable.

Students began storming out from wherever they had been watching the game. People were jumping up and down. In the courtyard, the crowd pulsated as the most energetic members gathered at the front of the group. At the back and side of the crowd, people were standing around watching, many recording the action on their smartphones.

The group grew rowdier. Some students began to throw rolls of toilet paper, which arced into the dark sky. Bottles and rocks whizzed by. Others attempted to tip a car. Roe saw a guy on the roof of the cafeteria trying to lead the crowd, clapping and pumping his fist, attempting to instill some order to the chanting. "Fuck the Giants" dominated the shouting. People also inexplicably chanted "USA! USA!" There were even some fans dressed in Giants gear. Roe described it as "complete chaos." Disgruntled fans climbed trees, provoking more feverish screams from the crowd. Some lit firecrackers. Others fought. Smoke plumes filled the air. It was later estimated that about 1,500 people had assembled.

This wasn't surprising. Big, emotional gatherings like this happened at UMass periodically. Between the World Series, the National Basketball Association Finals, and the National Hockey League's Stanley Cup, plenty of New England teams played for championships, and students regularly gathered to celebrate the outcome, one way or the other. This penchant for rowdy gathering wasn't limited only to sports. When U.S. forces killed Osama bin Laden and voters reelected President Obama, students rioted. Not to mention that UMass, nicknamed "ZooMass" by some, had a reputation for partying to uphold. Because of this, a large contingent of law enforcement, including UMass police, Amherst police, and the Massachusetts State Police, assembled on campus well before the end of that year's Super Bowl game.

They had their work cut out for them. To control the crowd, law enforcement—many dressed in riot gear—tossed grenades that emitted loud noises, blinding flashes, and smoke. With each thunderous boom, the crowd grew more excitable. "Fuck the police, fuck the police," chanted the mob.

About 15 minutes into the disturbance, a dispersal order came over the loud speaker. (A dispersal order means that you are subject to arrest if you don't leave the area.) Police converged on the crowd with dogs and pellet guns. Four mounted officers pushed forward, shouting "Move!" from atop their horses. "Assholes, Assholes," came the response. As the riot squad advanced, some students ran back. They stopped, turned, and tried to regain some of the lost ground. It looked like a dangerous game of rioter cat and mouse. One student tangled with a police officer on foot and was wrestled to the ground by several officers.

It was Roe's turn to make his feelings known. "Fuck the police!" he shouted to no one in particular. Suddenly someone grabbed him from behind. "Fuck the police?" asked a man wearing a Patriots sweatshirt who wouldn't let go of his arms. One of Roe's friends thought he was being assaulted, and she grabbed the arm of the attacker. The man quickly identified himself as an undercover officer. In the police report, it was alleged that Roe had also screamed, "Bring it on!" Roe denies making this statement.

Roe was livid, but he knew not to resist. He saw other students screaming and chanting profanities without consequences, yet he was the one getting jumped and led off by an undercover cop. As he was being taken to jail, he couldn't help but think that what had happened to him was a case of bad luck. Everyone was screaming and yelling. He just got nabbed for it.

That Monday, Roe attended his regular class, but it would be his last one ever at UMass. The following day, he headed to court, where he was arraigned and charged with failure to disperse and disorderly conduct. He had been one of 14 people, 13 of them UMass students, arrested. He pled not guilty.

Next stop was the dean's office, where he was handed a letter telling him that he was being expelled from school and needed to vacate his dorm by that evening. Rioting had gotten him kicked out of college. Roe and his family decided to dispute the university's right to move that quickly without due process, so they hired a lawyer, who filed a federal lawsuit that led to a quick settlement with the school. Cullen Roe is now a senior at the University of Scranton, planning to attend medical school. Between February 2012 and September 2014, more than 60 insurgents at UMass were arrested for rioting because of sporting and other events. "It's fun being part of the crowd and having the same energy as everyone else," said Roe, "but it isn't worth it."

ANATOMY OF A RIOT

The history of losing control on a large scale has deep and ancient roots. By most accounts, the first fan riot took place in ancient Pompeii in 59 A.D. During a gladiator match, fights broke out among rival fans in the arena of Pompeii. Chaos spilled from the terraces to the wooded area that surrounded the circus. Tacitus, a leading historian of the Roman Empire at the time, described the hostile actions of the spectators: "With the unruly spirit of townsfolk, they began with abusive language of each other; then they took up stones and at last weapons." Dozens were injured and killed. At least one fan lay wounded on the street.

Afterward, Emperor Nero punished the rioters with what is still, centuries later, regarded as the "sports death penalty"—cancellation of the season. "The authorities in Rome told the people in Pompeii there would be no more sports events for the foreseeable future," says Allen Guttmann, a retired professor of English and American studies at Amherst College. According to Guttmann, ten years passed before the Pompeians were permitted to stage another event in their beloved circus.

Guttmann is a well-known sports historian and former president of the North American Society for Sports History. He has also written several books on the history of athletics, including *Sports Spectators*, which was published in 1986. Guttmann lives in the hills of northwestern Massachusetts, just east of the Connecticut River and about an hour from ESPN's headquarters. Bookshelves line the walls of his basement from floor to ceiling. During my visit, he combed through his library to find an illustration of the almost 2,000-year-old mayhem. He was unable to locate it but mailed it to me later. It's a picture of a wall painting, also known as a fresco, now housed in an archeological museum in Naples, Italy. Stick figures engage in hand-to-hand combat inside the circular arena and outside on the grounds. Several fans lay wounded. Despite the stick figures, the brutality is evident.

If one is looking for an ancient example of a frenzied mob, gladiators are also a good choice. A symbol of the perversity of ancient Rome, they fought men (both free and condemned), as well as wild beasts, to the death, while bloodthirsty fans cheered them on. Although centuries have passed, some see a clear connection between then and now.

In 2012, after then Kansas City Chiefs quarterback Matt Cassel was knocked out during a game, hometown fans stood and cheered, voicing their frustration with the team. Eric Winston, his teammate at the time, blasted the crowd during a postgame interview. "If you were one of those people cheering, I want to let you know it's sickening," he said. "We are not gladiators, and this is not the Roman Coliseum."

According to Guttmann's research, chariot racing was actually the more popular spectacle for the ancient Greeks, Romans, and Byzantines. Predating the gladiators, chariot races drew spectators who were often more unruly than those who watched gladiators fight to the death. Chariot racing took place in a hippodrome or "circus." One of the biggest, the Circus Maximus, was a close neighbor to Rome's Coliseum. A historian from the first century, Dio Chrysostom, wrote of the crowd at a chariot race in Alexandria: "When they enter the stadium, it is as though they had found a cache of drugs; they forget themselves completely and shamelessly say and do the first thing that occurs to them."

Even Nero, emperor of Rome, was obsessed with chariot racing. According to various historians, he kicked his wife to death after she scolded him for coming home late from the races. Along with the domestic abuse came organized insurrection. "The circus factions rioted at a level that makes modern mobs seem almost nonviolent," says Guttmann. In Constantinople, race fans set the city's hippodrome on fire four times in the late fifth and early sixth centuries A.D., until the emperor replaced the wooden stands with a marble structure. In 532 A.D., 30,000 fans were killed, many inside the hippodrome, in what became known as the politically tinged "Nika riots." The chariot races were the main stage for the destruction, when fans of the Blue and Green racing teams rampaged for several days to protest against Emperor Justinian, burning down half of Constantinople. Nika meant "conquer," and fans shouted it to encourage the charioteers during competition. In this instance, the Blues and Greens shouted the word during the races to mark their displeasure with the emperor's rule. While chariot racing eventually disappeared as a popular sport, lethal riots certainly did not.

Fast forward a few thousand years. Half a century ago, Lima, Peru, was the scene of what remains one of the deadliest instances of sports rioting. On May 24, 1964, at a soccer match between Peru and Argentina, a late goal that would have sent Peru to the 1964 Summer Olympics Games in Tokyo was disallowed. Disorder erupted, and hundreds of fans were trampled in the ensuing stampede. Riots then broke out on the streets of Lima. The final toll was staggering, with more than 300 fatalities and more than 500 injured.

Forty years later, Africa's worst football tragedy took place in 2001, at the end of a league match in Ghana between Accra Hearts and Asante Kotoko, when Asante fans, whose team was losing, started tearing up chairs and throwing them onto the field. The police fired tear gas into the stands, and the resulting stampede led to the deaths of more than 125 fans. Imagine saying good-bye to a family member as they head out to a sporting event, only to have them never return home.

In modern times, some riots start in the stadium and worsen because of fences, overcrowded turnstiles, and aging infrastructure. Some erupt outside the event. Marauding bands of British hooligans have fought rival hooligans before and after matches in nearby neighborhoods, with violence sometimes spilling into train stations. Apparently, police escorts aren't just for VIPs and celebrities: British authorities have tried to keep the disorder from boiling over into full-fledged riots; one longstanding practice to control hooligan violence is to escort visiting fans to and from the train and stadium. British railway police say they have a robust strategy for containing chaos at the railway station, for instance, slapping hooligans with a rail ban.

Downtown areas often suffer at the hands of out-of-control rioters. When the National Football League's Denver Broncos won the Super Bowl in 1998, more than 25 people were arrested for smashing shop windows and overturning cars in the Mile High City. In Philadelphia, after a 28-year championship drought, some Phillies fans lost control after their 2008 World Series triumph, flipping cars, breaking store windows, and commandeering a fire truck on its way to an emergency call. Similar mayhem went down in Los Angeles with the Lakers faithful after the NBA Finals in 2009 and 2010. After the San Francisco Giants won the World Series in 2010, violence, arrests, and property destruction marked the city's celebration. At the ballpark, fans broke windows at the stadium store.

It's not just the big moneymaking sports that produce riots. Passions also become inflamed when it comes to lower-profile and women's sports. In July 2013, more than 20 people were arrested for rioting after the U.S. Open of Surfing in Huntington Beach, California. In the aftermath, fans tipped over portable toilets, broke store windows, and used a stop sign to smash the window of a bike shop on the main street. Several police officers were injured in the melee. In 2001, about 1,000 revelers at Purdue University gathered after the women's basketball team lost the national title game, flipping cars and burning vans. Eight people were arrested, including one who was charged with manufacturing an explosive. In 2007, 300 Greek fans brawled prior to a women's volleyball match, and one died of stab wounds and other injuries. It seems that no sport or region is immune to the plundering and violence.

THE MOTIVATING FACTORS

In the sports world, riots sometimes happen to challenge unpopular outcomes: During the 1909 Scottish Cup riots, rival football fans united to protest a match that had ended in a tie. Thousands of fans stormed the field, and it took more than two and a half hours to clear them from the premises.

When something isn't to their liking, fans will riot to make their feelings known. In 1955, Montreal Canadien loyalists were upset regarding the suspension of star player Maurice Richard for the rest of the season. Some saw his punishment for fighting as bias against the star's French Canadian heritage. During the Canadiens game at the Montreal Forum following the suspension, spectators threw food at the league president until the game was called off. Police turned tear gas on the crowd inside the stadium. Vandals caused hundreds of thousands of dollars of damage to the arena and local neighborhood. More than 60 rioters were arrested.

In the 1996 Cricket World Cup, during a semifinal match between India and Sri Lanka, a crowd of more than 100,000 was so frustrated by a losing score that they tossed projectiles onto the field and lit fires in the stands. Officials called the match and awarded the victory to Sri Lanka. An Indian batsman stood in the middle of the field and cried when his team was forced to forfeit.

Rioting is sometimes tied to strong feelings toward a high-profile coach. Pennsylvania State University students rioted when legendary coach Joe Paterno was fired as a result of accusations of covering up a pattern of child molestation by one of his former assistant football coaches. Fans also don't like what they perceive as rejection: Tennessee students rioted when head coach Lane Kiffin resigned, jilting their football team for a job at the University of Southern California.

THE JOY OF RIOTING

One of the more perplexing reasons to riot is joy. If you receive the Christmas present you wanted, chances are you won't burn down your Christmas tree to celebrate. But in the U.S. sports world, there is a counterintuitive notion that a big victory is a license for destruction in the winning community.

In the United States, most riots are triggered by wins and the drive to celebrate. When a team loses, fans usually go home and mope. In contrast, British hooligans and other international fans tend to riot out of frustration following a loss. This difference in reaction might be because of proximity. It's harder for a sporting event in the United States to attract significant numbers of fans of both teams because of the sheer size of the country. When the San Antonio Spurs play the Miami Heat in the NBA Finals, it's unlikely that Heat fans will show up en masse in San Antonio. In addition, the biggest events, for example, the Super Bowl or the Final Four, are often played at neutral sites. Compare that to British fans, who live in a country about the size of New York, making it much easier to support their team at both home and away matches. To avoid conflict, authorities usually isolate supporters from one another by seating them in separate sections of the stadium and sometimes stagger arrivals and departures.

In the United States, however, a culture has developed with postgame behavior in which celebratory fans stage some kind of public event to prove their devotion to a team. Researchers say that fans identify with the victory and partake in postgame violence, which allows them to participate more closely in the event. Testosterone, the aggression hormone, spikes in spectators whose team wins and dips when a team loses. Studies confirm that fans get a vicarious endocrinological lift—more testosterone—from watching their favorite team triumph.

These postgame riots are far from innocent celebrations. In 1990, eight people died in Detroit in riot-related violence, when the Pistons won the NBA Championship. When the Tigers won the World Series in 1984, another Detroit fan was killed during the ensuing mayhem. In Boston, a fan died after being hit by a drunk driver during the celebrations that followed the Patriots' Super Bowl victory in February 2004. Nine months after the Super Bowl death, the Red Sox beat the Yankees to capture the American League pennant on their way to their first World Series victory in 86 years. As fans basked in the win, a postgame partier, college student Victoria Snelgrove, was hit in the eye when police fired on the crowd with a projectile weapon. It turned out that type of gun wasn't designed to be aimed at a person's head. Snelgrove, who, according to police, was acting lawfully, was rushed to the hospital but lapsed into a coma and died. In 2008, after the Celtics won the NBA title and fans celebrated, a third Boston victim died after being arrested for public drinking. He stopped breathing while in custody.

Pundits decry the American phenomena of winning and rampaging with headlines that ask, "What's wrong with us?" University officials have called it a "crisis" on campus. Academics have studied the celebratory riot and developed a scientific framework to explain and predict it. Even the UMass riot after the Patriots lost was described as "celebratory" in nature more than anything else.

Robert Carrothers, an associate professor of sociology at Ohio Northern University, knows that news reports of sports mayhem mean that his phone will ring. In the late winter and early spring of 2014, five different universities experienced some form of rioting. Reporters—and even police—reached out to him after almost every incident to try to make sense of the disorder. The model Carrothers works with was first developed by his mentor, Jerry Lewis, now professor emeritus of sociology at Kent State University. Lewis was an eyewitness to the rioting at Kent State in 1970, which resulted in the fatal shooting of four students by the National Guard. He has spent almost half a century since then gathering data from other riots. Lewis and Carrothers define rioting as five or more people in a crowd of at least 100 who decide to rush the field, fight, lob projectiles, or commit arson.

Carrothers, a long-suffering Cleveland Indians fan, has grown adept at laying out the accepted criteria that explain these celebration riots. First, it depends how much is at stake. If the game involves a significant match-up, a closely contested battle, and a team that could bust out of a long championship drought, fans are primed to act out. The second factor is drinking. Throw alcohol into the mix, plus the next criteria of a natural gathering area like a downtown or campus setting, and the stage is set for trouble. "All of those factors, in a lot of ways, end up being very emotional," said Carrothers. "They think, 'We haven't had this for so long. I can't believe it's happening. The excitement's building and now we're in Game Seven, and that's the deciding game. We're in overtime and there's two minutes left and the game's still in doubt.' All of that is just ramping up the emotion."

Case in point: In 2012, the University of Kentucky Wildcats beat the Kansas Jayhawks to win the National Collegiate Athletic Association Men's Basketball Championship. Kentucky's eighth championship came after a 14-year drought and was the first for head coach John Calipari after three unsuccessful trips to the Final Four with UMass, Memphis, and another Kentucky squad. After the victory, well-lubricated and euphoric fans gathered in downtown Lexington to celebrate. The jubilation turned violent, and fans burned couches and destroyed cars. One man needed to have his foot amputated after being shot. Dozens were arrested.

The action played out online with a virtual play-by-play of the bedlam thanks to a real-time audio narration from the Lexington Police Department, courtesy of their police scanner, which was streamed to the Internet. Listeners heard the local dispatcher report people shooting fireworks out of a moving car and tossing rocks and bottles at police, as well as a person standing atop a moving vehicle as if surfing through the crowd. For a while that evening, the hashtag #LexingtonPoliceScanner was the number-one worldwide trending topic on Twitter. One tweeter called it the greatest postgame show ever. For some, monitoring the riot was just as entertaining as the basketball game. This glorification of violence might be part of the problem.

On the other side of the Atlantic, riots have recently been noted on the heels of exciting victories, which is a bit of a surprise if you follow the "only in America" celebratory riot theory. Algerian football fans rioted in the south of France to celebrate the unlikely win that propelled them into the quarterfinals of the 2014 World Cup. A year earlier, French football fans of the Paris Saint-Germain team rioted to celebrate the club's first league title in 19 years. Multiple arrests occurred in both cases.

In April 2014, University of Minnesota students rioted after an emotional semifinal win in the NCAA hockey tournament, or Frozen Four, as the tournament is known. Senior McKenzie Lagodinski wasn't much of a hockey fan, but that Thursday evening, she was off from her job at a pizza restaurant and hanging out with friends in Dinkytown, the lively neighborhood adjacent to the university. Lagodinski, an artist who wears her hair in dreadlocks, and her buddies caught the final moments of the game on television at Tony's Diner. With the score tied at 1–1, the Minnesota Golden Gophers faced off against rival North Dakota with less than ten seconds remaining in the game. Shorthanded, Minnesota won the faceoff and moved down the ice. With just .6 of a second left on the clock, Gopher defenseman Justin Holl somehow got the puck past North Dakota goalie Zane Gothberg. The Gophers had captured a berth in the hockey national championship against Union College in a quest for their sixth NCAA championship.

Excited fans immediately spilled onto the sidewalk, high-fiving one another. "It was all really fun, and everyone was just celebrating," said Lagodinski. "Everyone was just feeding off each other." But the revelry soon became frenzied. "Everyone was just so jacked up, and it just kind of turned negative so quickly." People were climbing lampposts and setting off fireworks. Someone tried to flip a car. Some were obviously extremely drunk. Others stood off to the side and watched. When the riot police arrived, their presence revved up the crowd. According to Lagodinski, "It turned into people thinking, 'Oh yeah, we are going to riot. We are going to burn stuff down. We just want to prove we can still riot,'" which she found disturbing.

Why were they rioting after the hockey game? "It's so silly," said Lagodinski, who told me she was trying to diffuse the situation by picking up trash. "I was definitely trying to draw attention but in a positive way to be like, 'Look here, police, we can riot but we can clean up after ourselves, too. We are good students.'" Research shows that some people in riots do act as Good Samaritans. Lagodinski said she was trying to calm the situation and that someone in the crowd called her a "grandma" and told her to go home.

The police, however, didn't see her as a Good Samaritan. She added, "I turned around, and I had six riot police running at me and throwing me to the ground. I wasn't trying to riot, in all honesty. I was just there. It was totally wrong place, wrong time." Police eventually turned tear gas on the crowd. The commotion lasted three hours, and in the end, ten students, including Lagodinski, were arrested, all but one for disorderly conduct.

But these days, Carrothers sees more and more people using sporting events as an excuse to riot, be it celebrating a win like the crowd in Dinkytown or mourning a loss. Losers engage in a strange mix of jubilant frustration. In 2014, after the NCAA basketball championships, fans of both teams rioted in their respective locations. The University of Connecticut's win kicked off a riot that caused damage throughout the campus, and fans of the losing University of Kentucky team erupted in downtown Lexington yet again. "The model works exactly the same, except it's with a loss," said Carrothers. Loser riots also took place at the University of Arizona during March Madness that same year. While University of Minnesota students went berserk after a last-second semifinal win in the NCAA hockey tournament, they rioted again after the finals two nights later, following a loss to Union College. The idea that Americans riot only out of joy is being tested. It seems as though Americans have morphed into equal opportunity rioters.

SOCIAL MEDIA: A NEW PARADIGM

The model for celebratory riots, during which Americans riot when their team wins, is getting turned on its side. Carrothers thinks social media is setting an expectation for this riotous behavior. "As opposed to ESPN showing five seconds of a clip from downtown wherever with 10,000 people in the streets, you're now getting almost a blow-by-blow on social media of what we're doing and how we're doing it and why we're doing it. That could be a sea change in this." He noted the explosion of "selfies" taken in front of burning cars and posted to the Internet:

> In the culture of fandom, there's the idea that if you don't do something extreme, then you really didn't care all that much about your team. Then you factor into that the selfie culture and you've got people who feel like they should be running on the field. They should be dancing on the streets. They should be setting a dumpster on fire, or something like that.

Social media is also credited with helping spread information about riot activities in the first place, telling people where their friends are and giving directions to hot spots. #Riot has become a recognizable postgame hashtag on Twitter when teams face off in meaningful contests.

Rioting seems to be a self-fulfilling prophecy as well. I once checked into a hotel in San Antonio, Texas, the night of Game Six of the NBA Finals, during which the hometown Spurs had the chance to eliminate the Miami Heat for the championship. The front desk clerk and I chatted about the certainty of riots in front of the hotel should the Spurs close out the series. The hotel was expecting it and had alerted guests. But the Heat won that game in overtime to send the series to a Game Seven, and no riots materialized. Sickly, I was disappointed. Was this the mark of a journalist jonesing for a big story or a voyeuristic fan who wanted to experience what it was like in the middle of a rioting crowd? After the game, the town was filled with small groups of fans wandering the streets and people honking their car horns in some sort of frustrated anticipation.

The intensity of a riot may depend on history. For example, a team may be playing an established rival or in a repeat circumstance that gave rise to a previous confrontation. In the mid-1980s, Kansas State football fans rioted after beating in-state rival University of Kansas. Two years later, fans, many of whom wore "Riotville" T-shirts to commemorate the previous victory, rioted again. They became known as the "Aggieville Riots," named for the entertainment district where they occurred.

The University of Minnesota has a history of turmoil after hockey games. Students had rioted in 2002 and 2003. And two nights after her arrest, McKenzie Lagodinski was back at work, serving pizza in Dinkytown, when the Gophers were trying to claim the championship, this time losing in the NCAA hockey tournament finals. Fans once again stormed the streets. "People were coming in at five, six, seven, before the game even started, saying how they are going to riot tonight," she said. Lagodinski noticed an even tougher response from law enforcement the second time around. "There was a lot more pellet shooting and helicopters and just no mercy, in a sense, the second night. It wasn't even about the game."

Carrothers wasn't surprised by Lagodinski's observations. Sociological research says that a group won't be as destructive until an out-group, for instance, the police, gets involved. "If police let the riot get started and then try to come in to stop it, they're just going to be seen as intruders. It's going to cause an escalation of the violence," stated Carrothers. Police may also turn their attention to bystanders as a way to control the situation. In the eyes of law enforcement, simply watching a riot oftentimes encourages it, even though a crackdown on the less active participants comes off as particularly brutal.

One of the most prolific riots in recent years took place on June 15, 2011, when turmoil took over downtown Vancouver and the streets filled with more than 100,000 fans after a frustrating loss in Game Seven of the Stanley Cup Finals between the Canucks and the Boston Bruins. In the 1990s, another riot had taken place when the Canucks lost in the Stanley Cup Finals to the New York Rangers. In fact, Vancouver was pummeled by fan mayhem long before that. Twice in the 1960s, after the Grey Cup, the Canadian Football League championship, riots broke out, and these incidents tallied more arrests than the hockey hooliganism. One of the distinguishing factors of the twenty-first-century chaos was the role of the Internet and social media.

On one of the longest days of the year, about 55,000 hockey-mad Canadians gathered in a public viewing area close to the arena so that they could watch the deciding game on outdoor large-screen televisions. One hundred thousand additional fans congregated downtown. Game Seven was "do-or-die," and the atmosphere was tense.

Canada is obsessed with hockey, much like the Brits and football. Images of children playing hockey once adorned the Canadian five-dollar bill. The prime minister published a history of the sport while in office. For the 2014 Olympic gold medal game, in which Canada played Sweden, the government allowed bars to open first thing in the morning throughout most of the country so that people could drink and watch the contest. In Vancouver, the Stanley Cup matchup was a game infused with the utmost meaning. Winning the cup would create national euphoria.

But the series closed with a devastating 4–0 shutout of the Canucks by the Bruins. Shortly before the end of the final game, activity in the streets turned ugly. In an expression of disappointment at their loss in a drawn-out and hard-fought series, fans began overturning cars and emergency vehicles, and setting them on fire. They also looted stores and attacked one another with fists and knives. More than 140 people needed medical attention. Police arrested approximately 100 people that evening, and damage was estimated at almost $4 million (Canadian).

Officials in Vancouver thought they had learned valuable security lessons from the 1994 riots and the 2006 Olympics, and this time they had enhanced security procedures and established checkpoints for access to fan areas. But some of the measures simply didn't work. According to an independent review commissioned by the government to determine what went wrong, people started gathering and drinking early. While alcohol sales had been cut off at 4:00 p.m. for Game Six, fans knew about this stipulation and were able to plan accordingly for Game Seven. As for temporary checkpoints at the outdoor viewing areas, this fan zone was almost one-quarter full of hockey fans by the time construction was completed on the barriers, basically defeating the purpose of building them at all.

Dave Teixeira watched the game at a pub in suburban Vancouver with friends. Teixeira, a communication and public relations executive in his early 40s, knew how crowded downtown Vancouver would be and was happy to avoid the crush. Earlier that day, he had noticed on social media that people were tweeting about getting ready for a fiery night. He was concerned about the inevitable violence. Suffering through the 4–0 shutout by the Bruins was rough for the fans in the pub. In downtown Vancouver, police reported that the crowd became rowdy even before the Bruins were officially crowned champion.

As soon as the game ended, the television channel Teixeira was watching instantly cut to the unfolding chaos outside the arena. Announcers had moved on from the game to give play-by-play of an agitated crowd. He also noticed that social media was erupting with images of the destruction. Many people downtown were watching the rioters with their smartphones in hand, posting videos, photos, and status updates about the rampaging and looting. More than 2,000 calls were made to 911 that evening. Photos and videos showed fans hurling newspaper boxes, sticking rags into gas tanks to ignite vehicles, and looting downtown stores. Even Good Samaritans who were trying to intervene and ward off the violence were attacked and beaten. The alleged criminal acts seemed endless.

After watching the coverage for about 20 minutes, Teixeira drove home from the pub, and an idea came to him. He started thinking that he could use his PR skills and knowledge of social media to help identify those responsible for the destruction. Barely sleeping that night, he came up with the idea for the crowd-sourcing site www.Canucksriot2011.com. According to Teixeira, "You had people implicating themselves. You'd have someone take a picture of themselves saying, 'Just started this epic fire.' I was able to use the geo-tagging to get exactly where they were and track that information. Then this person would wake up in the morning and go, 'Oh my God, I've just committed a crime, and I've documented it.'" His site called for people to identify rioters so that police could follow up. Referring to the twentysomethings that dominated the tweets, Instagrams, and YouTube videos being posted as the "the Jackass Generation," Teixeira felt the posts expressed a need to prove that any "jackass" could engage in outrageous activity that seemed to have no consequence. He saw a way to stop that.

The next day, the city tried to dig out. Local citizens came downtown with brooms to help clean up broken glass and other trash. Public furor grew. *Time* magazine's website encapsulated the damage with the headline, "Vancouver Riots: Hockey Fans Stick It to Their Own City." Overnight, Teixeira's site had garnered international attention, and he fielded media calls for days. People went to the site and connected the images to people they knew. While the intention of the site was to provide assistance to law enforcement, an Internet posse formed to publicly shame the rioters as well. Some on social media called for businesses to fire employees who were implicated, and several businesses followed suit.

His website (www.Canucksriot2011.com) wasn't the only crowdsourcing site to pop up in the name of electronic justice, but Teixeira maintained that his site was different because he curated the information to pass on to the police. It wasn't just "name and shame," it was "name and report."

The Vancouver police were criticized for the pace of their investigation. It took almost five months for the first batch of arrest recommendations to be handed out and more than two months for police to create their own identification website. According to authorities, they processed more than 5,000 hours of video evidence.

Teixeira says law enforcement credited him with helping identify about 150 people who were later arrested. "I had teachers turning in students. I had brothers and sisters turning each other in. I had ex-boyfriends and girlfriends turning each other in," he said. He called it a fascinating sociological study in revenge, adding, "It's not that I'm being vindictive; it's not that I'm being unreasonable; these are crimes, and I'm hoping that this site can live on as a bit of a warning to others who might want to commit these crimes."

More than three years later, as of July 2014, 298 rioters have been charged and 267 convicted. One lesson learned was that "there were too many people," according to the independent review, "not too few police." The report concludes that only better planning would eliminate a future riot and that the consumption of alcohol that night was "like gasoline on a fire." The authors of the report state a moral imperative for future celebrations: "The streets should not be surrendered to thugs and villains. People should be able to congregate downtown in harmony without the need for police on every corner."

THE PSYCHOLOGY OF A RIOT

Why do people riot? Sociologists point out several ingredients that can add up to a riotous stew. Fans crave involvement and attention, for example, the lone streaker who runs onto the field or the crowds of thousands who act out in unison at a stadium to do an organized cheer like the wave. According to Carrothers, there's much to be learned from what happened that evening in British Columbia. As an academic researcher, he points out that when 5,000 people riot, that's enough critical mass to be statistically significant.

The reason people riot starts with appearance. With the popularity of sports logo clothing, many of the perpetrators wear team jersey or colors, making it harder to pick them out of a group. In the Vancouver incident, more often than not, the young people involved were dressed in the Canucks' green and blue jerseys. Dressing this way breeds anonymity and can lead people to think that they can get away with bad behavior more easily because it will be harder for them to get caught.

With widespread chaos, it becomes easy to fall in and do whatever the crowd's doing. "It's something sociologists call 'social current,' a current that can run through a crowd like electricity, like energy, pick people up and have them do pretty atrocious things even though these are relatively normal people who wouldn't be acting this way if they were by themselves," explained Carrothers. Most of those arrested in Vancouver had no prior criminal record, and in court much of the behavior was described as impulsive and attributed to a "mob mentality."

In Vancouver, 22-year-old Timothy Lau was photographed standing atop an overturned and trashed green car. After the riot, he issued a public apology directed at the people of Vancouver, as well as three businesses, Hudson's Bay, Black & Lee, and Blenz Coffee, and the owners of six different vehicles. "Why I joined in the relentless stupidity of the mob, which was tearing apart the heart of Vancouver, is a mystery to me, but I know what I did was wrong and there is no excuse," he said. Sean Burkett, a high school student who was caught on tape slamming a police barricade through the window of a Hummer, was called by the judge in his appeals process a "follower rather than a leader."

Another rioter, Camille Cacnio, a honors student at the University of British Columbia, posted an online apology. "Being a part of the riot was simply to fulfill the adrenaline rush I was looking and hoping for," she wrote. Twenty-three-year-old Cacnio was caught on tape stealing two pairs of size 42 pants from Black & Lee, the formal clothing store that was ransacked by looters. "My train of thought at this point was that 'the place is already broken into, most of the contents of the store have already been stolen, so what difference does it make if I take a couple things?'"

Alternating between apology and manifesto, she tried to explain her actions: "In my immature, intoxicated perspective all I saw was that the riot was happening, and that it would continue happening with or without me." She cited a mob mentality behind her actions, claiming that she did not plan on taking part in the riot but got swept up in the moment. She also explained that she had subsequently suffered at the hands of a digital mob who castigated her online.

Most agree there can be incredible power within a crowd. The nineteenth-century father figure of crowd theory is Gustave Le Bon, author of *The Crowd: A Study of the Popular Mind*, a work first published in French in 1895, translated into multiple languages, and in its 26th printing in English alone. Le Bon saw the crowd as an irrational entity engaged in simple animal emotion. He describes a person in a crowd as a "grain of sand amid other grains of sand, which the wind stirs up at will." Analyzing the crowds of the French Revolution, for example, Le Bon, who was from an aristocratic background, feared their power and influence on social stability. The crowd, according to Le Bon, was highly suggestible and easily hypnotized by a powerful and persuasive leader. Both Hitler and Mussolini supposedly studied his work.

But modern crowd theory has discarded much of Le Bon's work and views the crowd as much more of a social phenomenon. Clark McPhail, professor emeritus of sociology at the University of Illinois at Urbana–Champaign, eschews even the use of the word *crowd* and prefers the phrase "collective behavior." Author of the 1991 book *The Myth of the Madding Crowd*, McPhail conducted fieldwork among large groups, for instance, the Promise Keepers, a religious organization, and fans at a high school basketball game. The myth referred to in the title of his book is the notion that individuals are transformed in a crowd and lose their individuality and capability for rational response. According to McPhail's research, crowds do not act in a uniform manner but are composed of small groups who engage in a variety of actions. For example, he observed that basketball fans at a high school state championship focused their gaze in the same direction only 3 percent of the time.

McPhail says that only a few of the participants in a riot engage in actual violence and that most people are observers rather than instigators or partakers. In a study published in 1994, entitled "The Dark Side of Purpose: Individual and Collective Violence in Riots," he writes that "riots are patchworks and kaleidoscopes of individual and collective, nonviolent and violent, alternating and varied action." He blames loss of control not so much on the power of a transformative mob, but on the use of alcohol and drugs and the physical constraints of a crowded gathering, factors certainly present in Vancouver and many other sports riots.

"Most participants are neither alone nor anonymous," writes McPhail in *The Myth of the Madding Crowd*, explaining that the role of anonymity is overstated, since people at riots are known within their own group. For McPhail, people know what they are doing in violent riots and should bear responsibility. It appears that for the young rioters from Vancouver, "mob mentality" is a bit of a copout and they should delve more deeply into their inner motivations and ability to handle booze and drugs.

The 1990 book *Among the Thugs*, written by Bill Buford, is one of the most stirring first-person accounts of life in the crowd. An American raised in Los Angeles, Buford moved to England in the late 1970s to edit a literary magazine. He developed a fascination with the world of football hooligans, being drawn in after witnessing a group of thugs rampage through a railway station while he was waiting for a train.

Intrigued by that experience, he embedded himself with Manchester United supporters for almost five years, spending Saturday afternoons with fans who sported such nicknames as "Robert the Sneak Thief," "Barmy Bernie," and "Steamin' Sammy." The thugs mixed their love for football with hearty servings of lager and indiscriminate brawls. Buford traveled with the crew and even got beat up with them, learning to crave what they craved: connection through violence.

It turns out Buford doesn't live too far from my parents in Lower Manhattan. One cold winter day, we arranged to share a sushi lunch. Balding, stubbly, and admittedly faintly hung over, he smiled when I explained that just about everyone says how much they love his book when I tell them I'm doing research on fan violence. He graciously accepted the compliment.

As we ate and talked, Buford was clearly transported back to his days in England. He first recalled the physical experience of being crushed in the crowd. "You couldn't really control whether you were going to go to the left, whether you were going to go to the right, whether you were going to go up, whether you were going to go down," Buford said. "You lose your fear when you give yourself up to being in the crowd. When it's not in your control, you just assume that it's going to be okay."

He then described the other members of the firm. The "thugs" Buford ran with were not Le Bon's suggestible grains of sand. Most had decent jobs, families, and homes, and weren't disenfranchised, disaffected, or unintelligent. He said they could be "normal, charming."

In his book, Buford dismisses theorists like Le Bon, as well as various politicians and historians who posit the crowd as being fickle, dirty, wild, and "not us." For him, it wasn't about angry followers with a uniform cause or blind allegiance. Buford's time with the thugs made him realize that he too got the same buzz and fix from the fighting as his hooligan friends. It wasn't that he didn't know what he was doing; he knew—and loved it. The crowd violence was "their drug," and in the midst of the mob, he could jettison a sense of self to be "of the crowd" for an "experience of absolute completeness." He loved it because of the connection to something greater than himself.

For Buford, researching the book established the primacy of the adrenaline moment. "Sport is that. Watching sport is that. Being in a crowd is that. Being in a crowd that's going off is that," Buford told me. Looking at it in today's context, he thoughtfully said,

> A lot of experiences are taken for granted. Things like shopping, the retail environment, the post office, a newspaper are all gone. We can all now watch virtually any sporting event we want to on any number of devices, and yet that access isn't eliminating the crowd. The crowd experience is still a high priority part of attending a sporting event.

Buford recalled playing in a high school football playoff game, during which fans stormed the field to fight: "A little girl was hitting me in the knee, saying, 'I hate you, I hate you, I hate you white man.'" The chaos resulted in the game being called before the end of regulation. Buford continued, "Every crowd experience rests on the simultaneity of focus of a large body of people on an event. The result is that people stop acting as individuals, and instead they act to reinforce the focus and the experience of being in that crowd."

As he talked about living in the hooligan moment, he got a wistful look in his eyes, as if recalling a great meal or sweet kiss. His appreciation of the adrenaline rush and thrill-seeking tendencies also explained his next major literary endeavor, his firsthand experience working in the kitchen of celebrity chef Mario Batali. The ones who are best in the kitchen "get off on the adrenaline," he said.

Buford's penchant for thrill-seeking is a personality characteristic that tracks with demographics of the typical sports fan. Psychology research from the 1980s shows that sensation-seeking, which is greater in men than women, peaks in the late teens and early 20s and gradually declines with age. A thrill seeker's quest for new experience can make him or her vulnerable to reckless behavior. In *Among the Thugs*, Buford asks the hundred-dollar question (not accounting for inflation, of course): Why do some young males riot every Saturday? The answer may be that it's in one's DNA.

But law enforcement often pushes the narrative of a deviant crowd separate from average citizenry. According to Carrothers, during the Vancouver riots, police and politicians at one point described the rioters as anarchists rather than sports fans. On the West Coast, anarchist groups have been known to participate in such organized disturbances as the Occupy movement and the infamous World Trade Organization riots.

Blaming the chaos on the "weirdos who are trying to bring down the society," said Carrothers, "gives you a better feeling about the sports fan." He continued, "Sports gives you an identity; it brings the community together. It's good economically for the community; there's nothing really bad about sports." Portraying perpetrators as outliers rather than everyday folk like the guy sitting next to you on the bleachers or in line behind you at the 7-Eleven may be comforting, but it is simply not true. As Buford described, being "of the crowd" is appealing and intoxicating for many.

After Paris rioted in 2013, during a parade to celebrate the Paris Saint-Germain title, authorities claimed that the "party was spoiled by a few hundred troublemakers who have nothing to do with football." Carrothers has seen this reaction before in cities like Los Angeles, when Laker fans rioted to celebrate the team's NBA Finals success:

The police chief both years came out and said, "We're chalking this up to a few bad apples and street gangs." I said, "Then you're going to get another riot the next time they win, because that's delusional." He's clearly putting his hands over his eyes and plugging his ears, because he doesn't want to see what the truth of the situation is. Are there gang members who were in the middle of that riot? Sure, just like there were anarchists in the middle of the riot in Vancouver. Doesn't mean they started it.

It may be time for the sports world to acknowledge that just about anyone can turn into a rioter.

For Carrothers, the conditions for a riot can surface in a slew of places—and there's no reason to think that rioting is endangered, no matter the efforts of law enforcement and others. In fact, there are plenty of fan bases starved for championships who fit the criteria. One place he's got his eye on is Chicago. He related, "If the Cubs ever win something, holy crap. Wrigleyville's in huge trouble. That's all residential. You're going to have people having their homes trashed."

2

FANDEMONIUM: UNFORGETTABLE MOMENTS IN FAN VIOLENCE

You get that liquid courage in you, and everybody wants to be part of the game.—John Green, fan credited with starting one of the biggest fan–player brawls in U.S. sports history

When sports fans riot in the United States, property usually suffers the most, but fans can't rule out the possibility of facing danger themselves. Wearing visiting team colors can put one at risk for more than good-natured ribbing from home-team fans. Flaunting support for the opposition has gotten fans viciously beaten, stabbed, shot, and even killed. While the American sports fan doesn't face the constant threat of hooligan gangs, we often face disruptions by individual troublemakers, who are most likely drunk. There are parents who fear bringing their children to sporting events and lament that games are no longer family friendly.

In August 2011, the San Francisco 49ers played host to their Bay Area rivals, the Oakland Raiders, in an annual preseason matchup that would become a seminal moment for fan violence. That night, the world saw the rivalry metastasize into fights both inside and outside the stadium. A friend of mine, a sportswriter who has covered both teams for more than a decade, said that as she went to work that night and passed by the tailgaters, there was a bad vibe in the parking lot. "People were picking fights, even women," she said. As members of the sports media, we very seldom think that it's going to be dangerous on our way to the "office," but it can be.

During the game, 70 fans were ejected from the stadium and one person was beaten unconscious in the men's room. Two men were shot in the parking lot afterward. All three were hospitalized for their injuries. "Nobody could have been prepared for what happened on Saturday night," said San Francisco Police chief Greg Suhr. Cell phone video of the fighting was posted to YouTube and licensed to television stations. Pundits throughout the country decried the behavior.

After that raucous evening, officials admitted that incidents among fans had been getting worse. They indefinitely suspended the popular preseason matchup, which had been played for more than ten years. Some of the chaos had been blamed on the fact that it was preseason, and season ticket holders had pawned their seats off on random attendees. The rivalry was shelved for two seasons, until the league scheduled a regular-season matchup to be played in Oakland in December 2014.

I was dispatched to San Francisco General Hospital to produce ESPN coverage from the trauma facility where the most seriously hurt were taken. For several days, we waited outside for news of the injured, but most of them kept a low profile after the melee. I heard whispers of gang activity and followed police investigations that languished and yielded little information. Some of the injured filed lawsuits against the 49ers, which have either been settled or continue to make their way through court. One of the shooting victims, who was discharged after several days, still lives with bullet fragments lodged in his body.

New policies were put into place—for instance, fans could no longer tailgate in the Candlestick Park parking lot once the game was underway. Still, at most 49ers games that season, more senseless incidents found their way onto the police blotter. The entire season became a window into bad fan behavior, yet few looked at it from that perspective. Most just focused on the 49ers' march to the playoffs and disregarded the frenzied pattern of violence.

In December 2011, when the Pittsburgh Steelers came to town, Manuel Austin, a 66-year-old Niners fan who was attending the game with his wife and son, asked a fan in front of him to sit down as the game got underway. According to various media interviews, that fan and several others jumped him, and he suffered several broken teeth, a concussion, and hearing loss. One fan was cited for misdemeanor battery.

While fighting can get a fan kicked out of a stadium, ticketed for bad behavior, and, on occasion, arrested, prosecution can be a challenge due to a lack of willing and impartial witnesses. Drunken stadium brawls rarely equate to aggravated assault (intent to rob or kill or use of a deadly weapon) or more serious felony charges.

A few weeks later, at a playoff game against New Orleans, Saints fan Don Moses brought his two daughters with him to San Francisco to watch the game. Dressed in Saints colors, the Moses family endured "F" bombs and other vulgarities, as well as threats, from 49ers fans throughout the entire game. Moses was so disturbed by the experience that he chastised the club in a letter to the *San Francisco Chronicle*. "Every 49ers fan, the team, and its owners should be ashamed and embarrassed to wear the red and gold today," he wrote. It seemed like it was getting too dangerous for visiting fans to even show up.

When the 49ers faced the New York Giants in the conference championship game later that season (the game in which the winner earns a trip to the Super Bowl), team owner Jed York took out a full-page ad in the *San Francisco Chronicle*, imploring fans to behave. York called for sportsmanship, respect, and class. Stakes were high. The winner would head to the Super Bowl. He reminded fans that they were ambassadors for the community and to treat fellow fans with sportsmanship. The fear of embarrassing violence was palpable. Fans were warned that undercover police would be patrolling the stands in Giants garb and that the police presence would be beefed up by 25 percent. More than 100 ticket holders were ejected from the game, double the count from the previous week. Arrests were slightly higher as well. Authorities used pepper spray on one fan after he allegedly assaulted a police officer. Could the increase in incidents and arrests be attributed to a beefed-up police presence and zero tolerance for misbehavior? Or was it because of the souped-up rivalry and presence of more miscreants? It's like the chicken and the egg. Which came first, the thugs or the cops? Were fans even more out of control at this game, or were police on overdrive, pouncing on any possible infraction?

Several months after the game, the *Sports Business Journal* surveyed fans and found that 40 percent of those polled didn't feel comfortable bringing children to NFL games—the type of statistic no team owner or league official likes to hear. Improving fan behavior was clearly an issue the league needed to address.

The league had, in fact, been grappling with fan violence for some time. Three years earlier, in 2008, it had instituted a Code of Fan Conduct, which prohibits fans from engaging in violence or irresponsible drunken behavior and using foul language, among other behaviors. The Code of Conduct gives teams the means to yank violators from the stadium in a systematic manner. NFL security chief Jeff Miller, a former commissioner of the Pennsylvania State Police, explained the impetus for the code. According to Miller, in 2006, during Roger Goodell's first season as NFL commissioner, Goodell attended different games, sitting in the stands and taking in the experience. Too many times he didn't like what he saw and eventually told Miller, "We need to take this from an R rating to a PG-13."

I attended my first NFL game well before the age of 13, as do many other fans. Shouldn't the NFL want to encourage a G rating for the sake of younger fans? "We want everyone to be able to come to our stadiums and enjoy the entire day," Commissioner Goodell said when the policy was unveiled. During an interview with Miller and his colleague, Ray DiNunzio, the NFL's director of strategic security programs and a former FBI assistant section chief in counterterrorism, the two told me that the atmosphere at stadiums is improving. "Fan behavior overall is getting better. Does that mean we've reached nirvana? No. We're nowhere near where I want to be. But we're going down the right path," said Miller.

Miller and DiNunzio cited a double-digit decline in arrests for the 2012 season and a texting service that allows fans to register complaints in real time. They said that fans have told them that the game-day experience is better and contended that it isn't fair to judge an entire stadium of people by a few knuckleheads and videotaped incidents magnified by social media. "It's a very small percentage of fans that go astray of the fan code of conduct," said DiNunzio. "We don't want to create requirements and restrict activity that impact the vast majority of law-abiding citizens."

Yet, horror stories still unfold. In 2011, a fan Tasered other fans during a dispute about the national anthem. Two years later, a fan was beaten to death in the parking lot at Arrowhead Stadium in Kansas City. According to little-known league statistics, that same season, security personnel confiscated approximately 30 knives per game, knives probably not used to cut up salami during a tailgate party.

"FIREMAN ED" RETIRES

The specter of violence was so threatening that even one of the most iconic, committed fans couldn't take it anymore. In 2012, 53-year-old New York City firefighter Ed Anzalone, aka "Fireman Ed," known for leading the New York Jets crowd in the chant "J-E-T-S, Jets, Jets, Jets," walked away from his famous game-day ritual, complaining about the game's corrosive atmosphere and mistreatment from the crowd. After 25 years, Fireman Ed quit being Fireman Ed.

I met Fireman Ed in 1999, as part of an assignment for ESPN, along with Tim McKernan, or "Barrel Man," a Broncos fan legend who has since died. Fireman Ed was decked out in his New York Jets jersey and a NYFD helmet painted green and white. Barrel Man, who resembled Santa with his long, white beard, wore nothing but an orange plastic barrel. We spent time at Ed's firehouse in Harlem and tried in vain to get Barrel Man to slide down the fire pole, as the plastic barrel got wedged in the shoot. Traveling downtown, we rode in a limousine because that was the only car we could find to accommodate the barrel. Even though the two men represented rival teams who were about to face one another in the conference championship, Fireman Ed and Barrel Man had a great time together.

But Fireman Ed would not last. When asked why he abandoned his super-fan persona, Anzalone says he had faced confrontation in the stands, parking lot, and even the bathroom, and he blames the belligerence on too much alcohol. "Drinking and football is a tough mix, to say the least," said Anzalone. "Some of the guys get real aggressive, and you blow them off and you walk away. But you're a human being. After a while, you're bound to get in a confrontation. I just said, 'I'm not going to embarrass myself, the New York City Fire Department, or my kids and family. Let me step away.'"

Two years prior to walking away, Anzalone got into a shoving incident with a Giants fan during a preseason game, an incident that was nationally televised and immortalized on YouTube. He was charged with simple assault, but the charges were dropped. The Giants fan was required to undergo anger-management counseling. Fireman Ed still attends games but sits in a different section on the other side of the stadium, leaving the J-E-T-S chant to others.

OPENING DAY

What happened to Bryan Stow is a stark reminder of how vulnerable a fan can be. On Opening Day of the 2011 baseball season at Dodger Stadium, Stow—a lifelong Giants fan from Santa Cruz who worked as a paramedic—was nearly beaten to death in the parking lot by Dodgers fans. The Giants were defending World Series champs, and the rivalry between the Giants and Dodgers is storied. Stow, a father of two, had traveled to Los Angeles with friends for the game, but from the time of their arrival at the ballpark, fans of the home team began taunting the group, clad in Giants apparel.

After the 2–1 Dodger victory, Stow's group was walking through the parking lot to catch a cab when they encountered 29-year-old Louie Sanchez and 30-year-old Marvin Norwood, dressed in Dodgers jerseys and acting belligerent. Witnesses testified that the ensuing attack was unprovoked and that the visitors kept trying to walk away from the menacing duo. One described Stow as trying to diffuse the situation. "We're ready to go home, it's just a game, leave us alone," he had said. But Sanchez blindsided Stow and knocked him to the ground with one punch. Stow immediately lost consciousness and hit the ground with a sickening thud. "It was just like a tree falling," one eyewitness said. Blood poured from Stow's ears. As he lay there motionless, Sanchez kicked his unconscious victim in the head. So did Norwood, who stood over Stow and, according to witnesses, asked, "Who else wants to fight?"

The beating lasted about 60 seconds. In that instant, Stow's life was forever changed. His skull was fractured, and he suffered permanent brain damage. Stow spent several months in a medically induced coma. He now uses a walker to get around, often wears an adult diaper, and struggles with memory loss. He has no memory of his beating. In a 2014 ESPN interview, he said that the one thing he regrets is that he didn't turn to see his attacker running toward him.

The sports world has not forgotten about Stow. As a testament to how his situation has resonated with others and how the Giants organization has embraced him, on a January Bay Area evening in 2014, a mostly middle-aged crowd gathered at a sold-out music venue in Marin County, co-owned by Bob Weir, a former member of the Grateful Dead. Music and baseball fans came to hear Tim Flannery, San Francisco Giant third base coach (now retired), play his brand of country folk music. Flannery refuses to let people forget about what happened to Stow. Since the beating, Flannery and his band, the Lunatic Fringe, have raised money during the off-season for Stow's medical bills. I attended the event, along with several other sports journalists who had gathered to hear what Flannery calls his "hillbilly" music. He's from Kentucky, so I guess he can say that.

Never a star, Flannery spent 11 seasons in the majors and hit only nine home runs, which he joked about with the crowd. As he plucked at his banjo, the crowd broke into a "Beat L.A." chant. Flannery released a new record, his 11th, and donated the proceeds to Stow's family for his care. "Selfishly, I do it because it makes me a better family man," Flannery said, citing the inspiring commitment of Stow's parents and siblings. After four sold-out shows, of which all ticket sales went to benefit Stow, Flannery presented the Stows with a check just short of $100,000.

Other members of the Giants community have also pitched in with the fund-raising. Pitcher Jeremy Affeldt matched the first $25,000 Flannery raised, and Will Clark, former Giants slugger and now a community ambassador, donated $10,000. Former Giants slugger Barry Bonds previously pledged to pay for Stow's two children to attend college, and pitcher Tim Lincecum donated $25,000 to pay for his care.

A few days before the January 2014 show, Flannery and I had a chance to chat. He was excited about how much attention he had been able to bring to Stow's predicament and expressed concern for security cuts that might have led to the beating. But he was also careful to explain that his performance was going to be about love, not blame. "This is about music. This is about trying to let a family know that a bunch of people still think about them and care," Flannery said. "But it's not my job to go after somebody and point fingers." The sports world supports countless philanthropic causes, and Flannery's heartfelt commitment is no exception. I asked him how bad he thought fan behavior had gotten. "I don't believe those guys are fans," Flannery said. "I believe those guys are gangsters and thugs."

Criminal court proceedings upheld Flannery's beliefs. After months of searching for the parking lot bullies in a public manhunt, during which police initially arrested the wrong man, Sanchez and Norwood, both of whom had criminal records, were apprehended. The two men were also accused of harassing other fans both inside and outside the stadium that day.

In a secret jailhouse recording, Sanchez was captured describing what happened. "I socked him, jumped him, and started beating him," he said to Norwood. Sanchez can also be heard describing the attack, and Norwood expresses no regret for backing him up.

Both men pled guilty to the attack in February 2014. Sanchez was sentenced to eight years for felony mayhem, Norwood four years for assault. In a Los Angeles courtroom, Superior Court Judge George Lomeli issued their sentence and angrily told the duo, "You are the biggest nightmare for people who attend public events." Judge Lomeli commented that he takes his son to college football games and that his "biggest fear is that we might run into people like you, who have no civility."

After two years in various hospitals and rehab centers, Stow's insurance would no longer pay for him to stay in a rehab facility. In the spring of 2013, he returned home to his family, who are now tasked with providing 24-hour care. Stow's lawyers, who filed a lawsuit on behalf of Stow and his children against the Dodgers, as well as Sanchez and Norwood and several other defendants, predicted that the family will need between $34 and $50 million to care for him for the rest of his life.

According to their claims in court, since 2009, the Dodgers have systematically cut back on a more expensive uniformed police presence, leaving fans vulnerable to unruliness and criminal activity. Owner Frank McCourt faced financial woes, in part because of a nasty and public divorce. The suit alleged that this affected funding for the Dodgers and that additional security personnel in the stadium and better lighting in the parking lot might have saved Bryan from the life he must now endure. The Dodgers' lawyers argued that Stow, a San Francisco fan wearing Giants gear, had been drinking heavily that day (he registered a blood alcohol level of nearly twice the legal limit) and, according to a witness, yelled at the Dodgers fans who had been taunting him and his friends throughout the game.

In the summer of 2014, after a five-week trial, a Los Angeles Superior Court jury awarded the Stows almost $18 million in damages, nearly $14 million of which was to be paid by the Dodgers—significantly less than the family had hoped for. Sanchez and Norwood were found to be partially responsible for Stow's pain and suffering and are on the hook for close to $2 million each. Several months after the verdict, Stow's legal team filed yet another lawsuit against the Dodgers and other parties, alleging fraudulent action with regard to his medical coverage.

Bryan Stow is a permanent reminder of the horrific and senseless violence that can take place at a sporting event. Stow's attorney, Tom Girardi, told me that since the verdict, he's gotten calls from four different law firms from throughout the country that represent stadium owners asking what they can do to avoid another "Bryan Stow" situation. Lou Marciani, who runs the National Center for Spectator Sports Safety and Security, told me the lesson to be learned is that the parking lot outside a stadium can be especially dangerous. For example, before a game, he pointed out that you usually "don't really get cranking with an in-game incident command center that soon and you're getting ready and your people are coming to work and getting set up for the game. You've got the whole four or five hours before the game that might be more vulnerable."

"Bryan Stow was obviously a significant incident," said John Skinner, director of security for Major League Baseball. While Skinner wouldn't comment directly on the Stow suit because of the litigation, he would talk about the delicate dance between funding and fan safety. "Most owners are visionaries, and they recognize that it's important to protect the safety of the game," added Skinner. Keeping people safe comes at a price. "Security is the big sucking sound sometimes. I hate to say that, but it is."

Most professional leagues hire former law enforcement officials to run their security operations. Skinner, for instance, previously worked in security for Minor League Baseball and in Florida as police chief of Port St. Lucie. For former police chiefs to FBI or secret service agents, it's a popular second career. These top cops spend time contending with fan violence, alcohol policy, and stadium procedure. Issues range from the more overt—MLB's plans to install metal detectors at each ballpark—to the more high-profile and threatening—working with Homeland Security to diffuse potential terrorist threats at the biggest events.

In professional baseball, fan unrest has been an issue for the game since its earliest days. In the beginning of the twentieth century, overcrowding, drunkenness, and antipathy toward players and umpires fueled bad fan behavior, often dubbed "rowdyism" in news reports. In 1896, during a postseason competition known as the Temple Cup, rowdy fans flung potatoes, apples, and eggs at players. When some tossed their coats on a player's head after he caught a fly ball to prevent him from throwing it back and making a play, the umpire called a do-over. In the early 1900s, baseball officials offered rewards for the identities of rowdy fans who threw projectiles onto the field. In a July 4, 1900, doubleheader, Chicago fans shot guns each time their team scored against the Philadelphia Phillies. The violence showed no sign of abating throughout time. In 1929, a glass bottle thrown in anger after a controversial umpiring decision killed a fan. An editorial in the *Cleveland Plain Dealer* several days later urged Cleveland to wake up and stop the unsportsmanlike outbursts: "Any man who will throw a bottle or any other life-endangering object from the midst of a crowd at any official or player is the rankest type of coward." It would take organized baseball 30 more years to ban glass bottles from the stands. Seems as though some lessons are only begrudgingly learned.

LIQUID COURAGE

In November 2004, the Indiana Pacers traveled to Detroit to play the Pistons in a rematch of the Eastern Conference Finals from the previous season. It was a combustible rivalry. In the spring, the Pistons had beaten the Pacers on the way to their first championship since 1990, the era when they were known for rough, intimidating play and brandished the nickname the "Bad Boys."

The Pacers came into the Palace of Auburn Hills looking to settle this grudge on national television. They took control of the game from the outset, capped by a 24-point effort from Ron Artest, who scored 17 points in the first quarter. Despite a lopsided score, the atmosphere oozed intensity. With 45.9 seconds left in the game, Indiana led, 97–82. As Pistons forward Ben Wallace went up for a layup, Artest fouled him hard from behind. Wallace shoved Artest with both hands, pressing against Artest's neck. To diffuse the situation, a referee pushed Artest toward the sideline, away from a still-agitated Wallace. In an unusual move, Artest laid down on the scorer's table and stretched out on his back, his head resting in his hands.

If you were watching a videotape of the incident, this is the point where you would make a face and quizzically say, "What the . . . ?" Artest's actions were defiant, weird, and confusing. He had crossed the line of what usually unfolds at a NBA game. Upsetting the usual decorum seemed to be a subliminal call to arms for fans to act out; some began to boo and shout profanities at Artest as he lay prone on the scorer's table. It didn't help that as he lay there, players from both teams were poised in suspended hostility, milling around the court, separated by assistant coaches, as the referees conferred and fans watched and waited for someone to take control.

John Green, a 39-year-old Pistons season ticket holder, was sitting in his usual spot a few rows up from the floor watching the bizarre situation unfold. He ended up getting into a boozy game of one-upmanship with his friend. "I was probably three sheets to the wind at that time, and I said, 'Man, I could nail him from right here,'" Green commented during a conversation with me. "And he said, 'Oh, no you couldn't! He's too far away.' I said, 'I'm telling you, I could do an underhand lob with this cup, with the way it's weighted with the ice in the bottom.' I held the cup in two fingers, my index finger, and my middle finger on the rim of the cup." The friends went back and forth, betting a drink for the winner. Green threw the cup, which nailed Artest right in the chest.

Known as an intense competitor with an erratic personality, Artest jumped up, charged into the stands, and punched the fan who threw the cup at him—or so he thought. When Green saw the wrong man being pummeled, he reacted. "I pulled Ron Artest off that kid." Green then threw his arms around Artest's neck, jamming him into a headlock. Pacers teammate Stephen Jackson followed Artest into the stands. The scene resembled a prison-yard fight, with fists flying and hands clawing at jerseys. It was ugly—and stayed ugly for far too long. Fans spilled onto the court. The Pacers' Jermaine O'Neal flattened one of them. Fans flung food at Indiana players. Someone tossed a chair at the visiting players as they tried to exit the court. Dubbed "Malice at the Palace," the brawl showcased the worst of player and fan behavior, with the players' misdeeds getting the brunt of the attention because they were well-known NBA players. But it wasn't just the players; some of the fans involved sounded like they were straight out of the bad fan hall of fame.

Charles Haddad, a 21-year-old Pistons fan, ventured onto the court during the brawl and was punched by several players. While he was charged with trespassing, he in turn filed a federal lawsuit against Pacer hoopsters O'Neal and guard Anthony Johnson. A jury decided that O'Neal's punch was justified and awarded Haddad no money.

According to testimony from the Palace's director of event operations, Tim Smith, Haddad, who paid $10,000 for his courtside seats, was known to Palace security for drinking too much and acting out. Earlier that season, he had allegedly threatened to pour a drink on Houston Rockets star Yao Ming. When confronted about the allegation, Haddad told the Pistons' employee that he was the "biggest Pistons fan in here and that nobody understood" that he just wanted to get involved just one time to "show everyone." When he made this comment, he patted his wallet. In addition, at halftime of the fateful game against the Pacers, security had already talked to Haddad about his behavior that night, and plans were in the works to permanently revoke his season tickets. Thanks to his decision to venture onto the court, he indeed lost his season tickets, and authorities also banned him from attending other events at the Palace.

Dave Gorcyca, the Oakland County prosecutor at the time, was tasked with deciding appropriate charges for the overzealous fans. "After John Green threw the cup, it almost turned into mob violence. Other fans started to engage in the brawl and going on the court," said Gorcyca, who watched video angle after video angle to identify the perpetrators. "Two others were on the floor and got in a fist fight. The whole situation just really escalated."

The game was called, and the Pacers quickly piled into their bus to avoid police officers trying to investigate. Green, who has a record riddled with several DUIs and a domestic violence charge, was identified by Gorcyca, who recognized him from the videotaped footage. They had once lived next door to one another. "I already knew his background," Gorcyca said in regard to the bizarre coincidence, continuing, "Quite frankly, it didn't surprise me. He had, at the time, quite the temper. I knew that for a fact, because occasionally the police would be called next door."

Five fans were charged with assault and battery. Green was the only one who ended up going to trial; he served 30 days of jail time and two years of probation after being convicted of punching Artest. All but one of the other fans pleaded guilty or no contest, and one case was dismissed. The five NBA players charged in the melee pleaded no contest, and each was sentenced to one year of probation and community service and fined $250. Nine players were suspended for varying amounts of time, and Artest was banned for the rest of the season, the longest suspension ever meted out by the NBA for an on-the-court incident.

I hadn't heard about the brawl until I was sitting in an airport in Mexico, on my way home from vacation and finally with cell phone service. When I turned my Blackberry on, this bizarre story unfolded in front of me electronically. Links to news stories, "Can you believe it?" e-mails from friends, and memos detailing coverage of the aftermath clogged my phone. It was a moment that shook the sports world and made people think hard about the power of the crowd.

Players fighting fans and fans fighting players was a terrible black mark for the league. Most of the security measures the NBA implemented after the incident were aimed at tamping down on fan excess, like establishing a code of conduct for fans (two and a half years before the NFL) and mandating a fourth-quarter ban on beer sales. The Pistons installed portable coverings over the tunnels that teams walk through to get to the court, separating fans from the players.

"I honestly believe this is mob mentality," Oakland County Circuit Court judge Rae Lee Chabot said as she was sentencing a fan who had thrown a chair during the fight. "It doesn't excuse it, but it does explain it." While the judicial system was once again relying on the mob mentality concept, Gorcyca saw it differently and described fans like Green and Haddad as likely being predisposed to trouble. He lamented, "All they needed was impetus, something to entice them to engage in that behavior."

Fans trying to hurt the athletes they've paid big money to see is a twisted way to show passion, but sometimes it works. You can find examples of fans agitating athletes in almost every sport and in almost every era.

Baseball's Ty Cobb beat up a disabled heckler in 1912. In the early 1990s, NBA star Charles Barkley spit at a fan who was launching racial epithets at him and unintentionally hit a little girl. Afterward, Barkley told *Sports Illustrated* that the spitting incident was the only regret of his career: "I wanted to win way too bad. I had to calm down." In 2005, the New York Yankees' Gary Sheffield went after a Red Sox fan who had thrown beer in his face as he was fielding a ball.

Infamous cup thrower John Green says he's calmed down since the Ron Artest incident. He works as a builder, moved to the other side of the state, and said he regularly attends Alcoholics Anonymous meetings and has kicked his booze habit. "I'll tell you what, this incident was probably the best thing that happened to me because it was one of the things that got me steering toward recovery," he said. Although he admitted to relapses, he added, "I just call them still doing field research."

Green and Artest, who subsequently changed his name to Metta World Peace, have become friends and sometimes make media appearances together. "I have to try to make something positive out of it," said Green. "That's what Ron did with me when he reached out to me." Green said Artest once invited him for Thanksgiving, but he couldn't make it.

Green summed up his proverbial 15 minutes of fame by saying, "That shit would never have happened if the whole crowd was sober. That's plain and simple. You'd have everybody sitting there watching the game, and holding hands and praying together at the beginning of the game, and then leaving."

He also provides his own assessment of fandom: "You've got a whole different crowd mentality there. You got a bunch of rock 'n' roll, party crazy people that go to sporting events, that live life to the fullest and are like thrill seekers or adventure seekers."

I later began wondering how Green was making out staying away from the booze. After a few months passed, I called him to continue our conversation. He refused to take my call.

3

FANS THROUGHOUT THE WORLD

It's the thugs that are destroying football.—Margaret Thatcher, prime minister of the United Kingdom, during a press conference held on May 30, 1985

I first learned that sports fans can be dangerous while traveling in Europe. I was with my friend Rob, who is British. We were in Milan, Italy, headed to the opening match of the 1990 FIFA World Cup. As we were walking the crowded streets toward San Siro stadium, which was gearing up to host more than 80,000 amped up fans in just a few short hours, Rob hovered over me, insisting I stay close to him. There were hooligans about and we weren't safe, he said. Looking back, I didn't know Rob that well. We had met a few days earlier on a ferry, when he told me he had liked the book I was reading. But I could tell he wasn't the overprotective or overly dramatic type. His fear was legitimate. I wasn't sure what to make of it and focused on the spectacle unfolding in front of me. I didn't witness any bloodshed that day, but the vibe was threatening.

Twenty years later, I instinctively knew my book had to examine violent fandom, not only in the United States, but throughout the world. It didn't take long to learn that some of the most stunning violence erupts in countries like Croatia, Argentina, and Algeria. England's notorious hooligans provided entrée into a world of organized rage—a rich psychological laboratory and thick compendium of historical embarrassments. I wanted to understand the thinking behind the fury of these fans and how fan violence and hatred reflect a country's history, preoccupations, politics, and national identity.

Few cultures are immune to fanaticism, and it's not hard to find disturbing anecdotes. During the summer of 2014, the top goal scorer for the Algerian league was killed on the field when a fan tossed a rock at his head. Officials suspended league play, and a violent sports culture in this African nation came to the fore.

Even in Japan, where there is a cultural premium on good manners, racist fans have, for decades, displayed ugliness toward white baseball players and Korean football players. During the same year that Japanese football supporters traveled to Brazil for the 2014 World Cup and cleaned up trash after matches, two top football teams were forced to play a match in an empty stadium as punishment for raising a "Japanese Only" banner.

Of course, I couldn't visit every country that suffers fan-induced mayhem. Such a feat would require an around-the-world ticket and a trust fund. But I could visit a couple key places. To understand how sports can go hand in hand with marauding gangs of thugs, I found myself in Antwerp, Belgium, in the fall of 2013, seated at an ancient wooden table across from a real-life hooligan. "We were just normal people with a not-so-normal hobby," explained Jan Van Cauwenbergh, a 47-year-old Belgian with sandy brown hair and a craggy face. Cauwenbergh, who works as a lifeguard, didn't attend university, but many of the Royal Antwerp supporters he associates with did. "People think you're all lower working class with no job, but that was not the case," said Cauwenbergh. "We had people who studied crime, people who studied journalism, people who ran their own businesses."

We visited in a wood-paneled pub called Den Engel, which dates from the 14th century. It's located in Antwerp's old market area, known as the Grote Markt, across a cobblestone square from the town's soaring cathedral. Den Engel has been in existence longer than most American cities. The atmosphere in the café is relaxed, and patrons know one another by name. If you go early in the day, you don't have to raise your voice to be heard.

Cauwenbergh, whose first language is Dutch, told me in accented English that at the age of 11 or 12, he and his friends basically formed a youth gang. That gang spent every Saturday living and breathing football and fighting. "It was a way of life," admitted Cauwenbergh. During the 1980s and 1990s, in a community racked by unemployment, he and his friends had the time to make hooliganism a full-time practice.

During our lengthy visit, he recounted his life as a member of X-Side, a notorious group of hooligans that had followed the Royal Antwerp Football Club throughout Europe for 30 years. His crew would often pile into cars, drive a few hours to Germany for a morning match, and then drive back home to watch Royal Antwerp in the afternoon. Drinking and fighting were a given. The fights were usually prearranged and took place a few hours before the football game and sometimes afterward. At home in Belgium and Germany, hooligan brawls tended to be weaponless. During a trip to Russia, however, Cauwenbergh said fans threw bottles, Molotov cocktails, and even gasoline at him. This fighting thrilled him, much as it had since his days on the playground, when he was young and admittedly blustery. My affable companion matter-of-factly detailed some of the results of his brawling: broken bones, stitches, and getting knocked unconscious, to name just a few. He complained that new rules and antihooliganism laws have diluted the experience of being a football supporter. Listening to Cauwenbergh, I realized that he didn't separate his passion for the sport on the field from his zest for violence off of it. It was part of the same continuum.

Cauwenbergh's identity is wrapped up in being a supporter. "When your favorite team scores an important goal, you can't describe how people become. It's a joy, it's deep, you can't compare it," he said. "It's indescribable." He told me that he's gotten more out of the group than just a legacy of football and violence. The gang he joined as a preteen, which he estimates to include about 150 to 200 members, is still part of his life. "We have a Christmas drink every year," he added.

In 2000, Cauwenbergh says he was arrested yet again after getting caught fighting on video shot from a Belgian police helicopter. By then in his 30s, he decided to write a book reflecting on his football fanaticism. Published in Dutch in 2004, the book, called *X-Side: Heersers Na De Wedstrijd*, which roughly translates to *X-Side: Postgame Warriors*, is a chronological history of his life as a hooligan, giving hair-raising accounts of violence, injury, and entanglements with the law. He's not the only one to memorialize football violence in print. There are more than 100 first-person hooligan titles on Amazon UK. It seems to be a popular genre.

We soon left the café to pick up his 12-year-old son Sebastian from football practice. Then he took me to Bosuilstadion, his mecca—the decaying soccer stadium where his team plays. He oozed pride as he pointed out the Spartan wooden benches on which he has spent most of his Saturdays. They were dilapidated and strained to hold almost 17,000 spectators.

As it turned out, Cauwenbergh was not permitted inside Bosuilstadion. He somewhat bashfully explained that he had been banned from attending games there after climbing the fence and running onto the field in an emotional frenzy during an October 2012 match. I asked him what caused him to flaunt the rules and invade the pitch, as football authorities refer to this type of behavior. He replied that he was drunk and in a highly emotional state after a surprising victory. During our conversation, he questioned, "I was 46 years old, why did I do it?"

Cauwenbergh later forwarded me copies of the photos from the closed-circuit television footage that had nailed him, showing him on the field in the crowd, surrounding the players, hugging them, and celebrating. He explained that he still comes to cheer on the squad, but in disguise. I'm imagining a Groucho Marx moustache or a man in a dress.

Royal Antwerp F.C. is one of the most popular clubs in Belgium, but it hasn't won a league title since 1957, and was relegated—or sent down to the second tier of competition—almost a decade ago. But Cauwenbergh's loyalty doesn't waver. He readily admitted that he's more committed to football than family, despite the profound disappointment of losing. "I still love my club," he said. "When a wife disappoints you over and over again, you separate. But you always stay with your club."

THE LEGACY AT HEYSEL

I could have picked almost any country to travel to and find a healthy dose of football fanatics. Why Belgium—land of multiple languages I don't speak, European Union bureaucrats, sybaritic chocolates, and an ancient brewing heritage that awes any beer aficionado? Chocolate and beer are actually a universal language I do speak. But I really went to Belgium, to Brussels, to visit Heysel, the site of one of the most tragic and ultimately pivotal outbreaks of spectator violence and death in the history of football.

On May 29, 1985, English football club Liverpool was seeking its fifth European Cup Championship against the Italian team Juventus. Brussels, the capitol of Belgium, had been chosen to host the final. Approximately one hour before the match, Liverpool fans, there to support the reigning European champions, were drinking and partying outside the stadium. Many had already clashed with police and were primed to seek revenge for a violent outbreak at the previous year's European Cup final in Rome. As spectators entered the stadium (many without a ticket), a large group of Liverpool fans ran toward the Juventus fans, who were standing in a designated neutral area. A frenzied riot ensued in the overcrowded terraces, or viewing areas. The Belgian police were unprepared and outmatched. Italian fans panicked and tried to run but were blocked by a concrete retaining wall. Fans near the wall were crushed, and the wall eventually collapsed. Thirty-nine fans died in the chaos, and several hundred were injured.

The shocking mayhem was immortalized on television, as most football supporters in a multitude of countries had tuned in for a hyped-up match. Inexplicably, the game kept going despite the disaster, authorities apparently concerned that canceling the match would incite further violence. The dead bodies were piled on the side of the pitch as the game carried on, remaining visible to fans and viewers. Juventus went on to win, 1–0, but at that point, the outcome was all but irrelevant. It's a score many do not remember.

Liverpool native Nicky Allt, 54, spent much of his youth following Liverpool FC, mostly for free, evading ticket takers, transportation tariffs, and authorities. He was at the match at Heysel, having crossed the English Channel with his crew. "I remember getting to Heysel and thinking, 'I've never seen a crowd like this.' There was just Liverpool fans everywhere," he said. "I've never seen so many people drunk and partying." According to Allt, the grounds were poorly policed, and the concrete was crumbling underfoot. He remembers both sets of fans picking up the concrete and chucking it like missiles at one another.

At the stadium, he watched the carnage from above the area where the Juventus fans were penned in: "The wall I sat upon was falling to bits. I thought it would buckle under our weight, but I wanted to keep my view high up for a game between two of the biggest football clubs in the world." That wall would eventually collapse, but Allt escaped harm. He said he knew something terrible was going to happen, commenting, "It was a bad vibe the minute you entered the stadium." Thousands were walking in and out of the grounds through large holes in the wall and unmanned gates. The Belgians were unprepared for and overwhelmed by the emotional crowd. "It was like putting a rock concert by the Beatles on at a scrap metal yard," Allt concluded.

Allt said he didn't engage in any fighting that day and stayed put until the chaos had calmed down. "I just saw people piled up, I didn't know people were dead," he stated. He saw the crush firsthand but never saw the wall actually collapse. He helped a stranger who had injured his leg and said he was unaware that people had died until he reached the boat to England.

Since the early 1970s, English hooligans had been wreaking havoc at home and throughout Europe. This time it had gone too far. British prime minister Margaret Thatcher declared war on the hooligan problem and resolved to bring some order to the chaos by instituting antihooligan laws. For five years, English teams were banned from competing anywhere in Europe. Liverpool was excluded for an additional three years, a term that would be reduced to one. Fourteen Liverpool fans were convicted of manslaughter and sentenced to three years in prison. The Thatcher crackdown kicked off an era of additional monitoring and targeted policing, measures some would call heavy-handed and repressive. The response contained but did not completely eradicate the problem.

The three countries involved—Belgium, England, and Italy—have a complicated relationship with the legacy of Heysel. Nicky Allt insisted that the source of the chaos was the Juventus fans who were spitting at the Brits. Some Italians feel that the British still haven't accepted enough responsibility. Eighteen months after the tragedy, a Belgian judicial report assigned blame not only to Liverpool fans, but also to Belgian authorities and the Union of European Football Associations, or UEFA, the governing body of European football. Several officials were convicted of criminal negligence: A three-month suspended sentence and fine were given to UEFA general secretary Hans Bangerter; a six-month suspended sentence was handed down to the head of the Belgian Football Association, Albert Roosens; and a three-month suspended sentence and small fine were given to Captain Johan Mahieu of the Belgian police, who was in charge of security that day.

Looking back, Allt saw Heysel as the end of an era. "We'd been on this roller coaster having this party, probably ten years since I left school, where we could go anywhere, do anything," he said. It suddenly just stopped. "Fences went up everywhere, bigger and higher. Police were watching everything."

Several other fires and riots shortly before and after the 1985 European Cup Championship helped seal the fate of unfettered football fanaticism and caused authorities to step up safety requirements at venues. Decaying stadiums proved to be a treacherous location for frenzied fans thirsting for a brawl.

Another tragedy took place at what was known as Hillsborough. Ninety-six Liverpool fans died and hundreds were injured in a stampede that took place during a 1989 match between Liverpool and Nottingham, held at Hillsborough stadium in Sheffield, England. In a lower terraced area, fans were split up into five pens separated by fences. These fences were built to keep spectators from running onto the field. With thousands of fans still at the turnstiles, pushing and shoving to get in, police sent more and more spectators into the already packed section. A few minutes after play had begun, one of the barriers collapsed, and people fell on top of one another. Some tried to climb their way out. Allt was there, too. "You could see people being crushed really badly, cause they were up against the fence at the time," he said. An official investigation resulted in the release of the Taylor Report, which established the main cause of the disaster as lack of police control.

But after 20 years and supplementary investigations, a more complicated truth has been exposed. Not only did various safety deficiencies and negligence by police and stadium authorities lead to the tragedy, but an orchestrated cover-up was also revealed. Police used the expectation of bad fan behavior as a scapegoat for their own negligence. An independent panel disclosed that statements of more than 100 officers were doctored to obscure the multiple failures that contributed to the death count.

After the incident, standing terraces—the sloped, fenced-off area where fans stood shoulder-to-shoulder, to form a living, breathing sea of humanity—were eliminated from all major footballs stadiums in the United Kingdom. According to Allt and other supporters, all-seated stadiums sapped the energy of the fans. "Once I sit down at a football game, my mind wanders," Allt stated. Authorities maintained that standing terraces were too dangerous for fans and too difficult to police.

Back in Belgium, Cauwenbergh echoed the disappointment about changes in the stadium experience, blaming features like all-seated stadiums and such newfound policies as no smoking, no alcohol in the stands, and steeper entrance prices. In 1998, Belgium passed sweeping antihooligan legislation that created a national "football unit" to oversee

law enforcement and mete out harsher sanctions for misbehavior. Cauwenbergh lamented that the "nice days of football" are behind him and
his crew.

Since the Heysel disaster, the stadium has been renovated and renamed King Baudouin Stadium, after the introverted fifth king of Belgium. The neighborhood and metro stop located on the outskirts of Brussels are still known as Heysel.

One October evening in 2013, I found myself strolling through this
neighborhood. The Belgian national team, known as the Red Devils, were
preparing to face the Wales national team in a relatively meaningless
World Cup qualifier, meaningless because the Red Devils had already
clinched their trip to the 2014 World Cup tournament in Brazil. It was the
first time the Red Devils were headed to the World Cup in more than a
decade, and Belgian fans were ecstatic. The country was thrilled that their
team had peaked in time for the biggest football competition in the world.

Pregame festivities were well under way. Belgian guys in their 20s
were congregating before the game in a grassy area under the Atomium, a
stainless steel building erected for the 1958 World's Fair but more closely
resembling a sculpture. Intended to resemble an iron crystal, magnified
165 billion times as a symbol of science and modernity, the Atomium was
named one of Europe's most bizarre buildings by CNN. Cocktail hour in
the shadow of a has-been science experiment was a curious choice, but no
one seemed to care. Football was what mattered.

Leaving the giant iron crystal behind, I headed to King Baudouin
Stadium. Heysel was a decrepit stadium in 1985, which certainly contributed to the chaos. Despite the postdisaster renovation, it is still decrepit.
With an unremarkable and generic design, it barely looks electrified. I
was supposed to meet a die-hard Belgian fan, a 36-year-old writer named
Jan De Jonghe, but I had already gone through the turnstiles and learned I
would not be allowed to pass into his section, which took me by surprise.
This would never happen in the United States. In fact, the last time I went
to the San Francisco Giants game with my cousins, none of us sat in our
assigned seats. While you may run into overzealous American ushers
who control access to the seats or exclusive premium areas, we usually
don't encounter fences that completely separate sections. In Belgium, I
couldn't even go to the bathroom in a different section. The stadium felt
like a cage, and I couldn't help but think what it would be like to be
penned in with a surging crowd and nowhere to go because barriers have

been erected on all sides. They have restricted movement as a fan safety measure, but it seemed to cage the fans—exactly what killed people at this location nearly 30 years ago. The only difference is that now the cage is not as small.

The play on the field reflected a lack of urgency, and the generic match ended in a 1–1 draw. A huge fireworks display lit up the sky after the contest, and the Belgian team lapped the field, waving to the enthusiastic crowd.

After the game, I e-mailed De Jonghe to apologize for my logistical miscue and ask what he thought about the match. His response was cautiously optimistic. "It is said that most football fans are fans against their will," he wrote back. "There is much truth in that saying. One becomes a fan as a child, and from there on fandom is maintained in sickness and in health." De Jonghe was hopeful for the team in the upcoming FIFA World Cup, assessing the Red Devils as the sixth-strongest team in the world. "Anything is possible in a knockout game of football," he maintained.

After the match, I went to look for a memorial to the Heysel tragedy. I knew of one but couldn't reach it without being ticketed for that section. I had already experienced how fans aren't allowed to walk the perimeter of the stadium, and it was getting old. I convinced an elderly female steward who seemed less like security and more like Mrs. Butterworth that I intended no harm and needed to sneak back into the stadium for my research. She was unsure of which monument I was referring to but granted me permission. After a few minutes of walking, I discovered a tall, stainless steel, abstract sculpture with 39 embedded lights, one for each fan who died. Designed by French artist Patrick Rimoux, the memorial incorporates Italian and Belgian stone and verses from the English poem "Funeral Blues" by W. H. Auden, to express the sorrow of the three nations. At the time of its installation, Rimoux had said the sculpture was meant "to commemorate the tragedy and to say 'don't forget.'" Everyone else streamed by without stopping, probably headed to catch the Metro before it shut down for the evening. I was the only visitor who paused.

The day after the match, Filip Van Doorslaer, marketing director for the Red Devils, met with me at his home to discuss my game-day experience. The 44-year-old Van Doorslaer looked to be someone who spends all of his time at the office; his apartment sported that blank wall, too-busy-to-decorate look and feel. He was too caught up in getting fans to embrace the Belgian national team, knowing it's a fickle relationship.

After being shut out of the international tournament scene for years, Belgian fans were frustrated. In 2012, a Belgian comedian came up with a scheme to auction off Belgian football fans after the Belgian national team failed to qualify for the European Football Championships, known as the Euros. Any team that felt its fan base was lacking passion could add the Belgians. About 15,000 orphaned Belgians were "sold" on eBay for a little more than 900 U.S. dollars, and the money was donated to UNICEF. After that stunt, Van Doorslaer knew the team had to improve. "We had to recreate the belief of the fans in the team," he said. They seemed to be succeeding, judging by the 46,000 spectators who had been in attendance the night before.

Van Doorslaer conceded that the on-the-field product I had seen at the qualifier was not the best, but he was pleased by the marketing implications. "Yesterday's game was more like a communion between the fans and the team, to share together this game as the moment where we celebrated qualification and not really a competitive game of football," he declared.

Like most European countries, Belgian officials will tell you they are on top of the scourge of hooliganism. While it's not as crazy as it was in the 1980s, European football still encounters fan disorder issues. Van Doorslaer stated that the biggest challenge with a game like the qualifier is the large number of spectators. An international match like that one is usually sanctioned by FIFA, the International Federation of Association Football, and tallies fewer incidents of fan violence because such a matchup draws more casual fans and invokes less passion than local rivalries. Authorities strictly monitor the hardcore fans.

But, in fact, during our café visit, Belgian hooligan Jan Van Cauwenbergh had shown me a text, in Dutch, that he received from a friend before the match, alerting him to a planned skirmish outside the stadium grounds; however, no Wales fans showed up, and the skirmish did not materialize.

"Nine and a half times out of ten, nothing happens. It's hard because the guys chicken out most of the time," Van Doorslaer said, rolling his eyes. "Police get word of it, and they just take out the two or three guys who are trying to set everything up." Old habits die hard.

I hadn't seen any police officers patrolling at the match. When I mentioned this lack of police presence to Van Doorslaer, he said they deploy undercover officers known as spotters, a shifting policy that depends on the opponent. According to Van Doorslaer, for matches against Eastern European teams like Croatia or Bosnia, uniformed police are necessary, and they automatically mobilize the riot squad. He said he considered the fans from those countries to be "savages" and backed up his disparagement with an anecdote from several years prior, when Belgium had faced the Bosnian national team in the industrial city of Zenica, about an hour from Sarajevo. Seventy Belgian VIPs and sponsors were slated to attend. Escorted by local security, Van Doorslaer went ahead to scout out the seats assigned to the Belgians, but those seats were already full and the squatters refused to budge. He waded into the section but had to retreat. "My whole back was blue from people hitting me. I didn't even have any colors of Belgium on me," he related. He knew that it was simply too dangerous for the Belgians to come to the stadium. Van Doorslaer added, "I called the boss and said, 'Go back to Sarajevo and watch the game on television.'"

"WE ARE ALL MONKEYS"

In the spring of 2014, most of the top-tier football leagues throughout the world were wrapping up their seasons so that players could join their national teams and prepare for the summer's World Cup in Brazil. During a single weekend, I scanned headlines that screamed of the unimaginable. A fan had been killed in Brazil and a police horse punched by a supporter in England. Three fans had been shot in Italy, one fatally. In Spain, fans had taunted black players by making monkey sounds. Was this just a typical weekend of competition for what is often called the most beautiful game in the world?

For the second week in a row in Spain's top tier of play, La Liga fans taunted a black player by making monkey noises, but the players refused to ignore the abuse. Pape Diop, a Senegalese midfielder playing for the Spanish team Levante, danced like a monkey when he heard fans making the racist noises.

The previous week, Barcelona's Dani Alves, a black player from Brazil, peeled and ate a banana that was tossed onto the field at him before proceeding with a corner kick. Out of that incident, the hashtag #somos-todosmacacos, translated as "We are all monkeys," was born and tweeted by Brazilian star forward Neymar.

Monkey chants and projectile bananas are just one form of reprehensible hate directed at opposing players. Some football fans have displayed swastikas and performed Nazi salutes to rile opposing teams, in what seems to be a show of support for extreme right-wing politics. In 2006, 60 Croatian fans stood in the stands, shoulder to shoulder, in the shape of a cross to form a human swastika during a friendly matchup with Italy. In 2013, a Nazi flag was displayed at a Russian league match between Spartak Moscow and Shinnik Yaroslavl.

Hate can also come in the form of antigay slurs. At a Champions League match, where the top European teams face off against one another, supporters of the German team Bayern Munich raised a banner with the phrase "Gay Gunners" and had a drawing of a cannon pointed at an opposing player's rear end.

I tried to unpack some of the hate during a visit to Italy in the spring of 2014. Italy's hardcore fans are called ultras, a term used in other countries as well that means "beyond" in Latin. The Italian version of hooligans, ultras assert their fanaticism through such expressive means as coordinated singing and elaborate banners that they unveil inside the stadium. In Italy, ultras sit together in the curved part of the stands at either end of the facility, known as the Curva.

To be a member of the ultra movement doesn't mean one automatically engages in violence or racist taunting, but intimidation is customary and violence looms over the entire Italian football establishment. Five thousand fans have been banned by the government from attending matches throughout the country because they have been labeled dangerous. Yet, they still manage to make trouble outside the grounds. According to statistics provided by the Italian government, injuries to spectators and police alike increased by almost 40 percent during the 2013–2014 season.

In Rome, I met with Mario Corsi, a lifelong fan of A.S. Roma, one of two teams in the city that play in Serie A (the top Italian league). Corsi hosts a highly rated football talk radio show, and I went to his studio to learn about Italian fandom. One of the day's topics was the racial invective that had been hurled at a black player from the Italian national team during a training session two days earlier. Corsi tried to give me some background, explaining that racist slurs are a way to get under the skin of opposing players. Through a translator, he interpreted the mindset for me: "I'm not racist from Monday to Friday, but come the weekend and the match, I become an asshole." According to Corsi, certain black players polarize the fans. He was referring to Mario Balotelli, who played for A.C Milan at the time. Balotelli is black, born to Ghanaian immigrants in Italy and raised in foster care by a white Italian family. He's the player who suffered the racist taunts at training camp. With his mohawk, Balotelli has always made headlines and is known for engaging in bold celebrations on the field. "It's not racism, it's because he's an asshole, upsetting the fans with his arrogance after he scores," said Corsi. To a Roma fan, players from Milan are the enemy.

It's no surprise that race is an incendiary topic on Corsi's radio program. Racial tension in Italy is not confined to football. A record number of immigrants from North African countries and others land on Italian shores each year, straining resources and pitting citizens against newcomers.

Corsi tried to downplay this tension in the sports world, commenting, "Two or three years ago, Roma fans chanted monkey sounds at a very white Swedish player that was playing against Roma just to make fun of the idea they are racist."

While Roma fans might have directed monkey chants as a joke toward a white player, they have also been documented slinging such chants at black players. In 2013, when Roma faced Milan, fans hurled racial abuse at Balotelli and his black teammate, Kevin-Prince Boateng. The match was halted for almost two minutes. Balotelli turned to the stands and raised his finger to his lips to shush the crowd. Two separate announcements were made via the loudspeaker, warning fans that the match could be cancelled if the behavior continued. Play resumed once the offending chants died down. A.C. Roma was fined €50,000 euros for the transgressions of the fans. FIFA and UEFA try to punish racial abuse with fines, match bans, and stadium closures but still face criticism for the persistence of hatred.

For Roberto Massucci, deputy director of the National Observatory on Sports Events, part of Italy's Ministry of the Interior, racism is a scourge because people are at their worst during a football match. "We arrest normal people. Young guys, a lot of them are good students. They come from a good family, but on Sunday, they change their behavior and abdicate any personal responsibility," said Massucci from his office in the historic Palazzo del Viminale near the main train station in Rome.

Most of the disorder that crosses his desk isn't related to hostility among fans of opposing teams. "The enemy is not the other supporters," stated Massucci. "It's the police. Fans think law enforcement is out to get them and destroy their enjoyment of the match."

Do the supporters agree with this assessment? My next stop was a law office in Rome, where I found myself sitting in the front room waiting for the one of the ultras' go-to defense attorneys, Lorenzo Contucci, to meet with me. Gun magazines graced sleek black shelves. Contucci is a criminal defense lawyer, after all.

An A.S. Roma fan, Contucci has represented hundreds of fans who have found themselves banned from matches for transgressions like throwing flares and fighting. Contucci arrived and welcomed my translator and me into his office. He concurred with Massucci, with whom he probably shares little other common ground. "The first enemy of the fans all over Italy actually is the police. Twenty years ago, it was the other supporters. Now, it's the police," Contucci contended.

But to Contucci, Massucci and the police have it wrong with regard to racism, and it's not just a question of normal people getting swept up in the excitement. In his view, there's no avoiding one's political leaning in the Curva. He elaborated, "If I am right wing, I am a right winger also in the stadium. If I am left wing, I am a left winger in the stadium, too." Racism flows from racists, but he too subscribes to the "Balotelli is a jerk" school of thought, bringing some of the harassment on himself because he is an "asshole."

Such measures as public awareness efforts, fines, stadium closures that force teams to play to empty seats, and even arrests are in place to try to stop the racism. But it seems that roadblocks persist at the highest levels.

In Italy, the newly elected leader of the Italian Football Association, which oversees amateur football in Italy, was investigated for referring to African players as banana eaters. At the 2014 World Cup, the FIFA official charged with keeping racist abuse out of the games publicly complained that his group wasn't properly staffed to investigate. During the month-long tournament, fans from multiple countries chanted gay slurs, attended matches wearing blackface make-up, and brandished banners with far-right symbols, acts that went unsanctioned by FIFA, despite a pledge of zero tolerance. Brazilian authorities did arrest two fans for hate speech after they chanted racist insults, violating Brazilian hate speech law.

There's a well-known ultra motto that says, "You will never understand if you're not one of us." As an American, I see how this can be true. I can't imagine fans in the United States systemically yelling racial epithets at players from the stands.

That doesn't mean there are no racial issues here. In the United States, we've had national moments of racial conflict—the Civil War, the Jim Crow era, desegregation in the 1960s, and the recent shootings of young African American men like Trayvon Martin in Florida and Michael Brown in Ferguson, Missouri. Law enforcement still stereotypes African Americans, and racial profiling of black motorists persists. Prejudice does manifest itself on the playing field. Americans have spewed racist and antigay venom and ethnic slurs. High school students in New York unfurled a confederate flag to taunt black players on an opposing team. And after watching P. K. Subban, a black player for the Montreal Canadiens, score a game-winning goal in double overtime, Boston Bruins fans sent, by one measure, more than 200 racist tweets voicing their displeasure with the outcome.

Nevertheless, I'd like to think that the United States is a more multicultural society, where monkey chants would not persevere. It's hard to imagine overt, organized displays of racial intolerance inside a stadium as part of the fabric of today's game, even at the hands of a vocal minority.

Radio show host Mario Corsi admitted that calling a black man a monkey is racist but said it's not as bad as being a member of the Ku Klux Klan. And he's right. In the United States, we don't have fans who walk around calling themselves weekend racists—you're either all in or all out. If true, it's a European custom I can't relate to, perhaps like the practice of not tipping wait staff.

A CULTURE OF *CAMPANILISMO*

To understand the passions that swirl in the hearts of fans outside the United States, history is a helpful starting point. Nationalist, ethnic, and political identities are imbedded in fandom, which isn't the case in the United States. In America, Republicans and Democrats often sit side by side, united by a sports team, but in other countries, fan groups can embrace specific political leanings and ideologies. Ultras in countries like Ukraine, Turkey, and Egypt have aligned to protest government.

Franjo Tudjman, the first president of independent Croatia, once remarked that "football victories shape a nation's identity as much as wars do." In 1990, a match between two rival Yugoslav teams, Red Star Belgrade and Dinamo Zagreb, erupted into thunderous violence and was shut down after only ten minutes of play. Police unleashed tear gas on the crowd, and more than 60 people were injured. The tension was considered a symbol of the burgeoning independence movement throughout the Balkan region, as the game pitted Croats (Dinamo Zagreb) against Serbs (Red Star Belgrade). A year later, the Yugoslav wars would officially start, followed by some of the world's most brutal bloodshed.

In Italy, the lines of rivalry are drawn according to region. "I am more Roman than Italian," Lorenzo Contucci explained to me, adding,

> We are a nation only since the nineteenth century, but we are barely a nation. A guy in Naples feels more Neapolitan than Italian, and if you go to Bergamo in the North you can't understand a word they say. In this kind of culture, it's more intense between football fans because we are very connected with our city.

The concept of *campanilismo*—the sense of belonging to one's hometown or province, more so than to the country as a whole—comes from the Italian word campanile, which translates to church tower, usually the most important and tallest building in a town. On the field, clashes are often rooted in historical rivalries that may date from the Middle Ages. "We fight against other teams because of the *campanilismo*," said Mario Corsi, the Roman radio show host.

TUSCAN TIFOSI

Parum-pum-pum, parum-pum-pum. The staccato beat of a drum bounced off the ancient masonry during my visit to the Renaissance city of Siena in the Tuscany region of Italy. A crowd had gathered to watch what looked like a marching band. As I navigated the narrow cobblestone streets, trying to get to Piazza del Campo, the town center, a group of men dressed in ceremonial garb paraded by me. They were wearing green velvet coats that stopped at their rears to reveal tights, with one leg green and one red. No pants. Some were banging on drums and some were waving giant flags in the same color scheme as their clothing. The band looked more court jester than college halftime, but their demeanor was serious. They were carrying on a centuries-old tradition.

Since 1597, Siena has been home to the oldest horse race in the world, Il Palio. Run twice a year, the Palio pits neighborhoods (in Italian, each neighborhood is known as a *contrada*) against one another in a smash-mouth battle for civic pride. Jockeys dressed in the elaborate colors and symbols of each *contrada* race bareback, making tight circles around the main square. A huge crowd swells in the center of the square, cheering from the depths of their cores.

There are 17 different *contrade*, but only ten compete in the race. Each is usually named for an animal, but other symbols are also used, for instance, a seashell or a tower. The marching band I ran into was from the *drago*, or dragon *contrada*. Golden dragons were etched onto their elaborate red and green flags.

I made it to the piazza where the Palio was scheduled to take place in a little more than a month. While Siena is known for its majestic horse race, it's also known for a floundering football team. That evening, A. C. Siena, a second-tier, or Serie B club, was taking on Padova in a last-ditch effort to qualify for the playoffs. I was headed to the Bar Manganelli, where football fans converge for pregame revelry. The top league, Serie A, had just finished its season, as the players had to get ready for the FIFA World Cup. Serie B still had a few more weeks to go.

Over drinks and bar snacks, three football fans explained to me in a mix of Italian and English the latest on the predicament of their team. Luciano Sardone works as a television anchor and would be covering the match later. Pietro Poggi owns a takeaway pizza restaurant across the piazza, and Simone Bernini sells water wholesale. I asked their *contrada*. Sardone is a tortoise, Poggi a goose, and Bernini a shell.

For years, Siena players wore jerseys emblazoned with the name of the team's sponsor, the oldest bank in the world, Monte dei Pacshi di Siena. A Sienese institution since 1472, and even older than the Palio, the bank's fortunes were intertwined with the city's, as profits were distributed in multiple civic channels. But with the financial crash of 2008 and an ongoing trading scandal, Monte dei Paschi nearly defaulted and had to be bailed out by the government. The bank pulled their sponsorship of the football team, and the team has since teetered on the edge of collapse.

For Siena's supporters, the biggest threat they face isn't a hostile police force or an aggressive cluster of opposing fans. It's that their beloved team may cease to exist if the ownership can't straighten out the team's finances. Winning the game and qualifying for the playoffs would put them one step closer to being promoted to Serie A. With Serie A comes television money that would help finance the team. If the team failed to advance and was forced to shut down, it would be an unspeakable tragedy for the fans, shredding to pieces their sense of identity and civic pride. The goose, tortoise, and shell scoffed when I tried to offer solace that the World Cup was coming up in a month. Siena is where their hearts are, not the Italian national team.

The bar's owner came over to chat. He was excited to share his past as an ultra from Verona, another Italian city to the north. He brought with him a hardbound book containing lavish photos and text in Italian that I couldn't really understand but that appeared to be a history of Veronese football fans. The photos illustrated a violent existence—he and his friends were depicted fighting and wielding batons, with some even wearing Nazi insignia. Verona has a history of a staunch right-wing fan base, and he expressed no shame about the Nazi symbols.

The piazza suddenly became packed, and I started thinking that there was no way all the people could be football fans; A.C. Siena doesn't draw that well. The locals—it looked to be the entire town—were gathering for an announcement of the final competitors for the Palio race. There were three spots remaining, chosen by lottery. There was no loudspeaker or celebrity stand-in to call out the winner. Rather, someone inside the town hall, which dates from the thirteenth century, thrust the flag of the chosen *contrade* out the window of the half stone, half brick building. The locals held their breath in the hope that their neighborhood would be picked. The *onda*, or wave; the *pantera*, or panther; and the *lupa*, the wolf, were chosen. Ecstatic shouts rang out. People from the winning *contrade* began to sing and cheer, reminiscent of football supporters. The marching bands were the first to depart the square after the ceremony. We soon followed and made our way to the football match.

In Siena, the football field, or ground, is located in a park-like setting, adjacent to town. A hotel and apartment building overlook the field. Siena wears white, Padova bright red. Two children sat in front of my translator and me, waving flags. They were nine and ten, and came with their uncle, who sat behind them, up higher. There were quite a few empty seats. The man who sat next to me explained in fragmented English that there are always empty seats and that people no longer come to the stadium since they put the games on television. A banner emblazoned with the phrase "In spite of everything: heart and fighting spirit," according to my translator, hung across from us. The supporters we met at the bar had disappeared into the crowd. Sardone had gone off to work, while Poggi and Bernini ventured off to sit in the ultra section.

As play unfolded, one man screamed that the visiting team was comprised of "fat men of shit." Another shouted that a Padova player had the ass of a married woman. My translator told me that she would have to go to church for a week to get over the curses we were hearing in the stands. In a heartening win, Siena got by Padova, 2–0. Both goals were scored by Alessandro Rosina, one in each half, keeping the team's playoff hopes alive.

But the team ultimately failed to make the playoffs. Six weeks later, A.C. Siena filed for bankruptcy and was promptly dissolved. More than 100 years of history were erased. The fans I had met were devastated. "Sore, offended, and hopeless" is how one describes himself in an e-mail. If reformed, the team will have to start at the bottom rungs of the Italian football system and work its way back up—a challenge for sure—but it has been done before. It's a sad death knell that rang from the campanile for A.C. Siena.

KNIVES IN THE HANDS OF BANDITS

While many countries have a reputation for vicious fans, the place where the conduct of football fans has proven the most deadly and uncontrollable is Latin America, with the violence usually coming at the hands of controversial fan groups.

Brazil, a country whose national identity is immersed in the game and that produces the best players in the world, has a sickening resume of fan violence. Crime and corruption rage on and often go unpunished. Combine this lawlessness with intense football fanaticism and stadiums become home to regular displays of unbridled thuggery.

In 2014, in the city of Recife, a fan was killed by a toilet bowl that had been ripped from a stadium bathroom and thrown at him by rival fans. That same year, approximately 100 supporters of Corinthians, a S ão Paulo team whose largest fan club totals almost 100,000 members, invaded the team's practice facility by cutting through a fence with wire cutters. Upset with the team's performance, fans went after several players with weapons. In June 2013, at an amateur game in the northern state of Maranhão, a referee stabbed a player to death on the field. In retaliation, the official was stoned by the crowd and then beheaded. Yes, beheaded.

With gruesome stories like these, Brazil leads the world with the number of fans killed at the hands of other fans in and around the stadium. In the 25-year period between 1988 and 2013, 234 people have died. The largest country in Latin America actually passed Europe's leader, Italy, in the lethal fan category almost two decades ago. In 2013 alone, 30 fans were killed. "These horrible statistics are what keeps fans from going to matches." said Juca Kfouri, one of the most respected Brazilian football journalists, who has been covering the sport for various outlets for more than 40 years. Through a translator, he explained that the "country struggles to fill its stadiums. Average attendance is 15,000, which is actually less than Major League Soccer in the U.S." Kfouri tried to explain the complex epidemic of violence in Brazil, saying, "Laws cannot control the uneducated masses when organized crime dominates. Football sadly reflects what is happening in wider society."

The fan groups are called Torcidas Organizadas. In the past, the original groups were well-intentioned, carrying flags and bringing musical instruments in support of the team, but Kfouri described the modern-day groups as "mafia." The *torcidas* are extremely influential and known for fighting with everyone, especially supporters of their own team who belong to rival *torcidas*. Some veer into criminal activity like drug dealing. Oftentimes intimately involved with the inner workings of the club, *torcidas* resell tickets, hawk products, and influence personnel decisions. When the team is flailing, players may find themselves under physical attack by these fans. According to Kfouri, their organizing principle is, "If you don't win, we will terrorize you."

Players rarely criticize the controversial fan groups for fear of antagonizing them, but in the spring of 2014, standout striker Fred (footballers in Brazil often go by just a first name), who plays for Fluminense and the

Brazilian national team, bravely spoke out after experiencing a threat firsthand. As he was getting into his car after training one day, he was surrounded by about 20 angry supporters. He finally extricated himself and sped off. "We need to look hard at these groups," Fred later posted on social media. "They're responsible for the majority of deaths in soccer, they get their team banned from playing at their own stadium, and they're infiltrated by *marginais* who drive ordinary fans away from games." He poetically explained, "The flags that fluttered in the stands before have been turned into knives in the hands of these bandits." Needless to say, the *torcidas* were not pleased with Fred's commentary.

Club management often looks the other way. "They depend a lot on the support of the organizadas to win political elections, so the clubs are scared to take action," explained Kfouri. "Fan groups regard police and the law with impunity. Brazil has never been able to put into practice measures that are proven to control fan violence." After the storming of the Corinthians training center, a judge discharged several of the fans involved, calling them "loyal supporters."

In Argentina, hardcore fandom is eerily similar to that in Brazil, with controversial fan groups, heavy-handed intimidation of players, and deadly outcomes. In that country's top league, known as Primera División, there were 15 football-related deaths in 2013. Since the founding of professional football in 1924 through the fall of 2014, 290 deaths have occurred in Argentina, according to the activist group Salvemos al Futbol (Save Our Football).

The deadliest incident took place in 1968, in the Superclásico, a century-old rivalry match played by football clubs Boca Juniors and River Plate, both located in the capital city of Buenos Aires. More than 70 fans died in a stampede at the exit, and some 500 were injured. Multiple explanations exist as to what happened, ranging from locked gates to fans fleeing burning flags and urine bombs, or the official version that it was simply an accident. Unlike Hillsborough in England, there was no investigation that brought meaningful change to stadium security and crowd management. Some say stadiums in Argentina have barely changed.

Most of the violence comes from organized gangs known as *barras bravas*, the Argentinean version of a vicious football ultra group. Kfouri said the disheartening statistics should be regarded as even more disturbing because Argentina is one-fifth the size of Brazil. Law enforcement tries to stem the violence but with minimal success. Almost 2,100 Argentine football fans who were identified as potential troublemakers were prohibited from traveling to Brazil for the 2014 World Cup. And for matches held in Buenos Aires for the 2014 season, visiting fans were banned from attending games by the country's football association because of fears of violence. If banning fans is what it takes to play matches free of violence and abuse, be it in Latin America or Europe, it leads one to ask, what exactly is the point?

According to the former director of Salvemos al Futbol, Monica Nizzardo, half of the representatives on the executive board of the organization have family members who have been victims of the violence. In a 2011 speech at a conference on sport and society, she told the audience that she dreamt of the extinction of her group. "That will be the day when the violent and corrupt people are finally behind bars, and we can feel safe inside any stadium, enjoying a sporting event in peace," she said.

"Football is popular because stupidity is popular," said Argentina's Jorge Luis Borges. Borges was one of Latin America's most profound literary voices. He died in 1986, and clearly was not much of a sports fan. Investigating these tales of fan violence makes it harder to dispute his sentiments—regardless of country.

4

YOUR BRAIN ON SPORTS

Those who can make you believe absurdities can make you commit atrocities.—Voltaire

One Sunday night in Seattle, during the 2013 season, Seahawk fans shrieked their way into the *Guinness Book of World Records* with the loudest crowd roar ever recorded (136.6 decibels) for a sporting event. But the record would not last: It was broken by Kansas City Chiefs fans, reset in Seattle later that season, and broken again the next season. Regardless, an official from Guinness described the racket as a "far louder, tribal kind of passion." Tribal. It's a throwaway term for people trying to understand fan behavior.

For Sunday Night Football's broadcast, veteran sideline reporter Michele Tafoya was standing on the edge of the field during that record-breaking game, gathering last-minute information. When retired Seahawk running back Shaun Alexander raised the flag, the din began and she braced herself. Having covered hundreds of football games in her career, she still found the atmosphere at CenturyLink Field unmatched. "It's the loudest environment I've ever been in," she said. "Period." For Tafoya to communicate with her producers, she had to speak louder than in any other stadium and remind them to talk even more clearly than they normally would. "To have that sense of hearing almost eliminated from the equation just makes it tougher on all sides," Tafoya added.

A group of sports fans gathered together is indeed tribal. But it makes sense. For millions of years, humans lived in groups, hunted together, and competed for limited resources. This wiring lives on in us as an evolutionary adaptation.

TRIBAL CONNECTIONS

In a 1988 book entitled *Tribes*, written by two Brits, Desmond Morris, a zoologist, and Peter Marsh, a psychologist, one must only turn to the third page to find a reference to football hooligans. The authors write that, "Sportsmen and their followers are the closest analogue we have today to the age-old human tribal hunters," underscoring the belief that our brain is literally primed to bond with our team and other fans.

Tribal bonding leads to hostility toward other tribes. "Regardless of whether the groups concerned are establishment-backed or rebels: foxhunters or football hooligans, commandos or criminals, trade unionists or terrorists, Boy Scouts or Hell's Angels," write Morris and Marsh, "all obey basically the same rules. We hate those who oppose us and praise those who support us."

When I moved across the country to California, I joined the transplanted New Yorker tribe, bonding with new friends over a mutual dislike of the Philadelphia Phillies, the Vancouver Canucks, and the Los Angeles Lakers. Our trash talk was tame compared to the fights, taunting, and torching of couches and other tales of fan misbehavior, but it was still aggressive, which may just be a preexisting condition of human nature. Our tribal ways wire us for aggression; we must protect ourselves from those outside our own group.

The ancient instinct of tribalism isn't the only trigger for sports fan violence. The fact that fans are watching brain-damaging sports can make a difference. While sports aren't quite bloodthirsty spectacles, as were the gladiator battles, there is an unrelenting brutality to football, hockey, boxing, and mixed martial arts. Combine other factors that can contribute to aggression, for instance, heat and alcohol, and the pump is primed for sports fans.

History shows varying viewpoints on the effect of watching sports. One of the earliest explorations of on-the-field and off-the-field aggression is the essay "The Why of the Fan," a Freudian treatise written by A. A. Brill in 1929. Brill claims that watching sports provides a sense of catharsis and drains aggressive impulses. An American pioneer, he was the original translator of Sigmund Freud's work into English and opened the first private psychoanalysis practice in the United States. Here was an important psychiatrist writing that fandom is good for the soul and will eradicate violent tendencies. In Brill's eyes, sports helped men "achieve exaltation, vicarious but real" and become "a better individual, a better citizen, a better husband and father." According to Brill, "no fight fan could be a criminal." He also notes that the Ku Klux Klan and lynchings flourished where sports were scarce. I'm not sure what methodology he used in the 1920s to come up with this misguided notion. At the time, Klan activity was strong, not just in the South, but also in the Midwest. Detroit, for example, was home to such Klan activities as cross burning, but it was also home to Major League Baseball's Tigers and a professional hockey franchise that would become the Detroit Red Wings. The Freudians should probably stick to sex.

THE NATURE VERSUS NURTURE LOOP

Nowadays, most psychologists see catharsis and its emotional purging as a myth, backed up by a half-century worth of data. Experts have learned that watching violent sports is not a safety valve for emotional release. Current psychology espouses that aggression is the product of both internal and external or environmental factors—nature and nurture. Behavior is shaped by social environment, which is how we can become good citizens or bad ones. Complex social behaviors like aggression are acquired by the direct experience of watching how others act, known as "social learning." In other words, watching brutal sports can instigate brutality in fans.

The man behind social learning theory is Stanford University psychology professor emeritus Albert Bandura. Bandura is 88 years old but far from retired. As I drive up to his home, in a leafy neighborhood that houses many Stanford faculty, an empty plastic tub sitting atop a wooden chair in his driveway catches my eye. Bandura recently underwent cataract surgery and has little vision in one eye but is still hard at work on his latest manuscript. He leaves handwritten pages for his assistants to retrieve for typing in the plastic tub since he never learned to type himself. He also delegates his e-mails to others.

Bandura is responsible for a landmark study using plastic clown dolls, which I remember as part of the curriculum in my freshman year of college psych class. Starting in the mid-1960s, he conducted studies of children playing with Bobo dolls, those cheap, five-foot-tall, inflatable plastic clown dolls. Adults hit, kicked, and yelled at the dolls in front of preschoolers. What followed was alarming, as the children went on to mimic the adult behavior and attack the dolls themselves.

According to Bandura, the aggression even carried over to other forms of play: "In their games with animals, they were fighting with each other, trucks were banging into each other. And they were more likely to pick up a gun and start shooting at the Bobo doll. So what it was doing was really activating much more general aggressive tendencies."

How does Bandura think this relates to the sports fan? He explained that the violence in sports and other forms of entertainment not only teaches people to be aggressive, but also rewards aggression and desensitizes and habituates people to it. "If you aren't upset by it that much, you're also reluctant to act on it if you see it," said Bandura. "That's how violence becomes an insidious norm."

He points to the research of another psychology professor, Leonard Berkowitz, now retired from the University of Wisconsin. Beginning in the mid-1960s, Berkowitz showed university students clips of a seven-minute fight scene from the 1949 boxing film *Champion*, in which star Kirk Douglas gets pummeled. In one experiment, a group viewed the brutal fight scene, while another group viewed a nonviolent track meet. In another, assistants running the test angered the subjects beforehand. Some of these instigators were referred to by the name "Kirk," like the star of the film, and some were more generically called "Bob."

Results showed that students who had watched the clip would readily administer electric shocks to others if they had been angered ahead of time and when there was a cue in the environment, for instance, a name similarity. The violent programming primed people for aggression. Other experiments have since produced similar results.

These scientific findings can be seen throughout the sports world. If violent media grooms people for aggression, imagine the effect of raw and unscripted live sports. Retired NFL player and FOX Sports 1 commentator Brendon Ayanbadejo explained his relationship with violence in the following way: "I wanna play at the edge. I wanna play violent. But I want to play controlled. I want to play right on the brink of insanity but controlled chaos." According to Ayanbadejo, "Fans have those same emotions and those same feelings when they're cheering for their teams." If the violent impulses exist for the athlete and fan alike, how much self-control can either exert?

While I was focused on sports fans learning crazy behavior from crazed competitors, Bandura tried to steer me to see the good that can come from mimicked behavior. "We often emphasize the negative," he told me. "The effect of efficacy on spectators, depending on how it's structured, can be exceedingly powerful in the positive way." For example, Bandura proudly explained his involvement in producing television dramas for social good in countries like Mexico and Nigeria. For these shows, writers create story lines that address such global issues as family planning and literacy. "My theory also puts a lot of emphasis on social modeling to produce change," he said. "We do a pretty thorough analysis—what are the problems people are struggling with, what are the impediments to change, how can we build their vision of a better future, and how can we inform, enable, and motivate them to take the steps to realize it." He cited a real-life increase in contraceptive sales in Mexico, which he interprets as a response to one of the story lines. What's becoming clear is how powerful the experience of watching others can be on spectator behavior. Thugs get a charge from the action they see on the field.

ETHICAL FREE AGENTS

Bandura is focusing his current work on what he calls "moral disengagement," and this is actually the subject of his next book. "There's a fantastic erosion of our morality across all of our institutions," he commented, adding that plenty of good people do evil things, even when they know better. Look no further than the tobacco or banking industries. Among the mechanisms of moral disengagement, "You minimize the seriousness of what you're doing," related Bandura. "Another is to diffuse responsibility—everyone is doing it!"

These are things I've heard from sports fans before with regard to questionable behavior. The first Vancouver Stanley Cup rioter from 2011 to be sentenced to jail time claimed he got "caught up in the moment," a moment shared with thousands of other rioters. The former hooligans I met stressed that they were football supporters first and downplayed most fighting as incidental.

Fan ugliness gets rationalized with a variety of phrases, for example, "bracketed morality," "cognitive dissonance," or—my favorite—the illustrative "Lucifer Effect," coined by another influential retired psychologist from Stanford, Philip Zimbardo. In the Bible, Lucifer was God's favorite angel. He fell from grace and ultimately turned into Satan.

Zimbardo is best known as the father of the notorious 1971 Stanford Prison Experiment, which created a simulated prison staffed with student volunteers to test the extent to which identity conforms to a specific social setting. Students randomly assigned to be prison guards became mean and controlling, while those assigned to the role of inmates became antiauthoritarian and withdrawn. The volunteers accepted their roles so completely that Zimbardo feared the outcome of his experiment and shut it down six days early. More than 30 years later, he published a book called *The Lucifer Effect*, in which he attempts to explain how good people do evil things. If you've ever read Dr. Seuss's book about Sneetches, which pits creatures with stars on their bellies against those who don't have them, you know what I mean.

According to Zimbardo, who testified in 2004 as an expert witness for one of the Abu Ghraib prison guards who was facing a court-martial, it's not a matter of a few "bad apples," but a "bad barrel"—the social setting and system contaminate the individual. He cautioned us to examine collective responsibility for atrocities. "If you want to change a person, you've got to change the situation," said Zimbardo in a 2008 Ted Talk. "If you want to change the situation, you've got to know where the power is, in the system." Extrapolating that to the sports world puts the blame for bad behavior on the sporting institutions themselves.

Florida State University social psychologist Roy Baumeister, author of *Evil: Inside Human Violence and Cruelty*, originated the phrase "The myth of pure evil." He says that most people who perpetrate evil do not see what they are doing as evil. Writes Baumeister, evil can be better understood if looked at from the perpetrator's point of view, not the victim's.

Most violence originates from everyday experiences. Baumeister lists "frustration, violent movies, poverty, hot weather, alcohol, and unfair treatment" as potential triggers. Since everyone experiences frustrations like these, the question then becomes, Why isn't evil even more of a norm? Baumeister's response is that "regardless of the root causes of violence, the immediate cause is often a breakdown of self-control." "To understand evil," Baumeister continues, "we must set aside the comfortable belief that we would never do anything wrong. Instead, we must begin to ask ourselves, what would it take for me to do such things?"

It dawned on me that sports already provides fans with a bit of an ethical wasteland and presents a well-equipped stage for fans to harness aggression, ignore customary ethical norms, and act out in inexplicable ways. Watching sports is a great way to escape reality. Marketers embrace this connection and run with it. Look at the ESPN ad campaign for Monday Night Football from a few years ago. Several television commercials in the series show fans who abandon their mundane jobs, in pest control or crane operation, for instance, so that they can get comfortable on the couch to watch that week's NFL matchup.

Fans can get away with lots of crazy behavior that wouldn't be accepted elsewhere. You can't interact with your coworkers or neighbors like you do with other fans. There are "fan norms"—wearing face paint or going shirtless to showcase your painted beer belly with the team colors—that just wouldn't fly at the office. That's got to be against company policy. If you incessantly taunt the guy next to you on the subway about his lousy chances of getting a seat, transit police would accuse you of harassment, but taunting a friend about his fantasy football shortcomings is considered acceptable. Picking on your neighbor via Twitter like you might pick on Kevin Durant would get you ostracized at the next block party.

No sporting contest exists unless it's under the watchful eye of an official like a referee or umpire. The message is that players and coaches will cheat unless policed. There are plenty of examples of cheating, for instance, flopping in basketball or soccer (where a player feigns injury with the hope of drawing a personal foul on an opponent), sneaking a sticky substance onto your hands in baseball, or the surreptitious videotaping of opponents during a NFL practice. These underlie a highly competitive spirit, a win-at-all-costs mentality.

And don't forget the powerful experience of a crowd, where it is easy to blend in and divest yourself from individual responsibility for behavior. In a throng of people, it may feel easier to morally disengage from one's actions. Seems to me that this isn't good news for the sports world. So far this portrait of the sports fan as aggressive, suggestible, and morally elastic seems unduly harsh. This can't be all there is—or can it? The message from science is that your personality definitely changes when you watch sports—and there isn't that much you can do about it.

In trying to understand the psychological underpinnings of the fan, I poured over scholarly research that closely studied the sports spectator. Throughout the years scientists have run brain scans on Yankee and Red Sox fans; measured testosterone levels in the saliva of Brazilians watching the World Cup; and recorded hundreds of occasions of what they term collective manipulation (clapping), collective verbalization (booing), and collective vertical locomotion (jumping).

Some great acronyms have been developed to explain fan behavior. To BIRG is to "bask in the reflected glory" of a team's success. Another acronym has its origins from the mid-1970s, when Robert Cialdini, a psychology and marketing professor at Arizona State University, noticed that students were more likely to wear clothing with team logos on Monday after a Saturday football victory than after a defeat. The same effect happened in speech; after a win, students talked about the team as though they were a part of that team. Pronoun of choice? "We." After a defeat, "we won" became "they lost." Subsequent research introduced the term *CORF*, meaning fans "cut off reflected failure" to distance themselves from a defeat.

SPORTS FANS 101

The academic most closely associated with fan psychology today is 51-year-old Daniel Wann. He is the rock star of his field, a psychology professor at Murray State University in Kentucky, who has consulted for professional leagues and Fortune 500 companies on fan psychology. He's authored or coauthored nearly 200 papers and three books on fan behavior dating to the late 1980s.

Eager to meet "The Man" himself, I found myself in a cab in Albuquerque, New Mexico, with a driver who swears he is Walter White, the chemistry-teacher-turned-meth-dealer main character from television's hit show *Breaking Bad*. He was wearing a black Walter White alter ego "Heisenberg" pork pie hat. It occurred to me that he was an example of a grown man worshipping an imaginary, dead character. Fandom is outsized everywhere.

I was in town to attend the Sports Marketing Association Conference. Although the name doesn't necessarily reflect it, it is an academic conference for wonks from the fields of sociology, psychology, marketing, and sports management who study sports fan behavior, a three-day affair held at the Hyatt Regency hotel in the heart of downtown Albuquerque. I met Wann for breakfast to talk about his latest research. Among other topics, I was particularly interested in what makes sports fans so crazy and just how pervasive moral disengagement can be.

After speaking with Wann on the phone a few times, researching his career and screening his various television appearances, I anointed him "King of the Questionnaire," because that is how he conducts much of his research, distributing online questionnaires to students who attend games, usually college basketball. For our meeting he was dressed like a college basketball coach, wearing a collared golf shirt with a Murray State logo and khakis. Growing up a die-hard Kansas City Royals fan, he told me that while attending graduate school at the University of Kansas, he met fellow social psychology students who complained of having to conduct boring research. Wann figured that investigating sports fans might help him get through his Ph.D. program, and he was right. He's the type of guy who, in his studies of sports fans, loves to share anecdotes like the one of a Dallas Cowboys fan who stole a television to watch a Cowboys playoff game but was arrested when he returned to the scene of the crime to steal the remote control.

His key concept is that of "team identification," the extent to which a fan feels psychologically connected to a team. The more "highly identified" a fan is, the more likely that fan is to engage in bizarre and sometimes abusive behavior. An example is the San Jose Sharks fan who removed her bra and threw it on the ice after a player scored three goals in one game, a feat known as a hat trick. She apparently forgot to wear a hat that day, the item most people choose to express their exuberance. The fan told a reporter, "It was a gorgeous red Victoria's Secret garment," and the red color complemented the Russian player who had scored the three goals. Now that's high identification.

Wann has worked to dispel the concept that "many die-hard fans are lonely, alienated people searching for self-esteem by identifying with a sports team." On the contrary, he said that commitment to a team raises feelings of self-worth and prevents depression. Winning raises confidence levels and the hormone testosterone, according to his research.

Losses promote pessimism and a hormonal drop. Yet, sports fans remain connected to their team despite a 50-50 chance that they will walk away from any given event disappointed. "The craziest thing about sports fans is that there are sports fans at all," Wann said, commending a fan's commitment to losing, as well as winning.

Between bites of breakfast and sips of coffee, Wann tried to explain the thoroughly bad fan, the ones he said are simply too wrapped up in the game for their own good. These fans are in the minority, but because their behavior stands out, they garner attention. "They are poops," he related, lowering his voice to a whisper. "Assholes. The technical term is 'dysfunctional fan.'" He said it is a personality type. "These are the same people who were bullies as children, the same ones that have very high levels of assertiveness and impulsivity."

In 2006, Wann, along with a professor of marketing from Baylor University, Kirk Wakefield, devised a scale to measure the asshole, or "dysfunctional fan." According to the paper they published, the results were "not a pretty picture." They learned that the dysfunctional fan is more likely to be the guy abusing the ref and thinking it is perfectly acceptable behavior. He's the fan who feels the need to drink at games and complains the most, often about the stadium food options. He's likely to travel for away games, where arguing with rival fans can fast track physical confrontation. Finally, the dysfunctional fan spends a significant part of his daily life watching, listening, and reading about his team. I say "his" because the dysfunctional fan is most likely male and single. In addition, the more dysfunctional a fan is, the less educated and lower income they are. According to Wakefield and Wann, "These individuals appear to make a career out of engaging in confrontational behaviors extending well beyond the arena or stadium walls on game days."

These types of fans may be true criminals. "We anticipate that future research may find that the antisocial behavior of dysfunctional sports fans is not confined to the stadium or arena—but that the sporting event context gives rise to circumstances where the true nature of the individual quickly rises to the surface," write the authors. I take that to mean if you think you are sitting next to a real knucklehead, stick with your gut and try to move away.

Wann has also conducted research examining the idea of moral disengagement amongst sports fans. In 1999, he explored fans' willingness to consider anonymous acts of aggression toward a rival team. He found that a sizable minority of basketball fans who strongly identified with a particular team would be willing to injure the star of the rival team prior to the championship game, provided that there was no chance of getting caught. A 2003 follow-up determined that these same fans would be willing to injure the rival team's star or coach *after* the championship game—to act purely out of hostility, rather than in an attempt to help their own team. Sounds like "Lucifer" is indeed lurking in the stands.

I asked Wann if fans are getting worse and if there is any scientific way to quantify the extent of the dysfunction. He smiled and replied that that's the most common question he's been asked in his 25 years of research and that people hate the answer: "The answer really is, 'We don't know.'"

But Wann did say that part of the reason sports fans seem to misbehave more these days is because misbehavior is becoming more acceptable at large. It is not uncommon to hear people complain that modern society doses out large portions of incivility and that our culture is adrift.

Take road rage, for example. I'm pretty sure that in the horse and buggy era, fewer people referred to one another as that favorite freeway insult, "douche bag." There are all sorts of culprits responsible for crassness: the frenetic pace of the digital world, consumerism, a general lack of self-restraint, the decline of heroes and role models, a gradual acceptance of profanity in day-to-day vocabulary. Wann connected the dots by saying, "It is absolutely logical to think that if society is becoming less civil, sports fans must be too."

He conceded that youth sport parents are some of the worst-behaved fans and explained his theory. If one of the best predictors of fan violence is team identification, most parents already have high levels of identification with their children, meaning they sink much of their identity into the achievements of their offspring. Wann said parents' level of identification with their children as athletes is likely increasing. Just look at the emphasis on youth sports in our country. "Fans think professional athletes are spoiled rich jerks so we don't idolize them as much," he continued. "Someone has to take their place, and for some it is their own children." Thus, it makes sense that if higher identification denotes higher aggression and parents' identification with their kids is on the rise, there should also be a rise of parental aggression at youth sporting events.

MOLDING YOUNG MINDS

There's no shortage of evidence for what Wann talked about. Instead of mere healthy competition, it's gotten rather intense on youth playing fields throughout the United States. In 2013, officials who oversaw high school sports in Kentucky issued a directive that postgame handshakes must be better supervised by schools because too many fights were breaking out when teams lined up for the ritual. In the mid-1990s, some schools in Ventura County, California, banned the practice for a month.

Kids get this attitude from their parents. Check out a youth sporting event and you'll likely come across parents misbehaving on the sidelines, pushing their kids to win and denigrating them when they don't. Fans or parents at youth sporting events can exhibit shocking behavior, which conditions the next generation of fans to follow in their footsteps and become poor sports.

A friend of mine once told me that his teenage daughter's soccer coach comes to each game armed with a supply of lollipops. Why? So that the coach can hand them out to parents and, in effect, silence them. My friend sheepishly admitted that it is a ploy to keep parents like him quiet. If he is sucking away on candy, he can't be yelling at his daughter for sucking in a different sense of the word.

Yelling is one thing, but sometimes parents go way beyond shouting in the stands. In Massachusetts, a dad tried to temporarily blind an opposing goalie by pointing a laser at her. Outside Chicago, a father issued death threats and threatened to rape a coach's family when the coach substituted another player for his daughter. Parents brawl at games, and police get summoned. Some youth sports leagues have banned parents from talking during games to try to clamp down on the problem. Some have banned parents from attending, period.

Sometimes the bad behavior proves fatal, and children bear witness to the violence. More than one child has seen the death of a parent at the hands of another adult. This happened in 2000, when Massachusetts hockey dad Thomas Junta beat fellow hockey dad Michael Costin to death. Costin was helping coach the youth hockey practice, and Junta attacked him while their sons watched. Junta would clearly be in my Sports Fan Gone Bad Hall of Fame, judging by how many people bring up "that hockey dad and his rink rage." Junta was convicted of involuntary manslaughter, served eight years in prison, and was released in 2010.

Junta's son Quinlan, who witnessed the attack and testified in his father's defense, faced criminal charges of his own for a vicious drug-related home invasion, during which he died of unknown causes in 2011. According to the *Boston Herald*, the priest who conducted the funeral service for Quinlan Junta, Father John Farrell, told the congregation, "We know why we're here, and we search for explanations." He told mourners, "Our enthusiasms and passions should never disgrace, degrade, demean, or destroy anyone else's dignity or worth." Costin's son, Michael Costin Jr., who also witnessed the attack, has since struggled with drug addiction and crime. He served time in jail for domestic violence, among other charges. According to Father Farrell's eulogy, "Violence is always personal."

Sadly, there is a perverse appetite for this type of sideline rage as entertainment. Look no further than Esquire Network's *Friday Night Tykes*, HBO's *Trophy Kids*, and *Sports Dads*, a show that ran on a cable network called Veria Living for 13 episodes in 2011. These shows explore the theme of out-of-control parents in youth sports. While you may have never heard of the Veria Living network, you have probably heard of the show's host, the man who practically invented look-at-me behavior on the playing field, NFL Hall of Famer Deion Sanders. Sanders fronted the short-lived *Sports Dads*, which carried the tag line, "Some Parents Need a Time-Out."

With *Friday Night Tykes*, the fledgling Esquire Network had a critical hit on their hands as soon as the program debuted. The show, set in San Antonio, Texas, follows five different teams of eight and nine year olds who participate in what they claim to be the most competitive youth football league in the country. Coaches push kids to play through pain and tackle hard, sometimes in conflict with best safety practices. If a kid vomits, they return to the field. Parents support the coaches in the name of toughening up their children and teaching them life skills. About halfway into the first season of the show, Illinois senator Dick Durbin, the second highest-ranking Democrat, wrote a letter to the network requesting that they immediately cancel the program because it glorifies violence. The Esquire Network refused to acquiesce.

The set of *Friday Night Tykes* is a football field, where executive producer Matt Marantz and his camera crew stand as dozens of boys run on the field with no particular aim, tearing up grass and tackling one another. Even though they have just finished playing a highly competitive game of tackle football, the boys are still full of energy and show few signs of slowing down.

The children's parents stand midfield, excitedly recapping the game that has just been played. According to Marantz, "They'll dissect every play and what went wrong and what went right. All the kid wants to know is where they're going for ice cream." He added, "The kids don't even remember five seconds after the game whether they won or lost. A lot of times, it means more to the parents than to the kids." He said this dynamic exists at every game.

For each of the program's two seasons, running from July through December, a camera crew documented the games, practice, as well as family time. "To me, the show is not about youth football or even about youth sports," said Marantz. He continued,

> At its heart, the show is about parenting. It's asking questions that every parent asks. "How do we want to raise our kids? How hard is too hard? How young is too young? How far is too far?" We all want to do what's best for our kids, and we all want our kids to succeed. We're all trying to figure out the formula that might equate to happiness and success.

No spectator at a sporting event cares more about an athlete than a parent watching his or her own child play, which creates a playing field ripe for bruised egos and sideline rage. But how do you draw conclusions about every youth sporting event throughout the entire United States? One widely quoted survey from 2003 queried 3,300 parents, coaches, youth sports administrators, and kids, and reported that more than 84 percent said they have witnessed parents acting violently—shouting, berating, using abusive language—toward coaches, officials, and children. Almost 80 percent of those surveyed reported that they had been the target of a violent or inappropriate act. A 2014 survey undertaken by Liberty Mutual Insurance revealed that 50 percent of parents and coaches believe that sportsmanship has worsened in youth sports since they were children.

Wann told me that researchers have even coined a name for the idea that parents become overly involved with kids in the hope that the kid is so talented that they bring home a college scholarship and ascend to a professional career: "Jackpot Theory." Of course, the chance of that happening is infinitesimal. According to the NCAA, less than 1 percent of high school athletes make it to the pros.

Greg Bach, vice president of communications for the National Alliance for Youth Sports (NAYS), said that parental behavior is getting increasingly worse—and he maintains archives of news stories about the bad behavior to prove it. Working for the alliance for more than 20 years, Bach thought the hockey dad case would serve as "a warning and a sign that things were going to change." But Bach said that didn't happen. When Costin was beaten to death, the organization was bombarded with more than 100 interview requests. A youth basketball coach at a seventh grade Amateur Athletic Union basketball game was later allegedly beaten to death by one of the referees after they argued over a call. NAYS didn't receive a single media inquiry. "I wonder if perhaps people are used to it," questioned Bach.

IT'S A MAN'S WORLD

Is bad fan behavior only found in bro-dom? When we think of the stereotypical sports fan, we think of the macho guy wearing a jersey, beer in hand, face red, and arms flailing about. As a producer for ESPN for almost 20 years, I wouldn't argue with this characterization. For this book, most of the studies I consulted focused on male fans. Vancouver police calculated that 89 percent of their rioters were male. All of my harassers from Ohio State were men. It's not that women aren't passionate fans—I'm not interested in denigrating my sisters—but when it comes to the ugly fan, more likely than not, he's a guy.

Throughout history, women have attended sporting events. Unmarried women were permitted at the ancient Olympic Games, and men and women could sit together at the chariot races of Rome. In the early days of professional baseball, women were often considered a civilizing force in the stands, with sportswriters observing that fans cleaned up their language when women were present. Boxing matches became fashionable in the 1920s, and women clamored to attend. When Jack Dempsey faced French fighter Georges Carpentier in 1921's heavily promoted "Fight of the Century," held in Jersey City, New Jersey, 2,000 women were on hand, including Teddy Roosevelt's eldest daughter.

THE FEMALE HOOLIGAN

Forty-year-old Lexi Alexander grew up among the thugs. Raised in Germany, she attended her first football match at the age of seven and immediately got hooked on the atmosphere. As a teen, she tagged along with her older brother while her mom was at work to watch their beloved Waldhof Mannheim play, which also involved running with a hooligan gang. She was one of the few females around. "There are not a lot of girls who want to hang out with guys who beat the shit out of each other," said Alexander.

In Alexander's eyes, hooliganism brought meaning to disconnected lives. "It was a constant, and for a lot of people this was the only constant in their life," she continued. "A kind of substitute family unity. That's really what it was." While she was no stranger to violence—she became a world champion martial artist and went on to work in Hollywood as a stuntwoman—she admitted that she steered clear of the fighting between rival football firms, opting to be more of an observer of the violence: "It was always me sitting on some wall taking pictures of a fight."

After some time, Alexander downshifted her thirst for the violence. "I realized how dangerous it was when I saw a bunch of our guys jump this poor guy who was by himself." In her late teens, she cooled her hooligan association. "It may look romantic for the first 40 minutes, but then it comes to a point when it doesn't and the reality of it hits you."

Alexander moved to the United States and became a filmmaker, garnering an Oscar nomination for a short film she directed. She also directed one of the most unnerving fictional accounts of fan violence with the 2005 film *Green Street Hooligans*. Cowritten with several others, including a former British hooligan, Alexander tells the story of an American who moves to England and embraces the dangerous pleasures of violence by joining a gang of thuggish West Ham supporters.

In the movie, the main character, Matt Buckner, played by Elijah Wood, explains the intoxicating allure of fighting: "I've never lived closer to danger, but I've never felt safer. I've never felt more confident, and people could spot it from a mile away." After the hooligan violence destroys relationships and claims lives, Buckner undergoes an awakening similar to Alexander's and walks away from the destruction.

THE TIES THAT BIND

There may be a reason that the intensity and aggression of hardcore fandom aren't as great for women. The phrase *male bonding* was first introduced in the late 1960s, when Lionel Tiger, a professor of anthropology now retired from Rutgers University, coined the term in his book *Men in Groups*. The book extrapolates on the tribal theme and hypothesizes that man's early ability to cooperatively hunt evolved into contemporary social patterns. In the distant past, men bonded over killing animals for food, while women gathered food. Men remain wired to bond, but since there's not a need to kill for sustenance, powerful alliances are formed in politics, war, work, sports, and secret societies. In a nutshell, men are more hardwired for fandom than women, and aggressive fandom at that. Moreover, male bonding is inextricably linked to aggression, as both are a product and cause of these strong ties. "To reduce opportunities for such aggression is to tamper with an ancient and central pattern of human behavior," writes Tiger.

MEN IN CRISIS

These days, men may have even more reason to wrap themselves in extreme fandom. Masculinity is in transition, according to various authors. Thirty years after *Men in Groups*, Tiger went onto to write *The Decline of Males*. His thesis is that with more women moving into the public sphere and gaining power in the workplace, men are struggling to redefine themselves. In an interview, he specifically cited sports (along with porn) as an outlet for men to express "their inherent maleness, which they may feel otherwise obligated to repress."

Sociologist Michael Kimmel writes about a new stage of life between adolescence and adulthood in his 2008 book *Guyland: The Perilous World Where Boys Become Men*. According to Kimmel, who teaches sociology at Stony Brook University, demographics show that adolescence starts earlier and adulthood later. People now put off marriage and childbearing. The median age for marriage is 27.4 years for men and 25.8 years for women. In the 1950s, it was about five years earlier for both.

One of the favored activities of this extended boyhood is watching sports, but there can be a dangerous toxicity attached to this zone. "Sports talk has become the reconstituted clubhouse, the last 'pure' all-male space in America," says Kimmel. "Men use sports to both hide their feelings and to express their feelings.

"In this topsy-turvy, Peter-Pan mindset, young men shirk the responsibilities of adulthood and remain fixated on the trappings of boyhood, while the boys they still are struggle heroically to prove that they are real men despite all evidence to the contrary," writes Kimmel. If this is the case, male sports fans have a whole new stage of life primed for misbehavior. According to Kimmel, "Like fraternity initiations and binge drinking, sports are sometimes another activity that almost-men engage in to prolong childhood and avoid becoming men—which we think means being sober, responsible, serious fathers and workers, unable to have fun."

While he's primarily talking about white, college-educated Peter Pans in the United States, Kimmel notes similar trends throughout the world— the "laddie" culture of Britain approximates "Guyland," as does the Italian version, known as "bamboccioni" or "mammoni," Mama's boys. "Guyland rests on a bed of middle-class entitlement, a privileged sense that you are special, that the world is there for you to take." Unlike women, he contends, even when men feel powerless, they still feel entitled to power. If you are applying this idea to fandom, it's a recipe for obnoxious behavior.

If aggressive fandom tends to pass women by, is it true that women suffer at the hands of fandom? Yes and no. The belief that intense fandom can harm women is slightly misguided. In an episode of the televised HBO comedy *Curb Your Enthusiasm*, main characters Cheryl and Larry argue after she returns from a trip because he's too distracted by a game on television to properly greet her. To make peace, Larry decides to buy her a bracelet at a jewelry store, but like all "Curb" story lines, Larry complicates matters for himself, and the bracelet solution takes several detours before it succeeds.

But football widowhood like this may be overblown. A research study on couples showed that while women may be less involved with the game, conflicts regarding viewing habits are usually easily resolved.

Another common belief is that intense fandom can be physically threatening to women. Super Bowl Sunday was long touted as the most violent day of the year for domestic violence victims, labeled the "day of dread" by activists and linked to a 40 percent rise in violent incidents. But a probe into that claim by the *Washington Post* in 1993 uncovered a faulty premise: The research was based on a slight increase in emergency room visits following wins by the Washington Redskins and had nothing to do with the Super Bowl.

While Super Bowl Sunday isn't as dangerous as once believed, a study published in 2011, in the *Quarterly Journal of Economics*, reports a connection between fandom and domestic violence. According to the work of UC Berkeley professor David Card and UC San Diego professor Gordon Dahl, a team's loss in a football game leads to a 10 percent rise in domestic violence. In an interview, Card expressed that rage especially spreads if the loss is an upset, comes at the hands of a bitter rival, or takes place during a playoff matchup. "There's a long-standing interest in the idea that an unexpected negative is very bad for your psyche and causes you to be in a really bad mood and to do lots of bad things," said Card.

Other research by Card and Dahl supports the notion that Super Bowl Sunday is a dangerous day, like many other celebratory days, including the Fourth of July, New Year's Eve, and St. Patrick's Day. "Super Bowl Sunday is a very bad day," contended Card, pointing out the potential danger of a festive occasion. "Any time when family members are together in the house, that's bad. After all, you can't beat up your wife if she's not in the building." Card and Dahl looked at Colorado towns and cities during a five-year period and determined that the rate of domestic violence incidents for Super Bowl Sunday was about 30 percent higher than the previous and following Sundays.

Card maintained that the results are noteworthy because of the study's specificity:

> If you're trying to study the effects of most other things on something like family violence, we don't see what any individual person is doing most of the time. But if you think about the exact time of a football game on a Sunday afternoon, you can be sure that a very large chunk of the local audience is watching that game.

SPORTS FANS 201

On the day that I attended the sports marketing conference, I sat in the audience as Wann presented a paper on whether college students remain hardcore fans of their high school teams once they graduate. About ten people gathered in a convention breakout room session to listen. Wann and his coauthors had surveyed almost 500 college students from several midsize universities, tasking them with completing their newly developed questionnaire on hometown influences. The research showed that college students who graduated earlier had lower levels of identification with their high school team, and college students who returned to their hometown had higher levels of identification.

I was a bit disappointed that his paper wasn't about fan aggression, but I learned it's a less sexy topic these days. Apparently trying to understand team identification is more of the trend. According to Wann, most of the research being conducted is about "increasing butts in the seats"—marketing to the fan. "If it's 1975 and you're a major league sports team, your fan base is built in," said Wann, adding, "In 2012, boy, you've got a lot of competition for a very scarce dollar. They're paying players more than they ever had to before. There's a lot more entertainment options for fans, not to mention the fact that they can just watch the game on television or on their computer." In fact, in the study about college students and high school teams, Wann makes branding suggestions for university sports marketers, recommending campaigns at high schools where collegiate stars once played. In the academic world, like so many others, you've got to go where the money is. I'm uncertain where that leaves the quest to understand and prevent fan violence.

5

BEER, HERE!

The beer consumer totally surrounds himself with sports. It's emotional, there's a connection. It's local. It's passionate.—Tony Ponturo, former vice president for Corporate Media and Sports Marketing, Anheuser-Busch

The theme of the 11th annual Beer Summit, a sold-out industry convention, was that the big beer brands are in trouble. Held at the Scottsdale desert resort the Phoenician—with its painterly views of the Sonoran desert, 27 holes of golf, and a pool lined with mother of pearl tiles—about 400 industry analysts and executives sat in a well air-conditioned meeting room, listening to dour statistics on who *isn't* drinking beer these days.

Speaker after speaker explained that for the last ten years, beer has been losing market share. Consumers 30 years of age and younger drank a third less beer in 2012 than 20 years earlier. That key demographic, the millennial generation, apparently disdains most domestic beers, even referring to them as "beer flavored water," as described in one of the presentations. Market research has shown that millennials are more likely to choose from a myriad of other drink options, like brown spirits and microbrew or craft beers made by small, independent brewers.

The man who organized the event was Harry Schuhmacher, the 45-year-old editor and publisher of the industry publication *Beer Business Daily*. Resembling Ernest Hemingway in both affect and wit, Schuhmacher had most of the attendees in a good mood with his shoot-from-the-hip style—despite the unfortunate stats he was tasked with disseminating. He was putting on a lively party for the attendees.

As part of his work, Schuhmacher is afforded behind-the-scenes access to the industry. Every year, he said, sports marketing becomes a more important and more integral part of the presentations he attends. "In the past, the sports marketing guy was kind of like an afterthought," Schuhmacher related. "Now, he's front and center."

Schuhmacher made it clear that for the beverage industry, sports marketing doesn't focus solely on making money at a game. Rather, it focuses on pushing product long-term. It's about association of a brand with game-day fun and team loyalty. The truth is concessions don't make that much money for the beer makers themselves, accounting for less than 1 percent of beer sales by volume in 2013, according to the Beer Institute. It's the concession companies and teams that stand to make the most money from food and drink at the stadium. These revenue figures are typically not disclosed by facility management, but there's little dispute they are a significant part of the income stream.

Schuhmacher grew up in Texas, the son of a beer distributor. He told me that he was five years old when he had his first taste of the family beverage. His grandfather, who was a newspaper publisher in San Antonio, used to drink Lone Star every weekend. Schuhmacher would shadow him as he watered his lawn on Saturday afternoons. "He thought nothing of handing me his beer at intervals and letting me take long pulls from it, even at a young age," said Schuhmacher. "I have always loved the taste of beer, and to this day that first cold sip reminds me of my grandfather." After working as a beer distributor himself for several years, Schuhmacher launched a subscription-only newsletter for the industry. Fifteen years later, he's a thought leader, parsing the drinking habits of young adult consumers the same ages as his own children.

BEER ON THE BRAIN

Sports and beer go hand in hand. In fact, a beer at the ballpark seems as American as the red, white, and blue. But things are changing for both fans and the beer industry. "Millennials are promiscuous drinkers," Schuhmacher commented. "The holy grail of beer marketers is to reach that 21- to 28-year-old drinker. They don't just drink beer, they don't even drink one brand of beer, they drink all brands and styles and then also all categories of alcohol, and they switch around a lot."

The percentage of craft beer sold at professional sporting events is growing. The same goes for spirits. At the stadiums, these options have a startling implication. Craft beer and spirits register a higher alcohol content than domestic beer brands. According to the nonprofit TEAM Coalition, which stands for Techniques for Effective Alcohol Management—comprised of the major professional and collegiate sports entities and initially funded by the Federal Highway and Transportation Commission—concessionaires try to dispense drinks with an equal amount of alcohol, which is why a craft beer may come in a smaller size.

Russ Simons, a leading facility management consultant and director at large of TEAM Coalition, said that the higher cost of a beer, no matter the brand, isn't much of an impediment: "People who want it are willing to pay for it." According to Simons, this dynamic translates to profit. "My sense is that profit has steadily grown as a percentage of revenue that's available back to the facility and/or the program over the course of the last ten years."

At the summit, attendees had beer on the brain. At the beginning of the day, I had a nonalcoholic breakfast with the CEO of Moosehead Beer. It's not verboten for a speaker to nurse a beer while he or she presents. And when attendees complain that they are ready for the happy hour, their impatience isn't dismissed. During the postsession cocktail hour, plenty of domestic premiums, along with craft choices, were served; Schuhmacher knows how to keep his clients happy. I didn't feel guilty about trading in a beer I didn't like for one I did. There were so few women in attendance that most of us naturally gravitated toward one another.

In one of the final presentations, a consultant forecasted a 1 percent decrease in volume per year for the next five years and that increasing profits would only get harder. The most vulnerable beers are what the speaker termed "aging brands"—the domestic premium beers like Bud, Miller, and Coors—once driven by the baby boomer generation and now apparently ignored by millennials. These are the brands most associated with the sports world.

For the last ten years, Bud Light has reigned as the number one brand in the United States. In 2010, Anheuser-Busch, the maker of Bud and Bud Light, paid a record $1.2 billion for its six-year deal for NFL rights, roughly twice the amount the previous sponsor, MillerCoors, had been paying. According to a Wall Street industry analyst I met at the summit, Anheuser-Busch walked away from the NFL sponsorship in 2001, because it thought the value was eroding. Coors took over (before merging with Miller), and Coors Light went on a ten-year run of unbroken market share gains and growth. Coors Light ended up being the number-two light beer brand in the United States. Anheuser-Busch got back in as soon as it could.

Now the leading beer brewer in the United States, Anheuser-Busch maintains a vast reach in the sports world. While competition for sports sponsorships is fierce, as of October 2014, the company brews the official beer of pro football, baseball, basketball, and golf. The 29 car in NAS-CAR, currently driven by Kevin Harvick, is emblazoned with the Budweiser logo, white script on a red background. Anheuser-Busch also inks marketing deals with individual teams to control what gets poured in the stadium.

What Anheuser-Busch doesn't have, others snap up. Crown Imports embraced boxing by sponsoring ESPN Friday Night Fights and Golden Boy promotions. Boxing viewership is off the charts for Hispanics, especially Mexican Americans. This connection with boxing is part of the reason why Crown (Corona, Corona Light, Modelo Especial) has clocked a 10 percent growth versus the industry's 1 percent decline.

These deals show that sporting events are the best advertising money can buy, meaning that the consumer is subject to a multipronged advertising attack for beer hinged on a sustained interest in the games, not just a game-day thirst. This ploy has become even more important during the past ten years because sporting events are one of the only remaining programs on television for which consumers actually watch commercials because they are tuned in to a live event. "The biggest nightmare is that sports become somehow less important to the young males' life," said Schuhmacher, citing that key demographic that brewers are trying to hold on to.

BUSINESS, BEER, AND BINGE DRINKING

The history of baseball ownership shows just how long beer and fandom have been intertwined. Brewer Jacob Ruppert was one of the first owners of the New York Yankees and the man responsible for bringing Babe Ruth to the Bronx. Anheuser-Busch owned the St. Louis Cardinals for more than 40 years; the team still plays in Busch Stadium. The Milwaukee Brewers embraced the city's brewing roots with their eponymous name and play in Miller Park. Coors played a key role in bringing baseball to Denver by investing in the Colorado Rockies expansion franchise. Having since sold their stake in the Rockies, Coors still possesses naming rights to their ballpark, Coors Field, a distinction that came with a $15 million price tag.

Drunken enthusiasm is an intrinsic part of the social fabric of the game. Others might call it binge drinking. Just ask Brandon Phillips, the Reds player who wrote the following inscription on a baseball to a fan who had been heckling him and other players throughout a game in June 2014. "Dear Drunk Guy, Thank You 4 All The Love and Support!! Now Take This Ball And Shut The Phuck Up!! :)"

I remember entering the Oakland Coliseum for a Raiders game once, and the line of discarded liquor bottles and beer cans outside the turnstiles could have stretched to Napa Valley. "Beer is about sociability, escape, and connection," one of the speakers proclaimed at the summit, which sounded exactly like the definition of fandom. According to social psychologist Daniel Wann, two of the eight most common motives for fandom are group affiliation and escape.

In December 2012, Minnesota Viking linebacker Chad Greenway called for fans to get drunk for a pivotal matchup against the Chicago Bears. "Hopefully, they're super-duper drunk," said Greenway, suggesting that they start drinking in the morning to maximize their support for the team. He backed off those comments several days later when interviewed on talk radio.

In 2013, Alabama head football coach Nick Saban scolded fans for leaving the stadium early and not upholding what he saw as the fan commitment. "All you have to do is come to the game, drink beer, do whatever you want, party in the parking lot," said Saban.

For a preseason women's basketball tournament that year, Louisville head coach Jeff Walz offered to buy beers for the first 2,500 fans as part of a $2 beer night promotion. "We're just trying to have a little bit of a good time here at the ballgame," Walz told the *Courier-Journal*.

RISKY BUSINESS

But what happens when fans have too much of a good time? "They're not going to take alcohol away because there's too much revenue, but how do we make it responsible drinking? How do we make sure that the fan behavior is managed?" asked Lou Marciani, director of the National Center for Spectator Sports Safety and Security, during an interview. Much of the reaction to fan misbehavior is to limit alcohol the next time around. Capping alcohol became a way to try and tame hooligans in England and overzealous Brazilian football fans. In Brazil, beer is banned at football games, but during the 2014 World Cup, FIFA forced stadiums to open their taps because of a lucrative sponsorship deal with Anheuser-Busch. In the United States, officials cut off beer sales by the seventh inning in baseball and usually by the end of the third quarter for football as a measure to control fan behavior. After fans rioted at the U.S. Open of Surfing in Southern California, organizers banned alcohol at the venue the following year.

"Alcohol matters, we know that. It's clear it facilitates aggression," said Dan Wann. "But it's not the only thing." Wann pointed to perfectly sober fans who yell obscenities and get into fights, as well as fans who sit in a stadium and get drunk and just fall asleep by the second quarter. Jerry Lewis, a riot specialist from Kent State, writes that there's plenty of excessive drinking without consistent street violence at events like Mardi Gras.

According to Gil Fried, a business school professor at the University of New Haven and chair of the Sports Management department there, studies show that about 5 to 8 percent of people in a stadium are above the legal limit for blood alcohol content—an alarming stat once you do the math. "When I take a look at that number, do I see a concern there? Yeah, because you're looking at close to 60,000, 70,000 people in a stadium. That is quite significant. Just looking at the sheer numbers, that could be several thousand people that are above the legal limit," stated Fried.

From stadium stampedes to foul-ball injury cases, Fried has testified in a number of high-profile lawsuits as an expert on liability, stadium security, and proper security procedures. He was one of the experts who testified for the Stow family against the Dodgers. Said Fried, potential risk is always present no matter how much planning has taken place. "I am definitely not of the opinion that you can eliminate all risk," he added.

One of those risks is when a drunk fan gets behind the wheel, something that happens far too often. Academic research shows that there are significantly more crashes and fatalities on game days than on nongame days in the same locations. A 2003 study looked at data for 27 Super Bowl Sundays and found that traffic fatalities increased after the game at a rate of more than 40 percent, exceeding the accident rate on New Year's Eve. Another study examined major sporting events during a span of eight years and determined that closer scores gave rise to significantly more fatal crashes. The authors of this 2011 investigation point out that the one good thing about a fan's team losing is that the drive home is safer.

In 1999, a New Jersey family was headed home from picking pumpkins when their car was hit head-on by a man who had been drinking beer during a Giants game at the Meadowlands. Antonia Verni, two years old at the time, was paralyzed from the neck down. The driver who was under the influence, Daniel Lanzaro, was found to have a blood alcohol level more than two times the legal limit and sentenced to five years in prison. Antonia's mother filed suit against the concession companies involved, the team, the league, and several other plaintiffs.

Fried testified for Aramark, the food service corporation, but it was a losing effort. A jury awarded the Verni family a record $135 million, but an appeals court set aside the award. Part of the argument during the appeal was centered on a culture of intoxication at Giants Stadium and whether it was relevant to the case. Before heading back to court, the concessionaire settled with the family for $25 million, about a fifth of the original jury award.

"One of the things that I was very clear about in the Verni case is that there could be a situation where a concessionaire or a stadium has not sold a person a single drink and they can get drunk in the facility," said Fried. "Other people could buy it for them. They could sneak material in. There's so many different ways that it can be done. If someone has a desire, it's almost impossible to stop them."

SERVE MORE ALCOHOL

When Oliver Luck became athletic director of West Virginia University in 2010, one of the pressing issues he had to deal with was vomit. Seriously. West Virginia had been grappling with too many "Code Vs," the term stadium security used for the vomiting at certain points in the first and third quarters, when fans started feeling the effects of binge drinking they had done at the pregame and halftime tailgates. Luck told assembled media,

> If the coarse behavior was leading to adults not taking kids to the games, because of language and other things, that's not a good sign. You potentially run the risk of losing a generation of fans. With our demographics, we can't afford to lose young fans. We need those folks to grow up on a steady diet of Mountaineer sports.

Luck, who is a former president of Major League Soccer's Houston Dynamo, developed a counterintuitive approach to the problem. University stadiums and arenas do not traditionally sell alcohol to fans because of the collegiate setting. His plan was to sell beer at sporting events, theorizing that controlling access to beer during the games would *curb* the binge drinking that was taking place during unregulated tailgate parties. Luck also eliminated what was known as the "pass through," which allowed fans to leave the stadium, tailgate, and come back. It was a risk that paid off: The move netted the school three quarters of a million dollars a season in sales and sponsorship, and the number of game-day arrests declined. During the first year of the policy, arrests for alcohol-related incidents dropped by 35 percent. Serving booze inside the stadium at West Virginia was considered a resounding success. The university police chief called it the best season he had ever worked there. Since solving the "Code V" challenge, Luck has moved on to a top executive role within the NCAA.

Other schools have taken note of this somewhat surprising success story—that selling more beer can improve game-day behavior. As athletic departments look for ways to increase revenue and keep fans in the stands, more and more schools buck tradition and serve alcohol inside stadiums and arenas. For the 2014 season, TEAM Coalition calculated that at least 30 NCAA schools served alcohol outside private suite areas. In the past three years, that number has risen by almost 50 percent. Many more institutions permit alcohol advertising at athletic events in signage, in programs, or on radio broadcasts.

Jill Pepper is executive director of TEAM Coalition. Pepper is aligned with Luck in this counterintuitive take on managing the game-day experience. One of her mantras is "serve more alcohol," because alcohol service, in her eyes, is actually the most responsible option. Serving alcoholic beverages inside the stadium allows for more regulation and management. If people only have access to alcohol at a tailgate, there is less oversight.

One of the programs TEAM promotes is responsible beverage service training for every employee at the stadium, not just those who serve alcohol. "The program looks at warning signs of impairment, absorption rate factors, venue policies, legal ramifications, intervention procedures, how to communicate the policies, enforce the policy, and make sure people are safe," said Pepper. In 2013, 50,000 venue-operating employees became TEAM certified. TEAM also organizes designated driver programs.

Nonetheless, according to researchers at the University of Minnesota's School of Public Health, efforts like these may be somewhat misguided. Traci Toomey was the lead investigator for several studies funded by the Robert Wood Johnson Foundation that surveyed drinking habits at sports stadiums throughout the United States, collecting data during a three-year period, from 2005 to 2007. Some of the findings were as follows:

- In a survey of 16 sports stadiums in five states, nearly three out of four people posing as a drunk fan and one out of five people trying to pass as an underage drinker without ID were able to purchase alcohol. While most sellers required IDs for a purchase, there was almost a 75 percent chance that a fan could keep buying booze when already intoxicated.
- The likelihood of illegal alcohol sales was higher in the seating areas than at concessions stands by 2.9 percent.
- A study of breathalyzed fans at baseball and football games found that those who tailgated before the game were 14 times more likely to have an elevated blood alcohol level when they left the game than those who didn't tailgate. "If they were drinking a lot before the game, it's going to continue to be a problem, even as they exit the game," said Toomey.

• As part of a separate study that looked at responsible server training of employees by their managers in 231 bars and restaurants, it was determined that after the training, sales to people who posed as drunk patrons returned to their original level after three months.

According to Toomey, reliance on this type of training doesn't really reduce problems. "It's just like all of the blame and all of the burden gets put onto these relatively low-wage earners," said Toomey. If they are on the payroll at all. In a widespread but little-known practice, at most sporting events (most, if not all, NFL stadiums, for example) concessionaires bring in volunteers to hawk food and drink as a fund-raising endeavor for nonprofit organizations. After going through training, volunteers receive a cut of the beer and hot dog sales for their group. There's debate and ongoing litigation regarding the effectiveness of this practice.

In Toomey's estimation, designated driver programs are also too reliant on individual responsibility and may, in fact, encourage more drinking in others. She said what needs to change is attitude, adding, "We have a binge drinking culture." Between bars and restaurants, community festivals and sports stadiums, the message that excessive drinking is okay is being clearly sent. "We do things in a way that says either we think it's okay to drink too much or we're actually encouraging people to drink too much." Toomey sees tailgating as the next frontier for alcohol management and would like to do more research in that area, working with stadiums to develop ways to manage the parking lot, which is often ground zero for binge drinking.

SKIRTING THE RULES ON SATURDAY AFTERNOONS

At Ohio State, drinking while tailgating is illegal. Even a red Solo cup filled with beer will technically get you a $100 citation because in Ohio, it's illegal to possess an open container of alcohol in public. You'd never know it, however, from looking around the parking lots outside Ohio Stadium on Saturdays when there is a football game. The Ohio State fan base, calculated by ESPN's statistical analyst Nate Silver to be the largest in the country, has elevated pregame partying to an art form. Tailgates stretch for miles each Saturday. There is no such thing as unoccupied concrete. One alum and devoted tailgater told me his eyes get bloodshot from the sea of red of fans dressed in team colors.

For almost 30 years, Richard Morman has been trying to control fan behavior at the school. When I first met him, he was deputy chief of police for Ohio State, and I was looking into Terrelle Pryor, the former OSU quarterback at the heart of the tattoo scandal. We met at the police station, and he was dressed in uniform. I was illegally parked outside. It's hard finding legal parking on a college campus.

According to Morman, "People come to tailgate, and some of the big games, I would say, we have 30,000 to 40,000 people out on those parking lots that have no intention of going to the game." Some people, he said, get there at 5:00 or 6:00 a.m. to stake out a good spot.

Ohio State doesn't serve alcohol inside the stadium, and Morman refused to accept the idea that selling more booze to regulate alcohol consumption would cut down on problem behavior: "If a beer costs eight or ten bucks, fans may overindulge at a tailgate because they don't want to pay ten dollars a beer."

What he said does work is alcohol enforcement. Fifty officers usually patrol the tailgating, walking the parking lots and keeping their eye out for underage drinkers and egregious misconduct. When they are understaffed, Morman said bad behavior increases, as do the number of incidents his officers must contend with. That same alum who told me about the bloodshot eyes also told me it's now more fun to tailgate at away games because he can drink more freely and not worry about getting caught in the parking lot. Since our interview, Morman has left his post at OSU to work for the school on a consulting basis.

Another football-mad Big Ten school that doesn't permit beer in the stadium is the University of Wisconsin, Madison. To combat excessive tailgating, they breathalyze fans. In 2007, the University of Wisconsin instituted a program they called "Show and Blow." A few years later, they changed the name to "Badger Alcohol Check" (BAC). Students who get caught misbehaving because of alcohol at football games have to pass a breathalyzer test to gain entrance to future games. For the three football seasons from 2011 to 2013, more than 100 students each season were required to participate. While hard facts aren't available, according to the school's administration, the program works. "Anecdotally we are aware of numerous students sharing that even as seniors they are attending a game sober for the first time. We can point to very few instances of recidivism within the program," contended Kevin Helmkamp, Wisconsin's associate dean of students. "At a minimum, students participating in BAC are not getting in trouble at the stadium a second time."

These drinking prohibitions usually only apply to the cheap seats. Most schools sell booze in their luxury suites. In fact, in the pros, seventh-inning and third-quarter cutoffs almost never apply in the high-rent, luxury suite, and club areas. That's the case at Wisconsin. In 2013, they netted more than $150,000 from alcohol sales in the suites, according to a public records request for sales figures.

A MELLOWER APPROACH

Baseball fan Joe Hodas was sitting in Coors Field, looking around and daydreaming. He texted his boss to say that perhaps their company would someday be a major sponsor of a sports arena. If the ballpark could display sponsorship from other local companies, why not his? They agreed that five to ten years was a good goal for such an ambition. That was during the spring of 2014, just a few months after Colorado legalized recreational marijuana for adults.

Hodas runs the marketing division of Dixie Elixirs & Edibles, a Denver-based company that manufactures and distributes cannabis products. Four months into the legalization of pot in Colorado, Dixie began producing product nonstop.

According to Hodas, marijuana is a better alternative than alcohol for the sports fan. "If you bump into somebody, it doesn't cause a fight. They turn around and say, 'Hey man, sorry, I didn't mean to bump into you,'" he asserted, mimicking the mellowness of stoner mentality and a mindset he thinks would lead to a safer stadium experience.

Research supports the widely accepted belief that marijuana's high is much mellower than the effects of a night of boozing. A 2003 study in the journal *Addictive Behaviors* notes that, "alcohol is clearly the drug with the most evidence to support a direct intoxication–violence relationship," and that "cannabis reduces likelihood of violence during intoxication." In fact, according to this study, there is a body of literature which shows that for chronic marijuana users, THC, the active ingredient in pot, actually caused a decrease in aggressive and violent behavior.

For the beer industry, legalized pot is perceived as yet another challenge to their bottom line. "As if we didn't have enough problems in our industry," Harry Schuhmacher pronounced at the Beer Summit. With the legalized cannabis industry in its infancy, it's too early to determine the fallout, but many of the executives in attendance echoed Schuhmacher's concern that alcohol will only lose market share to legalized marijuana.

Hodas has a term for people who feel this way: canna bigots. "Most of the research that's been done to date points to the fact that marijuana becomes a substitute for alcohol, rather than a complement," he said. "That's the big question, right? So if people consume marijuana, do they consume less alcohol, more alcohol, or the same amount of alcohol?"

Hodas failed to consider another possible scenario, one that might provide a surprise boon to beer sales at the stadium: that the legalization of pot will create a wider-spread stoner culture consisting of young men so mellow and so passive that they won't bother attending games, they'll just stay home and watch them on television, dude. Not something anyone trying to make money off the game wants to hear but maybe a comforting notion to anyone who has been confronted by a boozed-up sports fan.

CONTROLLING RAIDER NATION: A CASE STUDY

Controlling thousands of people amped up on booze and competition on game day can't be easy. A prime example is the Oakland Raiders, who maintain one of the worst reputations for fan behavior. Keeping Raider Nation under control keeps lots of folks busy. This is the team with a section in the south end zone known as the "Black Hole," whose occupants sport nicknames like "Violator," "Doctor Death," "Darth Raider," and "Gorilla Rilla," and dress in costume and face paint. This cauldron of intimidation is where the rowdiest fans are stationed, all within spitting distance of the field. Visiting fans know to stay away.

When Jeff Miller, the NFL's head of security, who started with the league in 2008, worked his first Monday Night game at the Coliseum, he was stunned at what he saw in terms of fan behavior, commenting, "It was terrible. It was just terrible what I saw outside the stadium. That's when I said, 'We've got to address this in a very intensive way here in Oakland.'"

Retired NFL cornerback and former president of the National Football League Players' Association (NFLPA) Domonique Foxworth forbid his family from wearing his jersey to the Coliseum when he traveled there to play as a rookie on the Broncos, after being warned by teammates about the fighting that goes on there. Another retired player, Donté Stallworth, told me about a Raiders fan who once laced into him. Stallworth said, "The guy's yelling at me and he's going off on me and he's flipping me off. I said 'You're going to yell like that in front of your kid?' He said something to the kid, and the kid flipped me off too."

Consider this illustrative history:

- On opening day of the 2012 season, the Raiders graced national television in a Monday Night Football doubleheader. A fight broke out in a men's room, during which two Raiders fans knocked one another out while at least ten fans watched and several shot video. The fight was posted on YouTube.
- In 2008, in another Monday Night Football matchup, a police officer was sucker punched in the face while trying to subdue a drunken fan at Gate C before the game. Three officers required medical treatment at the scene.
- In 2003, after the Raiders lost, 48–21, to Tampa Bay in Super Bowl XXXVII, a 50-block stretch of Oakland's International Avenue turned lawless, despite the presence of approximately 400 police officers. Incensed fans busted windows, looted stores, and torched cars, an example of Americans pissed off at a loss.
- When the Raiders played in Los Angeles, beer sales were banned for a game in 1990, after a fight sent a Steeler fan to intensive care. A 19-year-old Raider fan who claimed he had been an alcoholic since the age of 13 served a little less than three months behind bars for the beating.
- In 1980, fans booed their own starting quarterback, Dan Pastorini, when he went down with a broken leg.

Why such an outlaw fan base? Raider Nation emulates the image of the team, molded by the legendary late owner Al Davis. Davis himself was an outlaw, moving his team from Oakland to Los Angeles and back, suing the NFL multiple times. He was a master marketeer, introducing the silver and black uniforms and pirate logo in the early 1960s. This iconography captured the imagination of fans worldwide, was adopted by street gangs, and made black the uniform color of choice in sports.

Davis embraced the renegade persona, taking chances on players others would not. The fans ran with the image he created. Whether in Northern or Southern California, the Raiders' stadiums were located in urban and blue-collar areas, in the poor sections of town, the lowlands of Oakland and South Central Los Angeles. Nicknamed "Raider Nation," a trademarked term, Raider fans were known for dressing rough and acting rowdy, earning the aforementioned reputation of one of the worst fan bases in the NFL.

For the final game of the 2013 regular season, the Raiders allowed me to come see how team officials and law enforcement keep Raider Nation under control. I'm usually in the press box watching the action on the field, but for this game, I observed fan behavior in the parking lots, on the concourses, and from the seats.

According to Alameda County sheriff Greg Ahern, whose office shares jurisdiction with the Oakland Police Department for Raiders games, policing Raider football games is quite a job. "Alcohol keeps us busy. It's one of the main reasons for our work," Ahern said. He estimated that roughly 70 percent of ejections and arrests are alcohol related. Ahern grew up a Raider season ticket holder. When the Raiders came back from Los Angeles in 1995, he worked the games as a sergeant. As sheriff, he's in charge, but he's usually home watching on television while his staff handles game day.

Senior Raider executive Tom Blanda (no relation to Raider great George Blanda), a former marine, has worked for the Raiders for more than 20 years. He still looks like a marine, with a closely cropped haircut and trim physique. According to Blanda, the Raiders have had a number-one security rating since the NFL started reviewing compliance in 2009. (These numbers aren't a ranking but a measure of best security practices.) He said this number illustrates that labeling their fan base as rowdy is somewhat unfair.

The Raiders share the Coliseum itself with baseball's Oakland A's and the complex with the NBA's Golden State Warriors, who play inside Oracle Arena across the plaza. Blanda thinks baseball has it easier, since they have more games to work out kinks in security. With only eight regular-season home games, Blanda contended that NFL teams have a "small margin for error."

These days, monitoring Raider Nation is a huge undertaking, involving thousands of people. On Sunday morning at 9:00 a.m., more than four hours before kickoff, workers at the concrete bowl known as the Oakland-Alameda County Coliseum were readying for 50,000 football fans for the final game of a rudderless season. The Oakland Raiders had won only three games that year, and they were preparing to face their division rival, the Denver Broncos, who, led by superstar quarterback Peyton Manning, were expected to go far in the upcoming playoffs, unlike the Raiders. It's been more than a decade since Oakland has made the playoffs, and fans are used to it.

The parking lots were teeming with tailgaters, who were permitted to start lining up in front of the locked gates at 6:00 a.m. for an 8:00 a.m. entry. Game-day employees dressed in yellow windbreakers were directing traffic and watching the crowd file in. The Raiders' middling play apparently wasn't detracting from the tailgaters' enthusiasm for the traditional parking lot party.

My first stop was at a staff briefing in neighboring Oracle Arena, which was set up for a New Year's Eve rave. A stage had been erected where the basketball court was normally situated. Those entrusted with enforcing the rules were seated in the bottom rows of sections 102 and 103. There were about 200 people, mostly middle-aged African Americans. The room was divided into those wearing red windbreakers and those wearing yellow ones. Red meant that they had been hired by AEG, the company that runs operations for the complex, while those wearing yellow had been brought in by Landmark Event Staffing Services, an additional subcontractor who supplements AEG's hires.

Stadiums subcontract game-day security from outside companies for sporting events. Their role is to enforce rules. Sworn law enforcement intervenes if there is trouble, but those in windbreakers are the first line of defense. With the music blaring, many were dancing in their seats. Landmark seemed to be outdancing AEG.

Chris Sotiropulos, 25, was representing the Raiders at this meeting. He stood on the floor, mic in hand, and thanked the workers for their service. "Without you guys, we couldn't have the type of game day we do," said Sotiropulos, whose official title is ticket operations manager. "It's up to us that fans have a really great last game." The speech took less than 30 seconds. Supervisors then stepped in with more specific instructions.

Safety is a complex matter at NFL stadiums. At the Coliseum, the entire alphabet seemed to be involved. According to Sotiropulos, the Raiders hire an average of 185 police officers per game, a detail split between the Oakland Police Department and the Alameda County Sheriff's Office, along with 450 private security, split between AEG and Landmark.

"It is pretty standard from game to game. The only time it varies would be for a preseason game where attendance is drastically lower," said Sotiropulos. AEG supervisors staff the gates, as the Raider organization holds them more accountable. AEG workers patrol most of the stadium, including the end zones, while Landmark oversees the uppermost deck.

Greg Garrett, a former Raiders security staffer who is still involved on game day, pointed out that if the team draws 50,000 fans on game day, and 50 people get arrested or ejected from a given game, that's not even 1 percent; it's 1/10th of that. But another security official with him opined, "Imagine if no one put in any of the effort" overseeing the behavior.

At the south end of the parking lot, known as "Raiderville," the official tailgating section, meat was sizzling on the grills and fans were lining up to buy beer. Retired NFL players were arguing about pregame picks on gigantic television screens. Many fans were wearing the jersey of a favorite player, and several were dressed in costume or covered in spray paint. I noted a fan dressed in a helmet with plastic knives sticking out of it and another in black leather lace-up platform boots. There were more men in makeup than at a drag show.

Near some carnival-type games, an organization called "Fans against Violence" had set up at a table adorned with a black banner, some pamphlets, and a large plastic "number-one" finger. They were there to promote a message of peace.

Taking Back the Games

In 2012, 46-year-old Bay Area resident and Raider fan Kathy Samoun founded Fans against Violence. According to Samoun, hate is not a requirement of being a fan. "Why do you have to hate anybody just because you're a fan of the home team?" she asked. Motivated by the Bryan Stow beating and the notorious mélange of violence that took place at that 2011

Raiders–Niners preseason game, she started a blog, and a nonprofit soon followed.

Samoun is a petite but strong-looking woman, olive-skinned with dark, wavy hair. She designs rugs and is a mother of a 20-year-old and 7-year-old. She regards fan hostility as an adult form of bullying—and humor as an antidote. At a Raiders game several years ago, on her way out, she had seen some fans in New York Jets jerseys walking with their eyes cast downward and tentative body language. Samoun noticed the tension and shouted, "Good game! At least your quarterback is hot," referring to then-Jets quarterback Mark Sanchez. Everyone within earshot laughed, and according to Samoun, the mood relaxed. "Humor works," she pointed out.

This type of small gesture is one of her solutions. Samoun compared better fan behavior to recycling, implying that people can change. People's attitude toward garbage wasn't always what it is now. "If you throw a can away in the trash, you are now the devil," said Samoun.

At the final game of the previous season, the San Diego Chargers had called Samoun and asked her to bring "Fans against Violence" south. During the 2013 season, the group had maintained a presence at every San Diego home game. Her goal is to spread beyond Oakland and San Diego and have a chapter at every stadium.

When the Raiders hosted the Chargers, Samoun invited the San Diego volunteers to come to the game. When it was time for one of the visitors—who was dressed in a Chargers jersey, cape, crown, and mask—to use the bathroom, Samoun felt compelled to ask for help. "Can you just keep an eye, make sure he's okay?" she asked the security person posted outside the men's room.

Samoun stated that you'll always see a security person stationed outside the bathrooms, but she also said she realizes that this approach has its limitations. "I don't care if you post a security guard at every single section, you're not going to be able to watch every single fan," she conceded. Fans need to be aware of their surroundings and reach out for help if they need it. Bathrooms "are on our radar a lot," said Sheriff Ahern, because fans know there are no surveillance cameras inside, since that would be illegal.

Not many fans were stopping at the Fans against Violence table, so I headed back into the stadium. Each time I entered, I had to go through security. Workers were searching visitors by having them walk through metal detectors known as magnetometers, rather than checking them with hand wands. Each time I passed through, I registered a different result. By the end of the day, I had tripped security two out of four times in. I was told that magnetometers are good for detecting metal and not as good for detecting glass. I didn't have either on me, which made me wonder just how easy it is to exploit loopholes in the process.

Next stop was the Raiders Security Command Center, where the security and game-day operations have taken over a luxury suite on the loge level. Everyone had an assigned seat, with a computer monitor and a name plate identifying their agency. The front positions belonged to the Oakland Police Department and the Alameda County Sheriff's Office. In the second row sat representatives from the Raiders and AEG. The remaining rows consisted of spaces assigned to the FBI, Landmark Security, parking, paramedics, and concessions. In the back was a table stocked with snacks.

At the front of the room was a seating chart and a monitor of closed-circuit televisions, split into nine screens at once. Since it was pregame, we were mostly looking at parking lots and turnstiles, but there were also cameras throughout the interior of the stadium. Any seat could be isolated. There were 135 closed-circuit cameras in the coliseum and arena.

Matthew Pasco, director of information technology for the Raiders, was wearing a plastic earpiece in his left ear and sitting in the most forward position. What does Pasco dread? "When there is a blowout either way, that's when fans misbehave the most," he said.

Fans are provided with a number so they can text their location and issue if they need help; the texts come in to the command center. When the system was rolled out, most clubs provided a special code to text to a six-digit number. The Raiders' code was "OAK." Other clubs were more creative with their texting service. The Bengals let you text the code "JERK." In Green Bay, fans could text "FLAG" to the number provided. Many teams simply provide regular phone numbers to make it even easier.

According to Gil Fried, the texting system has its limits:

> They're a great idea, but it's like anything else, a tool. It's only as effective as how effectively it is used. Do they post the number in a prominent location? Some studies have taken a look at this and said should we place it on the scoreboard. Well, if we place it there in a prominent area, we might have to give up an ad.

So far on this day, mostly maintenance issues had registered on-screen in the command center. An elevator had gone out, which, if you've ever spent any time at the Coliseum, is as common as a long line at a ladies' room. Other incidents included an allergy attack and a broken magnetometer.

I was shooed out of the room before the game began—disappointing but typical when the media starts looking into security. Teams want you to know they are paying attention, but they don't want to tell you how they really do it.

There was less than an hour until kickoff. I walked by a designated driver booth, which was staffed by the California Highway Patrol and scantily clad women in high heels. If you signed the pledge, you got a coupon for a free nonalcoholic beverage. There was one of these booths at each gate.

The concourse that leads to the top of Gate C has a clear view of one of the entrance gates, and Sotiropulos instructed me to meet up with him there. I chatted with an officer from the Oakland Police Department as I waited and we watched the fans file in. While the Oakland Municipal Code technically forbids citizens from wearing a mask, it's clearly not a law enforced at the Coliseum. Fans wearing masks, face paint, and necklaces strung with plastic liquor bottles streamed by. People come up with the most imaginative places to plant a Raiders logo.

Sotiropulos, who sets his alarm for 4:45 a.m. each game day, arrived and scanned the crowd below. In a split second, he noticed seven people smoking. When asked if he worries that everything he sees is going to wind up on the Internet, recorded by a fan's cell phone, he said no, that he worries more about lawsuits, which is probably more relevant to the bottom line.

Fans who misbehave and get booted from the stadium receive a letter from Sotiropulos telling them the necessary actions they need to take to be permitted back inside the Coliseum. The letter explains that they must attend the NFL's version of "traffic school," a four-hour Fan Code of Conduct Class administered online. Sotiropulos gave me the link to try it out.

For a fee of $55, the course teaches fans about the stadium code of conduct, anger management, and the dangers of alcohol. The statistics cited by Mothers against Drunk Driving (MADD) are alarming. For example, "Over 1.46 million drivers were arrested in 2006 for driving under the influence of alcohol or narcotics. This is an arrest rate of one for every 139 licensed drivers in the United States." There's some touchy-feely stuff too. The course recommends that fans manage game-day stress by getting more sleep. It also suggests trying to show more empathy toward other fans.

The module is supposed to be customized for each club, but my test told me to "consider the costs of alcohol abuse while at your next Red Bulls game," which is the Major League Soccer club in New Jersey. I ignored the mistake and took the final quiz. Fans must score at least 70% to pass. I scored 25 out of 28, passing with room to spare. Since I took the course, the league has raised the fee to $250, which is more than some season tickets for Raiders games. According to Sotiropulos, $50 of that goes to Oakland's designated charity, MADD.

In the eyes of the Raider organization, fan behavior is improving. Local law enforcement concurs. "They wanted the rowdy people re-moved, the drunk people arrested, and they wanted to bring a better crowd to every game," said Ahern. "Our fan behavior has greatly im-proved since they first returned from Los Angeles." Ahern cited his arrest stats, which showed fewer problems in 2013 than 2012, although such statistics could reflect the crackdown on bad behavior. The league has seen progress as well. According to the NFL's Jeff Miller, "It's a much better environment there. Doesn't mean it's perfect. It's not perfect any-where."

Rowdy, drunken fans aren't going anywhere, no matter how many security guards stand outside bathrooms or how many text lines are in-stalled. Alcohol is too thoroughly tied to the emotional system of the game and profit margins of multiple industries. If alcohol consumption is tamped down on, will people still want to come to the game? How far is too far before sport loses the essence of what makes it fun? It's like the game of Whack-A-Mole: you hit one mole down and another pops up. It's exhausting.

For Sotiropulos, once the game started, he spent his time waiting for "splash calls." If someone gets vomited on, it's his job to attend to them. If they are season ticket holders, fans get treated a little better. He often gives them Raiders gear to change into.

6

THE VOICE OF THE FAN

Have you ever considered putting an attractive pic on your Facebook?—Message from an Ohio State fan to me on Facebook

Go back in your cage.—Another message from an Ohio State fan to me on Facebook

Throughout history, fans have been nothing if not outspoken. It seems that one false move against a favorite athlete has the potential to unleash a torrent of unwanted, and sometimes unjustified, responses. Just ask Martha Fleischman, the 62-year-old woman who, in 2006, hit Steelers quarterback Ben Roethlisberger with her car while he was riding his motorcycle. Fleischman quickly became an object of searing hatred. She said she received numerous letters from Steelers fans, lashing out at her for causing the accident, in which Pittsburgh's starting signal-caller broke several bones and suffered a concussion. In the mind of a sports fan, there is no tolerance for accidents.

If you are a whistleblower, for example, a professor who calls out a university for academically pandering to high-profile coaches and athletes, you might be tempted to enter into witness protection. Murray Sperber, while an English professor at Indiana University, was one of few to openly criticize popular basketball coach Bob Knight and accuse the university of leniency in dealing with Knight's behavioral transgressions. Fans didn't appreciate Sperber's outspokenness. At one point, he went to police because of threatening phone calls from Knight's supporters. He recalled the Saturday night he dined in a Mexican restaurant in Bloomington and was treated like a pariah by the other customers. "It was full and it was loud, and the only table was way in the back, so we started walking across and people looked at me and it got quieter and quieter," said Sperber. "It was eerie." The beleaguered professor wound up taking a leave of absence from the school and eventually moved to the West Coast. Sperber, in all likelihood, was the first college professor run out of town by sports fans.

FLAMES TO THE FIRE

Not surprisingly, it's the on-the-field officials who often bear the brunt of negative fanspeak. When replacement refs were called into service to officiate NFL games during a labor dispute in 2012, Lance Easley looked forward to the opportunity to pursue his hobby at a higher level. The 52-year-old Californian never dreamed he would work as a side judge on *Monday Night Football* for a Packers–Seahawks game in Seattle. But then again, he never imagined that he would make a ruling that would be endlessly scrutinized, ridiculed, and even credited for ending the lockout.

As the game clock ran out, Seattle quarterback Russell Wilson launched a Hail Mary pass deep into the end zone. Receiver Golden Tate and Green Bay safety M. D. Jennings leapt into the air; both got their hands on the ball and battled for possession. Easley eventually signaled a touchdown, handing the Seahawks a win and igniting bitter controversy over the call, as well as over the competence of the replacement refs. Three days later, the labor dispute was resolved, and regular refs were back on the job. Easley's contentious call may have been the last straw.

When he returned home a few days later, Easley received threatening phone calls and a suspicious package. He commented, "My wife picked it up and brought it in the house. I said, 'Oh, my God.' I gingerly put it back outside, and we called the police immediately, and they came down."

When the bomb squad opened it, the package contained cheese curds and a note from a Packers fan saying cheese heads will never forget. For more than a month, he needed a security guard at his full-time job as a bank vice president. Easley called it a "sad, sad statement" that people are "not getting better as human beings" and attributed recent health problems to the stress of his brief stint as an NFL ref. Meanwhile, he said his wife remains afraid to use her real name in public.

Cheese curds, although symbolic, would barely make it into a hall of fame of fan threats. There's a lot of "not nice" language in fandom, mostly attributed to an ethos of "it's just part of the game." Most female journalists in sports whom I know have been called whores at some point in their careers. Most African American men in sports, athletes and otherwise, have been called the "N" word. My colleague, ESPN and ABC college football analyst Kirk Herbstreit, an Ohio native and former starting quarterback and team captain for Ohio State, wound up moving his family from Columbus, Ohio, to Nashville, Tennessee. Why? Because some Ohio State fans incessantly trash talked him, sometimes even coming by his house after he made what they felt were unfavorable comments about his school. He was basically targeted for analyzing the team with objectivity.

For fans, online communication has added a pernicious dimension to the sports conversation. Since the mid-1990s and the days of dial-up Internet, fans have flocked to primitive online message boards, especially for recruiting discussions. Those were the days of Web 1.0. That was only the beginning, and things soon sped up. Twitter launched in 2006. That same year, anyone 13 years of age and older could sign up for a Facebook account, even though the social network had initially been designed for selected college students. The Internet is now packed with sharp-edged language and aggressive opinions in the form of Facebook status updates, tweets, blog comments, and message board posts. What we've got is a bully pulpit for a new age—online norms of conversation that veer toward diatribe rather than dialogue and ricochet through cyberspace, where they don't disappear.

Sports talk radio and 24-hour cable networks used to take the blame for much of the animosity in sports. Today social media and the blogosphere fan the flames of animosity on an ever-expanding scale. When a fight breaks out in the stands or parking lot, the mayhem is easily captured on a cell phone camera and sent directly to YouTube.

Replacement ref Lance Easley wasn't on Facebook or Twitter after his controversial call, but he blames social media for keeping him in the public eye and fomenting a punishing conversation. Not only do fans have access to a large amount of information, but they also have a staggering number of opportunities to target those who anger them. "There's so many ways that people can write and express themselves now. It's unbelievable," said Easley.

With all this opportunity, it's not just hate and harassment. Some athletes and fans say they love the direct connection they've established with one another. New York Giants starting running back Rashad Jennings, who has tens of thousands of Twitter followers and hopes for more, told me, "I try to use social media for myself to get the message out that I want, because I don't want anybody to tell my story."

Sometimes it's a deep connection that reveals an intimate thought or personal message. When Yankees superstar Derek Jeter first announced his retirement, he did it on Facebook rather than calling a news conference or giving an exclusive interview.

When Kobe Bryant tore his Achilles tendon and ended his season in 2013, he took to Facebook in a rare moment of vulnerability. "All the training and sacrifice just flew out the window with one step that I've done millions of times!" Bryant posted. In the same update, he asked, "Do I have the consistent will to overcome this thing?"

This connection offers meaning to many athletes. "You sign a bunch of autographs after the game or jerseys or something and people will tweet you and say, 'Hey I appreciate you. My son loved that jersey,'" said retired NFL safety Donte' Stallworth. "Before Twitter, there would have been none of that."

SOCIAL MEDIA MASHUP

Social media lets fans turn up their nose at geography, connecting fan bases across time zones and even continents. Fans don't need to go to the local sports bar to debate the merits of their favorite team's next opponent. Instead, they can jump on Reddit conversations known as "trash talk threads." A fan's computer or phone is like a sports bar that is always open, is always serving, and will never cut you off. But there's a dark side: Hostility can be anywhere and everywhere. It's hard to figure out when to close out your tab and go home.

Facebook ranks as the top social media network for 71 percent of online adults in the United States. According to the company's own stats, during the 2014 Winter Olympics, there were 45 million people worldwide posting, commenting, and liking content about the games. For the Super Bowl XLVIII matchup between the Seahawks and Broncos, 50 million people joined in the conversation. Twitter, with 18 percent of the adult online population, says Super Bowl XLVIII generated almost 25 million tweets. According to Nielsen Twitter TV ratings, 5.6 million people in the United States tweeted during the game. Contrast that to *Outside the Lines*, the ESPN show I produce for, which is considered an important voice in the sports world. In the summer of 2014, I felt fortunate that according to Nielsen's TV ratings, a tad more than 800,000 people watched one Sunday morning episode I worked on. While the visuals of television can create powerful visceral reaction, social media is scarily gargantuan in its reach.

Sam Laird knows more about social media and sports than anyone I've ever met. He's the sports reporter for *Mashable*, a top blog that covers social media news and calls itself the voice of digital culture. Twitter seems to be the platform of choice for the sports fan, which Laird attributes to a fan's "endless appetite for news and content" and Twitter's "never-ending stream." Laird, 29, sees social media as the "global water cooler" for the sports fan and shared some anecdotes with me.

He told me about the time that the Portland Trail Blazers' Damian Lillard, the 2013 NBA Rookie of the Year, blew off a fan who asked for an autograph while shopping at a local mall. After Lillard tweeted that he regretted brushing off the fan, he got a response from the fan, saying he understood. They arranged to meet back at the mall, and after hanging out the fan tweeted a photo of the two of them together.

Laird also told me about a marriage born on Twitter. The official Red Sox feed tweeted a birthday shout-out to a Massachusetts woman named Shannon Armitage in 2011. Cody Anderson, a Red Sox fan from Illinois, began following her. An online courtship soon began and escalated to real life. Cody and Shannon were married at Fenway Park on Opening Day 2014, the same day the Red Sox received their 2013 World Series rings. That must have warmed the hearts of those in the Twitter executive suites.

VIRTUAL FANS

Social media has also given rise to a kind of cyberspace autograph chasing—fans begging athletes to acknowledge them on Twitter. A retweet or follow from the famous signals accomplishment. Using Twitter, a Cleveland Browns fan begged Browns running back Ben Tate to retweet him because if he got the retweet, his brother would buy him Tate's jersey. Tate agreed, and the jersey was on its way.

Most agree that online commenting has been hijacked by the obnoxious. In 2013, ESPN.com changed its comments policy in hopes of improving online discourse by enforcing accountability. Commenters are now required to log in with their Facebook accounts and presumably their real identities. Other publications have also tried to clean up commenting chaos with similar measures. *Popular Science* magazine, for one, chose to turn off comments altogether. It turns out that science was too polarizing for the masses to engage in reasonable conversation. Other publications moderate comments and must approve what gets posted.

More bad taste: relentlessly calling out an athlete for an on-the-field mistake. Screw up and social media rains down on you. Performance glitches polarize. Former Giants running back Brandon Jacobs suffered death threats for failing a fantasy football fan. When the 49ers' Kyle Williams fumbled two punt returns in the 2012 NFC Championship Game, he immediately took a beating on social media, including tweets with nasty messages, with some people expressing the hope that he would die. After a difficult loss, the Montreal Impact's Davy Arnaud received the message, "I hope your family dies in a fire." He responded to the message, saying, "WOW. I know we lost and I made a mistake but I deserve this?" In 2011, then-Marlins outfielder Scott Cousins faced threats after a home plate collision with Giants star catcher Buster Posey, which broke Posey's leg and ended his season.

Twitter trolls attack family members, too. The son of Lakers coach Mike Brown, Elijah, a high school student at the time, got nasty messages when the Lakers started out poorly in 2012, with fans tweeting that they were praying his dad would get fired. After her husband Steve missed a game-winning shot in a playoff game with the Lakers, Kristen Blake told reporters that she had to block more than 500 followers and their vitriol, which included the message, "I hope your family gets murdered."

"You can go from irrational thought to statement so quickly, without any sort of filter," Laird said. "It just takes a second to take your phone out and write it, or to type these thoughts as they come into your brain on your computer." Something done in haste can easily have a long-lasting impact. Who hasn't sent an angry e-mail in the heat of the moment only to regret it shortly afterward?

Nice is the outlier on Twitter, but it does happen sometimes. Louise Groomer is a 56-year-old woman who works for a volunteer ambulance service in a remote part of southern Oregon. A NASCAR fan for 14 years, she said she hasn't missed watching a race on television since 2001, although some she records and watches later. One Tuesday night in early December 2013, Groomer was on her couch perusing Twitter on her iPad. One of her favorite NASCAR drivers, Kevin Harvick, was tweeting from his private jet. Fans were begging him to follow them. Groomer decided to jump in, tweeting, "Please, will you follow me?" It took about a minute or so for him to respond that he would. Harvick clicked "follow," and Groomer was stunned, wondering if it was a practical joke. According to Harvick, Groomer's use of the word *please* is what led to the follow, while other fans had rudely demanded a follow. Groomer followed a different script.

A few minutes later, Harvick sent her a direct message, inviting her to the Daytona 500. "I grabbed my iPad, turned on the light, and I ran into the bedroom," said Groomer. "Honey, honey, we're going to the Daytona 500," she shouted at her husband, who was hard of hearing. "He thought the house was on fire or something."

So what effect does social media have on sports fans themselves? According to Ravi Chandra, a clinical psychiatrist who blogs for *Psychology Today*, people struggle with the tone of communication on social media. Chandra studied this area while doing research for a book that looks at how social networks influence our minds and hearts. He often hears complaints about social media connections from patients. "You lose the visual cues of being with another person," Chandra said. "When you are face to face with somebody, it tends to kind of pull you into a relationship and also provide a social context; it can also maybe suppress some of the more aggressive impulses that you have." Mark Cuban, the outspoken owner of the Dallas Mavericks, calls this phenomenon "Twitter courage."

Anonymity makes it easier to abandon inhibitions. "Any time you don't have to be accountable for your actions," Chandra stated, "it's another disinhibiting factor." He has also noticed that people can sometimes forge new identities online. "I've seen a disconnect between the real self and the persona that you're projecting online and that you have to assume in order to push your opinions." All of that can create an unforgiving space.

Late-night talk show host Jimmy Kimmel pokes fun at social media nastiness in a regular segment where celebrities and athletes read mean tweets about themselves. The Dallas Cowboys followed his lead and produced their own video, which opens with a fan who wrote, "I want the Cowboys to be the pallbearers at my funeral so they can let me down one last time." After reading this tweet, quarterback Tony Romo asked for the guy's number.

Why so much negativity in cyberspace? Communication research suggests that people express negative opinions more emphatically than positive ones. As an example, look at a study of political beliefs by George Bizer, a psychology professor at Union College, which was published in the journal *Political Psychology*. It shows that voters who were led to frame their opinions in terms of whom they *opposed* were more likely to campaign and vote for their preferred candidate. During an interview, Bizer said this is part of a broader negativity bias in human nature. "Negativity in life causes us to act," commented Bizer. "We are hardwired for this."

Negativity yields action. I can only be bothered to write Yelp reviews when I get bad service and am pissed off, but my Yelp reviews seem mild compared to the harsh Twitter death threats that get directed at athletes who screw up.

George Atallah, assistant executive director of external affairs for the NFL Players Association, called death threats from Twitter and other platforms a "major issue." "It is very easy for a social media user to engage in hostile and threatening behavior," Atallah said. "There is very little in the way of analyzing legitimate threats versus unseemly behavior." As a spokesman for the union during the contentious 2011 NFL lockout, his own life was cyber threatened. And he revealed to me that many more NFL players get threatened than the number reported in the media.

Perhaps the threats are just an inevitable part of the way we communicate now. In fact, *Mashable's* Laird conceded that he can even "sympathize with the people who write the death threats in a way." He said that without any filter, "it's easy to write something you don't mean in the heat of the moment." Various pundits opine that online threats are meaningless, saying they should simply be ignored and that it's the media that legitimizes them.

Nevertheless, the Secret Service says they take these types of threats extremely seriously. Death threats on Twitter directed at President Obama have resulted in prosecution and conviction. In the sports world, hostility sometimes merits the involvement of authorities. During a losing streak in 2013, former Texans quarterback Matt Schaub faced an issue with angry fans offline when they came by his home to upbraid the struggling signal caller. According to the Houston Police Department, they investigated the situation, and private security monitored it as well. The frustrated fans eventually backed off from their unsolicited visits. Ralph Cindrich, an agent who represents NFL players in contract negotiations, got the FBI, among other organizations, involved when he received online threats via Twitter after an inflammatory conversation about Alabama football head coach Nick Saban and NCAA president Mark Emmert on sports talk radio. But for now, threats to those in the sports world seem to elicit a mishmash of alarm and responses often cloaked in secrecy.

Most of these cases don't progress far unless the threat conveys imminent and specific harm. Oftentimes the legal system isn't equipped to handle hi-tech threats. People are quick to cite First Amendment protections when regulatory suggestions related to Internet speech are discussed. A 2012 survey from the National Cyber Security Alliance and McAfee found that one in five Americans have been affected by cyberstalking, harassing e-mails, and other undesired contact online. The online bullying of young people and the cyber harassment and cyberstalking of women now merit sustained attention from both government and industry.

But there can also be a laissez-faire attitude of "this is how the Internet works," especially if you are a public figure, for instance, a politician, journalist, or athlete, since public figures are entitled to less protection of their reputations under the law. One NFL player told me, "That's part of football. That's part of anything where you're scrutinized."

At Twitter, the company stands firmly behind its commitment to freedom of expression with a "tweets must flow" ethos. Since real identities are not required to register for the service, the anonymity of Twitter protects users when they make unpopular political statements, as well as abusive threats. As Del Harvey, Twitter's head of trust and safety, said in a 2014 videotaped TED Talk, the majority of users are positive people reaching out to connect and share, but "there's no denying people do weird things." The scale of Twitter makes for a vast challenge. In 2014, the service clocked 500 million tweets each day, and Harvey conceded that the odds for harmful communication are actually high because a "one in a million chance happens 500 times a day."

According to Danielle Citron, a University of Maryland law professor and author of *Hate Crimes in Cyberspace*, after a number of women in the United Kingdom were threatened on the site with rape and murder during the summer of 2013, Twitter eventually responded to media criticism and online petitions by rolling out an in-tweet "report abuse" button. (Complaints previously had to be lodged by using a separate, less accessible form.) But Twitter standards remain relatively impenetrable for those who request that content be taken down or what identifying characteristics of accounts will be revealed—unless you've got a subpoena.

Unlike Twitter, Facebook requires people to register using their real names (although this policy is under review for some groups) and prohibits hate speech on the site; however, Facebook also cites scale problems in policing communication. Citron explains that the company has publicly wrestled with complaints from advertisers and community members about pro-rape pages and anti-Semitic groups, two examples of troublesome content at one point hosted on the site.

In a conference room at Facebook's vast Silicon Valley campus, Arturo Bejar, Facebook's director of engineering, got specific to the sports world, explaining how stadium-speak comes off differently online, away from the arena. Bejar formerly worked at Yahoo, in charge of online security, where his title was literally Chief Paranoid. "We're in this age where technology has taken what has been interactions reserved for different places into this larger context," he said. Bejar added that at the same time, this process has removed the element of reflection and other tools that we draw upon to relate to one another.

To improve the process of reporting inappropriate content, Bejar's team at Facebook studies what they call "compassion research," drawing from academia, to understand how to make interactions between people more pleasant and give them the proper tools to report when the interaction becomes unpleasant. According to Bejar, while content may not technically violate Facebook community standards, it can still upset people. If Facebook can provide an arena for explanation, he said the tension may be diffused.

While this seems more applicable to teenagers who suffer online bullying, Facebook must grapple with the inflammatory power of sports speak. In countries like Brazil, Italy, and India, Facebook has found that fans get insulted when they see sports stars being mocked and flag it with some regularity. Bejar shared the example of someone drawing horns on a picture of the coach of the Brazilian national football team and posting their artwork. Some Brazilians have been so offended that they reported it as hate speech. That's taking sports hero worship awfully seriously.

Remember my assignment in Columbus, Ohio? If you recall, I was there to report on a scandal within the Ohio State University football program. When I alienated some of the Ohio State fan base with my investigative reporting there, my hometown, phone number, and e-mail address were posted on the Internet. My home voice mail soon filled with messages of anger and profanity. My Facebook and Twitter accounts erupted with nasty correspondence from strangers complaining that our coverage was slanted and sensational. I wound up blocking tweets from an anonymous Ohio State fan with the Twitter handle @OSU (Ohio State) Blacklist after he assigned two hashtags to me: #keepwomenoutofsports and #kankles. The attention to my ankles was simply odd.

On Facebook, I got messages from people I didn't know ripping my profile picture and complaining about my work. Many pointedly told me I wasn't welcome in Ohio. Degrading my appearance was integral to most of the messages.

I was directed by ESPN's corporate security to file a complaint with police. At midnight, a patrol car came by my house to investigate, but there was really nothing they could do since no one had directly threatened to rape or murder me. How comforting. Sadly, none of this treatment was exceptional. People with regular bylines and on-air segments get it much worse than I did.

Despite the lack of hospitality in the past, I returned to Columbus, Ohio, to do more reporting for this book, but before I tried to hobnob with any cyber hooligans, I got tickets to the annual Ohio State spring game, which is really a glorified practice. My friend, who is a local television executive, and I, along with 61,000 other fans, showed up on the second Saturday of April to watch a mix of starters and backups scrimmage other starters and backups. Most spectators were dressed in OSU red, and everyone was sporting a different T-shirt or jersey, a testament to the marketing prowess of the football team. It was hard to spot two people wearing the same item. Alcohol was not being sold inside the stadium, per university policy. Ice cream was winning as the refreshment of choice.

There was nothing on the line that day, except for third stringers fighting to become second stringers and second stringers looking to move up to the first team. No one seemed to mind. My friend and I basked in the sunshine. The first nice weather of spring was more exciting than the messy play that ended in a meaningless 17–7 score, the Gray over the Scarlet. I spotted a man walking up the stadium steps with a young boy who looked to be about nine years old. The man was wearing a "Mark May is a Douche" T-shirt. There's the hostility directed at media who criticize the football program; Mark May is a college football commentator for ESPN. I wondered what that guy had told his kid about the meaning of the slogan.

The day after the game, I went to work. Since messages from Facebook users are supposedly tied to actual identities, I did my best sleuthing and tracked down some of my own harassers from three-year-old Facebook messages. At the time, I knew it would be a mistake to respond, but I had grown curious about what motivated these fans.

It turned out that most of my harassers didn't actually live in town, which shows just how far the Ohio State fan base extends. After the game, I reached one fan on the phone who is now living in Miami. Sean Eilertson, who graduated from Ohio State in 2013, said he didn't really remember much about contacting me with a message entitled "honesty and integrity regarding your investigation." He bristled at my contention that his line, "I simply advise you to do what's right and if you don't, realize that Buckeye Nation will not show you mercy," felt vaguely threatening. He told me that he was just explaining the power of a large fan base and that "it is all in the fun of sports."

Two days later, it was time for a house call. My friend Scott, a photographer who lives north of Columbus, kindly agreed to come with me. As a local, he felt guilty about the way some fans had treated me. He even apologized to me on behalf of more civilized Ohioans.

We were in search of a fan whom we'll call "Tommy," a 2011 Ohio State grad still living near campus in Columbus. After knocking on the front door of where we thought he lived, a woman answered. I explained as best as I could the premise of my visit, and she said she'd get "Tommy" for us. As we waited outside, I whispered Tommy's Facebook message to Scott: "He's the guy who told me I was 'not even on the same level as a prostitute' and 'a disgrace to journalism.'" Since "Tommy" majored in journalism at Ohio State, he must know. I looked around. The paint was peeling on the gray porch, and it was dotted with dilapidated chairs, a snow shovel, and a cat carrier. A guy who looked to be in his 20s came to the door, wearing a backward baseball cap and sweatpants.

"Hey, my name is Justine." I asked him, "Are you 'Tommy?'"

"What do you want?" he asked. I told him I just wanted to talk with him. He exploded, "You are a shit journalist, you are a fucking, fucking you went out of your way to write a shit piece on people who are innocent. We knew all about it. Get the fuck off my porch."

I tried for some sort of conversation, but he wouldn't have it. "Get the fuck off . . . get the fuck off. You and the *Outside the Lines* people can go suck shit."

The next day, on the Internet, "Tommy" blogged about the visit and conceded that he probably hadn't handled it in the best way. He and others in the comment section of the blog expressed curiosity as to why I was there, but in his heart, I know he knows the truth: I had tried to tell him the reason for my visit, but he wouldn't listen. Funny how he was so forthcoming on Facebook and the blog with his opinion but fled from an in-person conversation. Was rational conversation just too much to ask? Maybe so.

Sports creates a stark dichotomy between winning and losing, good guy and bad guy. To "Tommy," I was wrong and he was right. In this black-and-white sports world, there's not a lot of room for gray. Jerry Jones, owner of the Dallas Cowboys, said he wants fans to either love the Cowboys or hate them. "I understand the importance of having passion involved, and not apathy," Jones said in a television interview I produced. "If we're not the most popular team, we're always the most hated team."

7

THE ART OF NOISE

If you talk trash and you're sorry, it doesn't matter.—NFL defensive
end Justin Tuck

It was a brisk Saturday evening in mid-December 2013, and I had pur-
chased a ticket for Missouri's men's basketball game against Western
Michigan in Columbia. I'm usually part of the credentialed media scrum,
sitting in a press row with a pass dangling from my neck, but that night I
was posing as a fan to observe the Mizzou student fan group, the Antlers,
whose seats are behind the basket, a few rows up from the floor. I was
undercover because the Antlers were under fire. They were the only ones
who knew that ESPN was there, gathering information for an upcoming
story and trying to determine if the administration was overreacting to
their antics.

The arena was half full. Most students had gone home for the break,
and since it was a nonconference game, a low-key crowd was expected.
About 15 Antlers showed up a full 90 minutes before tip-off to tease the
opposing team during warm-ups. Pregame is their prime time. Competing
sounds couldn't block out their taunts because most other fans hadn't
even gotten into their cars to head to the game yet. Other fans couldn't
block the view of their crazy outfits: One Antler was wearing a fuchsia
polyester dress that was ripping at the shoulders because he was too broad
for its seams. The rest of them were outfitted in navy and yellow T-shirts,
with sophomoric nicknames emblazoned on the back, for instance, "Sir
Loin," "Leprechaunorrhea," and "Rectum Ralph." These names matched
their brand of humor, as they took turns saying "penis" into our micro-

phone, hidden from everyone but them, to see if we were listening. Of course we were. We wanted to see how the administration and other fans would react to their antics.

It was this potty humor that had landed them in the hot seat. Just a quarter of the way into the 2013–2014 season, the Antlers had been ejected from two games for what the administration called inappropriate behavior and sexually suggestive language—verbal hooliganism, if you will. About 15 years ago, the Antlers had been suspended for an entire season and banned from the arena for generally poor behavior.

As they do for all games, the group came armed with taunts customized for the evening's opponents. "Why do you have a hairline like a 40-year-old?" they yelled at a player from Western Michigan. But looking too young is also a case for ribbing. Number 22 got one word hurled at him: "Puberty!" They'll make use of any characteristic they can exploit. Even as the arena filled in and the game got going, the Antlers sucked the white noise out of the space; they were the loudest fans by far, cheering madly in support of the home team, working up a sweat before the first whistle. Between chants of "Let's Go Tigers," obligatory ref razzing, and dancing in place to the arena soundtrack, they picked on individual opponents. "Hey 32, you look like Tyler Perry," hooted one. "Katy Perry," snorted another Antler. And in the name of distraction, non sequiturs abound. "Austin Richie is ticklish!" Richie, a guard, is number 22 for Western Michigan. They had already accused him of suffering from hormonal deficiencies.

BIG SPORTS, BIG CHEERS

Pick a college campus, any Division I college campus. Big-time sports have big-time cheering sections. Students sit together in preassigned seating areas that carry names like the Quarry, the Bench, the Nest, or the Trough. You'll see the faithful rowdies at football and basketball games—and sometimes at hockey, soccer, or baseball matchups—dressed in school colors, saturated in body paint or wearing outrageous costumes and coming together with hopes of making their turf an intimidating stop for visiting teams with their vigorous taunts.

In the late 1880s, the Princeton Pep Club organized student cheering in the stands. From the beginning, the stadium was mostly filled with students. This was before the stands were regularly shared with adults from elaborate alumni networks and local communities. As early as 1916, students at University of Michigan football games sat together and formed a giant "M" with paper cards as a sign of spirit. According to Murray Sperber, the professor who was run out of Bloomington, Indiana, who also happens to be a Notre Dame historian, hateful cheer was part of the game in 1924, when Notre Dame traveled to play Nebraska. At that matchup, the students, along with townspeople in Lincoln, organized anti-Catholic chants in the stands. Notre Dame refused to visit Nebraska after that, and it would be 20 years until they faced one another on the football field again.

College basketball took a bit longer to capture the imaginations of the student fans. Oklahoma State claims to have had one of the first student sections, in the 1950s, in their basketball arena, Gallagher Hall. In 1957, leaders of the University of San Francisco's "rooting section" wore letter-man cardigans and guided fellow students in cheers. Student sections as we know them today, often called an "insult row," generally gelled as the twentieth century drew to a close. The enclosed space and intimacy of the arena means that cheering pulsates within earshot of the majority of the crowd. Signs and costumes pop from the stands, especially during free throws, and television cameras easily magnify the experience. These ele-ments contribute to the allure of the student section.

Nowadays students employ a strategic mix of dedication, diversion, and distraction. The best antics often go viral. You can count on a display of homemade signs that insult everything, from a school's reputation to a coach's intelligence or player's looks. If a player has had a run-in with the legal system, be it a speeding ticket or suspected drug use, fans will make sure those themes are on the day's cheer menu.

Paired with this high-decibel speech are highly creative visuals. San Diego State's student section, the Show, is credited with the first use of big heads—giant cardboard photo cutouts—as free throw distractions. Fans wave them behind the backboard as an opposing player steps up to the line to shoot a freebie. In 2002, the Show unveiled its debut Michael Jackson big head with the hopes of psyching out opposing players with its randomness.

Free throw distractions have morphed into sophisticated art projects. We see a pop culture arms race that picks the image of a celebrity, often controversial, to make a statement as a cardboard cutout, 3-D rendering, or life-size puppet. The goal? To mess with the heads of opposing players, coaches, and refs to help win the game. Of course, antics aren't just limited to arenas. Student groups have been known to hack websites, call opposing teams' hotel rooms in the middle of the night, and send pizzas.

CRAZIES AND ANTLERS

What do you get when you mix a smart, sophisticated, and resourceful student body; a consistently high-caliber team; and fans who will camp out overnight for weeks on end to get game tickets? The Cameron Crazies of Duke University. This famous, or infamous, group is named for its home court, Cameron Indoor Arena. The number of blue and white-clad members fluctuates at about a thousand. The Crazies aren't even close to being the biggest—Indiana University has been known to fill its student section with 7,800 devotees, the University of Kentucky with 4,500, and the University of Louisville with 2,300. The Crazies aren't as big as these other groups—Cameron only holds 9,314 fans—but they are certainly the most famous.

The origins of the Cameron Crazies are hazy. The name seems to date from the mid-1980s, and with the name came scrutiny. Credited with popularizing the chant "airball" for players who miss the backboard, net, and rim on a shot, the Crazies elevated the personal taunt to an art form. In 1984, after an opposing player who was being accused of sexual assault took the floor and was pelted with panties and condoms, Duke president Terry Sanford, a former North Carolina governor and U.S. senator, sent a letter to the student body chastising their trash talk. He warned students that they were getting a reputation for crudeness, profanity, and cheap shots. Sanford told students that he'd hate for people to think they were stupid at Duke, an elite private school with rigorous academic standards. He signed the letter "Uncle Terry," and it became facetiously known as the "avuncular" letter. In response, students reacted to bad calls with the ever-so-polite retort, "We beg to differ." Throughout the years, the Crazies have harassed an alleged plagiarizer with taunts of "copy machine" and got on retired NBA big man Shaquille O'Neal when he played for Louisiana State University, chanting that O'Neal (at 7'1" and almost 300 pounds) had a "big ol' butt."

In 2003, a Cameron Crazy wearing nothing but a royal blue Speedo gyrated under the basket with moves worthy of a professional pole dancer to try to break the focus of a University of North Carolina player who was at the line shooting free throws. UNC guard Jackie Manuel missed both attempts. Afterward, Mike Krzyzewski, Duke's iconic head coach and master of discipline, banned the practice, suggesting there was no need to be running around in one's underwear. As for the "Speedo Guy," well, he became a pastor. Most students now remain clothed for games, but the one-off tomfoolery of the student in the Speedo lives on in infamy. The university likes to say that the Cameron Crazies "are copied but never matched." But in reality, the Crazies follow historical precedent.

THE ORIGINS OF TRASH TALK

I traveled to Rome to visit the Circus Maximus. Morning joggers were running laps on a dusty path. The Rolling Stones were in the process of planning a concert at the location, amid objections that the expected onslaught of music aficionados would ruin the historic site. I'm not sure how it can get more ruined than it already appears. There are no remains of the concrete stands or chariot race course, just dirt, overgrown grass, and litter. Despite its underwhelming appearance, the Circus Maximus holds an important place in the history of sports and fandom.

The Circus Maximus was the Yankee Stadium, Michigan Stadium, and AT&T Stadium (home of the Dallas Cowboys) of its day, seating more fans than the three facilities combined—a quarter of a million spectators for the beloved races. That's five times the number of spectators that fit inside the Roman Coliseum to cheer on the gladiators.

I walked the grounds with a trained archeologist and tour guide, Livia Galante, a native of Rome who explained that at one time there were five hippodromes, or horse-racing stadiums, in Rome, which points to the immense popularity of these contests. At Circus Maximus, which was used for the first six centuries A.D., 12 charioteers, representing either the red, white, blue, or green team, would emerge from starting gates at the curved end of the circus. They galloped their horses around a long, skinny oval bisected by stone turning posts, and the first chariot to complete seven laps was the winner. Fans dressed in the colors of their favorite team.

The fans were so passionate about the competition, Galante said, that they placed curses on rival charioteers. She directed me to an archeological museum near Rome's main train station, where lead "curse tablets," or *defixiones*, hung. But upon my arrival, after wandering in circles, I discovered that part of the museum was closed for renovation—perhaps I am slightly cursed—and I could only view the mid-fourth-century trash talking in a book. They had put the mystical curse tablets away.

According to the museum's employees, who seemed to regard me as a nuisance and begrudgingly pulled out a guidebook in Italian, which my translator helped me muddle through, these tablets reveal how ancient fans cursed their opponents. Etched in ancient Greek and Latin on delicate and decrepit metal sheets were various taunts, sometimes cursing individual charioteers, sometimes wishing harm on the horses. In one tablet, the creator pragmatically wishes for the starting gate to fail. Another calls for the gods to make a rival charioteer bedridden and suffer an evil death. One pointedly proposes amputating a competitor's foot. Fans buried these tablets at the Circus, sometimes under the starting line. Although the defixiones are ancient history and stored in dusty museums, the sentiments track with today: Fans are committed to all forms of intimidation, believing they've figured out how to make a difference.

LARGE CORNED BEEF SANDWICHES

Most universities work with an official student section, which at Mizzou is known as the "Zoo Crew." The Antlers, on the other hand, are unofficial and unsanctioned, and number about 30 rebellious fans. "I think we are the best fan group in the country," said Emmett Delaney, the head Antler, or Grand Poobah, as he is called. Delaney was in his junior year, majoring in finance. Two members of the Antlers from his high school recruited him. "I think we have the same effect, if not greater, than the Cameron Crazies," Delany stated for our TV camera. "We do it like a special forces team, small but effective."

Current Antlers select the new members. If you want to be an Antler, you have to prove your Mizzou basketball knowledge, as well as your creativity, during the application process. During the interview, Delaney said questions range from the predictable to something like, "If you were the candy Mike and Ike's, what color would you be?" This year, a little more than half the Antler applicants made the cut.

A month after the Western Michigan game, I was back in Columbia, Missouri. Invited into the Antler's inner sanctum long before game time, I took my camera crew to a student apartment with cheap wall-to-wall carpeting and hand-me-down college furnishings. Not much adorned the walls except a giant team logo sticker and an American flag. Even though two months had passed since the holiday, a small plastic Christmas tree sat atop the mantle, along with a gray plastic decorative keg of Coors.

A bunch of 18 to 21-year-olds were debating how to spell the word "*crimson.*" They weren't picking paint chips or fighting over crayons, but rather trying to come up with the best way to taunt the day's opposing players, the Alabama Crimson Tide, as they crafted signs to take into the arena. They were going for clever, not crass, to avoid having the signs confiscated—or worse—getting ejected again. Of course, the difference between clever and crass is subject to interpretation. "Sometimes we have signs that are just so outrageous, they don't mean anything," Mason Bartlett, an Antler majoring in art history, told me. "The event staff is like, 'What does that mean?' And we are like, 'I don't know,' and so they're like, 'We are taking that for sure.'"

As a freshman, Bartlett applied for a job at a gas station. During the interview, he was asked if there were certain days he would need off. When Bartlett said he was an Antler and that he needed all home basketball games off, the woman interviewing him ended the interview. Bartlett did not get the job.

Along with the signs, the Antlers were carrying a cutout photo of Katherine Webb (Miss Alabama 2012 and girlfriend, now wife, of then Alabama quarterback A. J. McCarron) on poster board. They also had their stat sheets, which are well-crafted research and statistical notes on the opponent. Many student sections embrace this often-devious tool. The Antlers know what works and have a few members assigned to stat sheet patrol. "Their job is to look up the team's roster and get Facebooks, Twitters, criminal histories," Delaney said. "If the guy's got a parking ticket we're gonna know about it."

When University of Mississippi guard Marshall Henderson was found with less than one-tenth of a gram of cocaine in his car, he avoided prosecution, but not ridicule. When the Rebels played Missouri, one Antler showed up at the game with pancake powder all over his face, simulating "white face," if you will. Delaney pointed out that Henderson was averaging 22 points a game that season, and he had 11 against Mizzou, evidence to the Antlers of a job well done.

Sophomore Julian Vizitei was majoring in education. He was known, thanks to the color of his hair, to answer to the nickname the "Pudgy Ginger." Growing up, his family attended Mizzou basketball games. He said his mother hoped he'd join the pep band, but he opted for the Antlers. He beamed as he told the story of how he got under the skin of an opposing player. "I had a guy yell at me once when he was walking off the court," related Vizitei, who was probably the loudest Antler of the season. "He said, 'I don't like the redheaded kid.'"

The Antlers' efforts were focused on heckling inside the arena, but they recounted an outside mission from the previous year. When Arkansas's basketball team got on their bus to take them from the airport to the hotel, three Antlers got in their cars and drove about 20 miles an hour in front of the bus. The Grand Poobah proudly explained that it took the bus more than an hour for a trip that normally takes 30 minutes. As for the standard pizza delivery to the hotel room? "We're college kids, we can't afford to buy a pizza for every game we have," Delaney admitted. "We kind of save that kind of stuff for the bigger games."

The Antlers have done an admirable job of embracing the latest cultural zeitgeist in sports. For Alabama games, some of the guys dress in costume, which includes the fuchsia dress again, a Davy Crockett coonskin cap, a Richie Incognito jersey, and Ray-Ban sunglasses. Incognito was the NFL player at the center of a bullying scandal among Miami Dolphins players and was indefinitely suspended from the game. The Antler wearing the turquoise Dolphins jersey with Incognito's number 68 told me "he got it cheap."

The Antlers have identified a favorite target. "Trevor Releford plays for Alabama, his brother [Travis] used to play for Kansas," commented Delaney with glee. "Travis was a lot better so we call him Travis, and his mom hates it!"

The unauthorized Antlers sit in the arena just behind the university-approved student fan group the Zoo Crew. Once upon a time, the Antlers had courtside seats, but their behavior got them moved back from the floor. They now trawl a mid-section ghetto. For the Alabama game, I had two video cameras trained on the Antlers. People often amp up their behavior when they know they are being taped, but judging from previous descriptions, I felt pretty good that we were documenting raw Antler activity.

A raspy scream came from Delaney's rotund frame: "Hey Travis, I've eaten corned beef sandwiches bigger than you." A non sequitur, for sure, lobbed at the Releford kid. I couldn't tell if his mother was at the game. The Alabama player didn't acknowledge the comment, which is pretty standard. It's rare to see a player admit that the teasing works.

Although much of a typical college student's social activity is fueled by alcohol, Delaney said that isn't the case with the Antlers. At football games, students often tailgate into oblivion, but for basketball, they mostly lay off the booze, at least until postgame. For the Antlers, it's a rule. "We're already acting rambunctious, and if event staff sees these drunk idiots over there, we just look stupid," said Delaney. "But if we all blow zeroes, we are just wild and crazy guys having fun." Good point.

Why are the Antlers called the Antlers? Missouri's team is known as the Tigers, so there's no jungle connection there. During the third quarter of every game, the Antlers raise their hands to their temples and pantomime having antlers, while standing and twirling in their section as the band plays the "Missouri Waltz," the state's official song. It's sort of like a more madcap seventh-inning stretch. In its infancy, people were spotted doing this dance from across the arena, and observers thought it looked like a 1976 *Saturday Night Live* skit featuring Lily Tomlin. A nom de theater was born.

In the mid-1970s, it was apparently easy to spot the Antlers. "Basketball was like a mausoleum on bingo night. There was nothing going on," said Jeff Gordon, a sportswriter for the *St. Louis-Post Dispatch* and one of the Missouri students who founded the Antlers almost 40 years ago. "We were just a bunch of guys going there and having a good time, and you could have an impact."

Norm Stewart, who was Missouri's head coach at the time, adored the Antlers and thought they meant eight to ten points a game to his team. But opposing coaches? Not so much. The Antlers once put the head of a real hog on a stick outside the arena and taunted Arkansas coach Nolan Richardson. "I was long gone from the school, but the pigs head on a stick?" said Gordon with a grin. He praised the prank by posing a rhetorical question: "Why wouldn't you?"

Antler Mason Bartlett contended that the current coaching staff had also expressed support. "Hey guys . . . keep coming," then-Missouri head coach Frank Haith told the Antlers, according to Bartlett. "We really appreciate it."

In 2001, one of the Antlers ran onto the court, tackled University of Illinois mascot Chief Illiniwek, and was arrested. "From time to time, they would step over a line in the eyes of the administration and then have to fight their way back in," Gordon related. "So many different kids have gone through all that, and yet today, here they are still going strong."

But the Antlers' lack of etiquette is too much for the current administration. Almost as soon as the season got underway, complaints started rolling in to the athletic department about offensive heckling. E-mails obtained through a public records request revealed the nature of the grievances. A math professor wrote that when a visiting player was injured, the Antlers could be heard urging the trainer to "check his hymen." An arena employee explained that at a women's basketball game, the Antlers teased the opposing players about their weight. "You're used to being around energy and excitement and enthusiasm and support," said Mike Alden, Missouri's athletic director for the past 16 years, in an interview with ESPN. "But certainly some of those will make you step back and take a little bit of pause." Alden since announced he planned to retire as of August 2015.

In November, Delaney, as the head of the Antlers, was called to a meeting with school administrators at the Student Center. He dressed in a suit and tie. They told him they had a problem with things the Antlers had been saying in the arena and on Twitter, and he was handed a list that detailed more than 20 crude chants heard at recent games. The administrators told him that the Antlers were in serious trouble.

Delaney said he regretted that the list was accurate—with references to herpes, tampons, abortions, and a request for spectators at a game against Southeastern Louisiana to raise their hands if they thought Hurricane Katrina was a good thing. But Delaney said the Antlers had already agreed amongst themselves to clean up and tone down, even before the meeting.

The next day, at a game against Gardner-Webb, a small private university in North Carolina, the Antlers launched into a chant that wasn't on the list. "We had this chant that when a team comes out of the locker room, we yell, 'Scum scum scum, go back to where you're from,' three times, and then we say 'and die,'" Delaney said. "With administration being on our back, I was like, guys, we'll say 'and cry.' It sounds the same, and I think that kinda got to half the guys and the other half didn't hear it."

But the chant drew the ire of the authorities, and the Antlers were promptly ejected from the game before it began. When they asked the campus police and athletic department staffers who had expelled them why they were being asked to leave, they said they were told, "You know why." "I couldn't believe it," said Julian Vizitei, one of the most vocal Antlers. "They took us to the hospitality room, which wasn't very hospitable." Escorted from the arena floor, the Antlers gave their names to a police officer, who also checked their IDs. Each Antler was issued a temporary trespassing warning.

Two days later, at a game versus Indiana University–Purdue University Indianapolis, the Antlers tried again. According to the group, they chanted the words "*sportsmanship*" and "*respect*" until the second half, when again they thought they could rely on an Antler classic, where they chant, "Pelvic thrust, churn the butter, step to the right, cop a feel," and then squeeze their neighbor's shoulder. But that didn't work either, and they were booted once again. Said Delaney, "They told us to cop a feel is sexual conduct and won't be tolerated." As they were being escorted out of the arena for the second straight game, the Antlers waved to the people in the crowd, some of whom were booing.

Alden said it doesn't matter that these particular chants weren't on the list the Antlers initially received. "When you're taking a look at personal attacks on people, or different things that certainly are inconsistent with the values that you have as an institution, it's common sense," he stated, indicating that members of the rogue group should have known not to use those cheers.

"I understand they have a job to do," Delaney said. But for some reason, the powers that be are clamping down more than they did in the past. As to why, "Your guess is as good as mine," he added.

Since then, the Antlers have toned it down, survived their version of "double secret probation," and avoided ejection. For the Alabama game, they razzed the school and individual players, steering clear of inflammatory chants. One of the signs they held up read, "Tuscalosers," a play on the University of Alabama's location, Tuscaloosa. But, in fact, the Antlers said that a sign with the same phrase was actually confiscated by arena security last season, a move that seems to underscore Delaney's sentiment about ever-changing standards.

Despite the drama, the Antlers never veer from their love for Mizzou basketball. The Tigers beat the visitors by 21 points. A postgame celebration of chicken wings and beer followed, with some laughs recapping highlights of the game, for example, the Travis/Trevor taunt and how friends kept coming up to them to tell them that ESPN should "show more hockey highlights."

"We're the best fans the team has," Delaney declared. Win or lose, scrutiny or not, the Antlers' passion burns strong. Delaney said no matter what, he'll always cheer for his beloved Tigers.

THE PIT CREW

Almost 2,000 miles to the northwest, in Eugene, Oregon, the University of Oregon's official student section, the Pit Crew, brings a different brand of raucous behavior, and I was there a few weeks after my final visit with the Antlers to document the scene with my ESPN camera crew and correspondent. They are a little more corporate, a lot bigger—the Crew averages 1,500 students a game—and definitely better dressed. They should be. The University of Oregon's biggest booster is Nike founder, Portland royalty, and Oregon alum Phil Knight, whose company helps outfit the Pit Crew. A few years ago, the most dedicated student fans got their own Pit Crew sneakers.

At the mid-February game, the Pit Crew was doing everything it could to distract the archrival Washington Huskies. The lower stands were swelling with screaming students, decked out in yellow Pit Crew T-shirts. I sat courtside, in front of the "Pit." Directly behind me was senior Cody Karlin. "I love being loud and crazy," revealed Karlin in a television interview. "I guess that's just kinda who I am. In a hectic college environment, it's good to have that outlet." Loud and crazy was an accurate description. The section throbbed with shrieks and feet stomping on the bleacher seats.

Karlin dresses in an apron and tucks his light brown, curly hair into a chef's hat for each game. Why? Why not? Any distraction, Karlin explained, can help. He pointed to the influence the Pit Crew can have. "People really start to get into the game in the last couple of minutes, especially in a close game," stated Karlin. "The energy is tangible, and I think it really makes a difference on the court."

Helping the team is a common refrain among the die-hards of any student section. Guys who can't play funnel their energy into extreme cheering. Sort of like that line from the movie *Grease*: "If you can't be an athlete, be an athletic supporter."

Home team players and coaches appreciate the effort. Later in the season, Oregon head coach Dana Altman made the rounds on campus, visiting the library, rec center, and frat houses to make his plea for students to come out and cheer for their team.

Earlier in the day, Karlin and company had bought the domain name of a Washington student fan website, UWDawgpack.com, and redirected it to UOPitcrew.com. This digital prank meant that Washington students trying to find out the latest information online from other student fans would instead be accessing information about Oregon's Pit Crew. Score one for the Ducks.

Score two for the Ducks on how many student fans showed up for the game against Washington. The Pit Crew dominated the space under one of the backboards and the entire side behind the TV announcers. The Crew's cheers ranged from, "We are going to beat the Duck out of you!" to a taunt directed at a UW player named Andrew Andrews: "Two first na-ames!" As they clapped in unison, next came, "Ric-ky Bob-by!" a reference to the Will Ferrell movie *Talladega Nights*. They were hoping that the taunts would be enough to startle Andrews.

The Pit Crew boasts a rich resume of pranks. In 2005, they taunted Washington's 5'9" point guard, Nate Robinson, with photos of pint-sized actor Gary Coleman, chanting "Ga-ry Cole-man" when Robinson took the floor. Fans have also been known to try to rattle shorter players by chanting "Webster," after the 1980s TV show featuring another small actor, Emmanuel Lewis.

Pit Crew members will admit that they have crossed the line at times. In 2002, they repeatedly yelled "deadbeat dad" and "your son hates you" at University of Southern California coach Henry Bibby, who was estranged from his son, Mike, a NBA player. The elder Bibby told reporters at the time they were the "rudest fans" he had ever seen.

In 2008, when the University of California, Los Angeles, came to play in Eugene, the Bruins roster included Kevin Love, who was raised in Oregon but, as a top high school recruit, had chosen the Bruins over the Ducks. His return to his home state was tinged with rancor. Students held up signs displaying his cell phone number and calling him fat. In the stands, fans tossed popcorn at his family and called his grandmother a whore.

Looking back at the incident almost a decade later, Love recalled that he actually got death threats. "There's certain times where it really does cross the line, and being a fan can be taken a little bit too far," he said as part of our television story. "It's sad, you don't want to see that in sports." Probably the meanest moment in student section history? In 1988, students from Arizona State University chanted "PLO, PLO" to distract Arizona guard Steve Kerr, whose father had been assassinated in Lebanon by terrorists.

Despite the hostility, Love claimed his game wasn't affected. Indeed, UCLA won, 80–75, and Love racked up 26 points and 18 rebounds.

If Love thrived on the attention from Oregon supporters, former USC player Gabe Pruitt may have wilted under it against Cal. In 2006, Pruitt faced humiliation at the hands of the Berkeley student section. During a time when cyber flirting was new and uncharted, and a mere two years after the launch of Facebook, a Cal student posed as a potential date named "Victoria" and began exchanging Instant Messages with Pruitt the week before a pivotal USC–Cal game. The conversation quickly turned personal. With the handle "SexyBruin Babe," "Victoria" told Pruitt "he was so hot." In a later conversation, Pruitt suggested that his digital paramour "dream about him." Pruitt planned to meet up with Victoria after the game once he got back to Los Angeles.

But at Cal's sold-out Haas Pavilion, just moments into pregame warm-ups, "Victoria" was exposed as a hoax. Students circulated a flyer with Pruitt's number, the Instant Message conversation, and photos Pruitt had sent Victoria. By the time the national anthem was being played, Pruitt realized what was going on. Throughout the entire game, chants of "Victoria" rang out. So did the chant "Gabe got punked," as well as recitations of Pruitt's cell phone number. He went 3-for-13. The *New York Times* magazine included the antic in its "Year in Ideas" issue with the title "NCAA Psyop."

Former Cal student Steve Kenyon, a freshman at the time, was the brains behind the idea. On a warm San Francisco spring day, I met him at his office at the University of San Francisco, where he worked as director of marketing for the Dons' athletic department. His office is actually a trailer across from the basketball gym, and while it is furnished with a phone, desk, and computer, it is also storage for mascot headgear and a megaphone.

Until our meeting, he had never publicly explained the prank. Among the University of San Francisco gear, Kenyon unloaded his Cal story. First came the origin of the pseudonym—his parents had planned on naming him "Victoria" if he was born a girl. The point was to distract an opposing player, something Kenyon had been trying to do during the entire season from his seat close to the floor. "Coaches would step in front, between me and the player, to be just like, 'Hey come on. Stop talking to this guy.'" Pruitt wasn't even the first USC player Kenyon had tried to lure into a prank outside the arena, but he was the first to take the bait. Kenyon argued that he was just trying to give Cal a competitive advantage.

"You can make more of an impact in college basketball as a fan than you can in any other sport in the world," claimed Kenyon. He went on to explain that the disconnect between the athlete and the fan is "so much greater in football than it is in basketball." In football, Kenyon said, "the players are in the zone, they are literally in a helmet. They can't hear anybody." Some football fans would disagree. Look at Seattle Seahawks or Kansas City Chiefs fans and how they orchestrate a loud, intimidating environment for every home game.

For the first half, Kenyon sat in his usual seat, waving a large poster of the photo Pruitt had sent of himself, wearing only boxer shorts and flexing his muscles. In most circles, displaying oversized photos of half-dressed people in public is considered deviant behavior, but in that venue, no one batted an eye.

About midway through the game, arena employees yanked Kenyon out of his seat and into a hallway. As it turned out, his phone number had been circulated on the chat flyer as well, and as he sat in the student section cheering, he heard his phone ring. In retrospect, he assumed someone was trying to confirm his identity. Arena employees didn't seem overly concerned with the prank itself, just that Pruitt's phone number had been made public. Kenyon said he was ultimately told, "Great job, go back out there and have fun," and sent back to his seat.

Kenyon recounted a conversation he had after the game with a starter for the Cal team, who told him the student section's spirit absolutely made a difference, as Cal beat USC by 11 and headed into the postseason hoping for their first NCAA tournament berth in several years. On the bubble for the tournament, the Bears' definitive win over the Trojans gave them a total of 12 conference wins and brought them one step closer to success.

Despite the fact that he was underage, Kenyon said he celebrated at a favorite campus bar and was hailed as a hero for his antics. The bash after the Cal–USC game, he explained, was epic. "It was a killer, killer post-game celebration."

Aside from some angry Trojan boosters online, Kenyon faced no re-percussions for his prank. What could Cal do? What rules had he broken? But jest can and often does have consequences, especially when it in-volves four-letter words. In this case, the Internet reverberated as word of the prank began to spread, and Kenyon faced backlash. He said he got messages from USC fans threatening to physically harm him and have him prosecuted. Several days later, Kenyon went back online to apolo-gize to Pruitt via Instant Message. "I'm sorry if people have been calling you and bothering your personal life," he typed.

Pruitt actually complimented the prank, writing back, "I expect that on the road, so it's fun."

Kenyon described his motivation for the online apology: "I wanted to just clear it up a little bit. I was worried that Gabe himself was actually going to try and push the legal." He said he was shocked by Pruitt's thick skin. With a lack of long-term repercussions, this outcome allowed the "Victoria" prank to go down in fan intimidation history rather than serve as a warning to the limits of cyber stalking an opponent.

THE ANATOMY OF BAD WORDS

Slightly more than a decade ago, the University of Maryland came under pressure to address a pattern of profane heckling. In 2004, during a na-tionally televised basketball game on ESPN between archrivals Duke and Maryland, Maryland students showered Duke player J. J. Redick with chants of "fuck you J. J." You could hear the hostile clamor on television.

Redick would become Duke's all-time leading scorer and, throughout his college career, be targeted by opposing fans, whether playing at Ma-ryland, Florida State, or Temple. There was something about Redick that earned him the reputation as the most hated player in college basketball at the time—his skill, his swagger. At one point, his parents were forced to change their home phone number, and Redick had to trade in his cell number.

Redick radiated arrogance on the court, which is no way to endear yourself to a student section. He admitted he thrived on the teasing, telling the *Washington Post*, "I'm able to internalize all the hateful things that are said to me, and it gets my competitive juices going." Redick scored 26 points against Maryland, and Duke won, 68–60.

At Maryland, heckling Redick as public enemy number one became performance art. In addition to the profanity-laced tirades, students held up signs that said, "I hate you J. J." and wore T-shirts printed with "F#$# you J. J."

After the profanity used by fans during the Duke game, criticism mounted, and Maryland sought legal guidance. They had endured an embarrassing incident a few years earlier, when the mother of Duke player Carlos Boozer was hit in the head by a water bottle thrown by a student and required medical attention.

The issue this time was whether the school could boot students from the arena for bad behavior, like cursing out Redick. Could Maryland place limits on student speech at the games considering that the university is a public institution and the games are played in a public facility? According to the U.S. Constitution, the university was obligated to protect free speech, for instance, the use of the word *fuck*. The "F word" is not considered obscene, as the legal definition of obscenity only refers to hardcore sexual conduct. Also, while universities play special roles in educating young people, they also have to support an open exchange of ideas.

When it comes to controlling verbal sludge, there's more leeway at a private school. For example, at Boston University, in 2006, after BU hockey fans jettisoned the classic chant "Rough 'em up" for "Fuck 'em up," the university prohibited cursing in its rink. According to a spokesman for the school, 15 students were thrown out of the hockey arena during the first three years of the policy, but no one has been tossed since, and excessive swearing no longer seems to be a problem.

But since the majority of schools in Division I sports are public, it's a different standard. To that end, Maryland's president consulted with the state attorney general's office on the school's options. John K. Anderson, an assistant attorney general for the state, responded by citing a landmark free speech case from 1971, *Cohen v. California*, which addressed a person wearing a "Fuck the Draft" button on a jacket. The U.S. Supreme Court ruled in a 5–4 decision that states cannot prohibit certain words from the public's vocabulary. "One man's vulgarity," Justice John Marshall Harlan writes in the majority opinion, "is another's lyric."

According to Anderson, the university had the authority to control the chaos as long as the restrictions did not include criminal punishments. Because children were present at the arena, the university could have forced fans to alter communication to avoid offending "captive" spectators. This is known as the "captive auditor" doctrine. If steps would have been taken to draft a carefully worded policy that was publicized and enforced in a specific way, Maryland might have had a way to clamp down on the cursing, counseled Anderson.

Several months after the incidents, a student task force promised that students would show some self-control and improve their behavior. Brian Ullmann, a spokesman for the school, explained that it is difficult for the administration to dictate behavior and that it's "more impactful if it is peer to peer."

It didn't hurt to have someone from the basketball team involved. The next season, Maryland head coach Gary Williams spoke to fans about their word choices, and the students instituted a T-shirt exchange, during which one could trade in a X-rated shirt for something PG-13. When Redick and Duke rolled onto campus for the next year's game, complaints about profanity declined, and Maryland beat the Blue Devils in overtime.

A PRAGMATIC APPROACH

While Maryland ultimately wasn't willing to use legal muscle to control the jeering, one athletic administrator found a way to use the rules of the game. Karl Benson is now commissioner of the Sun Belt Conference, the third collegiate athletic conference he has presided over in his career. When he was commissioner of the Western Athletic Conference from 1994 to 2012, New Mexico State students were known to consistently chant "Nice shot, asshole" at opponents.

From his office in New Orleans's Superdome, Benson told me and my crew, "It was something that they had done for years and just kind of accepted as tradition." He came up with a process: If fans yelled that chant, the section would be warned. If they yelled it again, a technical foul would be called on their team, and the opposing team would head to the line and get to attempt two free throws. It worked, according to Benson, who said, "The very next game when the shot occurred, the students in unison chanted, 'Nice shot Karl Benson.'"

"You never want to discourage students and eliminate student crowds. But there is a line," Benson added. When asked how to define that line, Benson suggested it's anything that's profane, sexist, or racial in nature. "You know when something is acceptable, because you know you chuckle," he said. "You know when it's inappropriate when you say, 'You gotta be kidding me.' The idea that just because you pay to get into a game you can say anything is being tested right now."

Despite graduating from Mizzou's journalism school, Ken Paulson had never heard of the Antlers. Paulson is now dean of the College of Mass Communication at Middle Tennessee State University and head of the First Amendment Center, an organization dedicated to the study of free expression. He's also a former editor in chief of *USA Today*. Paulson reminded me that even hate speech is constitutionally protected, and that principle trickles down to student sections. They have the right to cheer, chant, and taunt almost anything they want.

"If they said, 'kill the ref' and they meant it, yes, you can bounce them out of there. But that is different," Paulson said. "You can express yourself any way you want to as crudely and rudely as you choose to as long as you're not interfering with the game or creating some kind of a disturbance to be violent or disruptive."

Paulson doesn't see many student speech issues that get pursued, since student sections don't have lawyers on retainer and aren't ready to take on large public universities in test cases. Paulson said no potential litigant is "going to get into a courtroom for less than $10,000," and it is unlikely that the language is worth $10,000 to them. But he said the Antlers probably would have had a case. "I'm amazed Mizzou went to the students and took them out of the game. They have no legal standard to do that," related Paulson, "no matter what they (the students) are saying."

One issue was the involvement of campus cops. Grand Poobah Delaney recalled a heavier police presence in the Antlers' section right before they were ejected. Once they were removed and sent to the hospitality room, the Antlers were left to the police. Documents from a public records request show that the Mizzou administration expressed concern about police involvement and warned that police and event staff were prohibited from physically touching spectators with regard to verbal issues.

Some legal scholars say universities have developed a basketball arena for commercial purposes and not public discourse, meaning free speech laws don't apply. Professional arenas fall into that category. Unlike a public school, for instance, the government does not run Yankee Stadium. Plus, universities have codes of conduct and mission statements that may be applied to speech. As for the Maryland assistant attorney general's contention that the heckling could harm children in the audience, a legal scenario known as "captive auditors," Paulson disagreed. "People attend voluntarily," he said. "A captive audience is a public school classroom. The law says you must be there. That's a captive auditor. It's not a captive audience when people pay admission to get into a place."

I asked Paulson about signs. "You can control the size and you can control whether they have signs, but you can't control what they're saying," he replied.

Maryland's Ullmann stated that he finds signage even more worrisome because they could easily pop up on television under the basket during a foul shot. One sign he wishes students hadn't made was displayed at a game against Oral Roberts University in the first round of the NIT: "Why stop at Oral? Let's go all the way." But Maryland lawyers told him there was nothing he could do unless someone complained that they couldn't see the game. The University of Illinois avoids the issue by banning signs and banners altogether, which, as Paulson acknowledged, is permissible.

Paulson countered with the belief that you can influence student section behavior by employing the right strategy. "Asking them to quiet down, asking them to be more respectful, and asking them to leave is perfectly consistent with the First Amendment," he declared. The challenge, of course, is when people don't take the hint.

Paulson listed other ways schools can manage arenas, including controlling both the size of banners people bring in and where they sit. "The biggest issue is when there are 60 young men typically sitting together, chanting the same thing, and creating havoc in an arena." Paulson suggested simply splitting up the student section. "Create a policy where you've got four tickets here, six tickets here, two tickets there. Or sit them right next to the band and make sure the drummers and the trombone players are right next to them," he suggested.

Duke's president wasn't the only one to write to the student body, chastising them about their behavior. The athletic director and head foot-ball coach sent an e-mail to students at the University of Wisconsin asking them to tone down their vulgarity. The Big Ten Conference has been threatening student sections with dissolution for bad behavior for more than 12 years and has handed out a handful of warnings, which is the first strike in a three-strike program. The conference has never called a second strike on students. When I asked, they refused to release the number of first-time warnings issued.

But as Karl Benson mentioned, the chance that a student section would get exiled into oblivion is minute. No one wants to clamp down on students so that they are driven from the arena. Repercussions would be felt not only at the gate, but with alumni giving, with the media, and even in recruiting. Unless, of course, it is a small group of rogue Missouri hoops fans with a history of trouble and a childish vocabulary that prove to be an easy target for a publicity-conscious administration.

8

THE AGE OF ENTITLEMENT

How We Are Shaping a
New Generation of Sports Fans

Fans provide time and hearts for the sport of sports and for the business of sports.—Stephen A. Greyser, Harvard Business School professor

There's no question that sports is a massive business. Look no further than the corporate names of stadiums, mass marketing of teams, or generously compensated athletes. Not to mention the crazy money for Super Bowl ads, massive sales of merchandise from hats to jerseys, and the inflated prices for the food available at games. The powers that be know that there's big money to be made off this passion. That beer-guzzling, jersey-wearing guy headed to his buddy's house to watch football all day isn't only a sports fan, he's a fruitful revenue stream. Fans in the United States spent $14.3 billion on sports logo apparel alone in 2013, according to the Sports Business Research Network, a data research firm. No wonder marketers are paying attention.

A NEW DEMOGRAPHIC

This idea of the fan as a revenue stream doesn't only exist in the United States. Gabriele Marcotti covers soccer/football in various languages for several outlets, including ESPN. Born in Italy and currently living in England, he has witnessed the transformation of the game in England. English football, with its top-level Premier League, once mostly known for working-class passions, spectator violence, and decrepit stadiums, is wildly popular with a mainstream, international audience. This translates into big transactions. Billionaire owners pluck the best players in the world to compete, and people from throughout the world religiously follow teams like Manchester United, Arsenal, and Chelsea. Television rights are highly lucrative, and the competition to secure these contracts is fierce.

"The Premier League is very commercially successful," said Marcotti. "They're very smart about saying, 'Oh look, we defeated hooliganism.' But they defeated hooliganism in part because of draconian measures and largely because they simply raised ticket prices to such a degree that working-class people can't afford a ticket." He noted, "The Premier League fans are the oldest in Europe," because many fans, especially the younger set, are priced out.

It's sad for people like Nicky Allt, the Liverpool supporter and retired hooligan. For him and others like him, passion for a football team explains one's identity. That passion is not to be milked as a revenue opportunity. "These are cultural assets, these are people's lives, they've grown up with these things," said Allt. Along with rampant commercialization comes the loss of the sport and perhaps the identity these fans once knew.

Allt and other grassroots guardians of football tradition are left behind as fandom morphs into something he no longer recognizes. "People are not as fanatical as they used to be," he added. "They're sort of looking at their teams as franchises and brands."

Allt isn't alone in his feeling of alienation. Marcotti told me that fans in Italy, Germany, and the Netherlands are protesting what they see as the overcommercialization of football by raising banners that say, "Against Modern Football." Whether these banners are raised at Champions League, Europa League, or local league matches, the message is the same: Too much greed is ruining the game. They are arguing that owners don't have the fan's best interest at heart.

What does it mean to be a fan against modern football? "They're against too many games on television and high ticket prices," stated Marcotti. "They're against owners and agents taking money out and being greedy. They see themselves as a pure manifestation of fandom."

A similar feeling of being left behind has also arisen in the United States. "The crowd's changed," declared Ed Anzalone, aka "Fireman Ed," the former high-profile Jets fan. He blames the price of the game and especially the personal seat licenses, known as PSLs, like the ones the Giants and Jets sold in advance of opening their new stadium in the Meadowlands in 2010. About half of the teams in the league sell PSLs. It's a one-time fee that allows you to buy season tickets, and the money funds stadium construction. But the PSLs don't come cheap. The best seat in the house to watch the Dallas Cowboys play at their new stadium, opened in 2009, required a fee of $150,000, and that's before plunking down any money for the actual ticket.

"Even the people that do go to the games, they feel like they've been taken advantage of, and they feel like they're owed something," Anzalone told me. For Jets games at New Jersey's MetLife Stadium, PSL fees are required for two-thirds of the seats and range from $4,000 to $30,000. "You've got families that were there for 90 years that no longer go to the games because they got priced out. They said, 'Oh, we'll give you a ticket, but you'll be upstairs.'"

With a changing fan base, attitudes shift. "I don't think people have the respect they once had. As the years have gone on, I think it's more of a 'me' society, and everybody feels entitled," lamented Anzalone. "I don't think it's just in the stands, I think it's in society in general, when you're driving a car, when you're online for a product. I don't think the courtesy is there that used to be years ago."

A CULTURE OF RUDENESS

After the brutal beating of San Francisco Giants fan Bryan Stow, Jorge Costa, the team's senior vice president for ballpark operations, told *USA Today*, "People are taking ownership of events in a different way. . . . It's not the team won or lost; it's *he* won or lost. You see a difference in fans' need for acceptance and self-glorification, maybe in ways you didn't see before."

When you've paid money for a game, there is a sense that acting out is socially acceptable. This free-for-all includes screaming nasty insults at players, throwing objects on the field, nudity, and even sex in the stands. (Whatever you do, don't Google "sex at stadiums.") In the name of research, Daniel Wann, the Murray State psychologist, compiled a list of items thrown onto the field by rowdy fans during two Yankee playoff games in the mid-1990s. It includes a softball, a shot glass, personal electronics, a golf ball, plastic bottles, beer cans, a sanitary napkin dispenser, and small change. Fans have also been documented tossing urine bombs from hillsides during the Tour de France and the stands at Penn State's Beaver Stadium.

Good luck to anyone who asks another fan to tone down his or her behavior. During the summer of 2013, a Pittsburgh Pirates security guard lost his finger when it got caught in a fence during a scuffle after a woman refused to leave the ballpark when she got caught smoking in her seat.

People deplore a widespread epidemic of rudeness that permeates well beyond the culture of sports. Stigma and shame once shaped behavior, decorum was expected. But with the 1960s and 1970s, conformity gave way to self-expression, which began an all-out assault on the more button-upped standards of an earlier time. Now, bizarre and brazen acts garner attention and often lack consequences. Polls show that the majority of Americans believe popular culture has gotten cruder.

In modern times, humiliation functions as entertainment. Think of the most popular shows that have become television staples during the last decade. Examples include "Bridalplasty," where brides-to-be compete to win plastic surgery in time for their weddings; "Wolfboy, Divorced and Looking for Love," the tale of a man suffering from a disorder that makes his face hairy like—you guessed it—a wolf; and "The Littlest Groom," which chronicles the dating life of a dwarf and others.

Think of politics. There was a day when politicians used to refrain from calling one another outright liars. That changed when a U.S. representative shouted, "You lie!" at President Obama during a speech to Congress, forever coarsening political discourse. Today attacks on integrity are the norm. One recent poll found that 72 percent of Americans believe politics have become uncivil.

Think of the acceptance of profane language in the public arena, from Meryl Streep at the Golden Globes in 2012, when she cursed after forgetting to bring her glasses onstage, to Lady Gaga when she used profanity on *Saturday Night Live*. I'm not pointing fingers; I've been known to use the same choice language when I drop my bus transfer or someone cuts me off while I'm driving. Studies show that profanity is getting worse, especially in media directed at children. The Parents Television Council found that prime-time profanity increased almost 70 percent from 2005 to 2010. And researchers at Brigham Young University found that curse words are pervasive in adolescent best sellers.

We can see these changes in popular culture: In the 1950s, television shows would not depict married couples like Lucy and Ricky Ricardo of *I Love Lucy* sleeping in the same bed. President Clinton insisted he didn't inhale when he smoked pot. Yet, several years later, President Obama casually admitted to snorting cocaine in his memoir.

Trust in the government, church, local newspaper, and banks has disintegrated. Family and community don't provide the same structure they once did. "It's something much deeper and more existentially disruptive: the near total failure of each pillar institution of our society," writes MSNBC host and liberal pundit Chris Hayes in his book *Twilight of the Elites*. "We now operate in a world in which we can assume neither competence nor good faith from the authorities, and the consequences of this simple, devastating realization is the defining feature of American life at the end of this low, dishonest decade." In the book, Hayes cites poll after poll that illustrate America's loss of faith in public institutions during the last 20 years.

During this time, we've had pedophile priests, lying politicians, and corrupt executives. In this context, it's no wonder people have also lost faith in sports leaders. "While people feel like they *know* an actor, they feel like they *own* a sports star," writer Phoef Sutton told the *New York Daily News*. Sutton wrote the screenplay for the movie *The Fan*, starring Robert De Niro as a deranged baseball aficionado. "There's a sense of civic connection. And when they fail, it's almost like an elected official is letting them down," he said in that same interview.

And let them down is right. In the past decade, athletes have disappointed us. Many of baseball's notable sluggers were exposed as steroid users. Lance Armstrong's seven consecutive Tour de France victories from 1999 to 2005 were exposed as fabrications fueled by drugs. Former track star and fastest woman in the world Marion Jones served jail time for lying about her use of performance-enhancing drugs.

The National Football League has faced major litigation because of allegations that it suppressed the seriousness of concussions, jeopardizing the health of its players. Penn State University covered up the relationship of a pedophile coach to its football program, and the school president and other administrators faced criminal charges. The NFL is also under fire for its handling of domestic abuse. In 2014, football player Ray Rice was caught on security video punching his fiancé, now wife, who fell to the floor unconscious in an elevator before he dragged her out. The NFL knew of the incident and suspended Rice for two games; however, the widespread release of the video by the website TMZ created an uproar, prompting the league to suspend him indefinitely. His team, the Baltimore Ravens, immediately cut him. The league's indefinite suspension was eventually overturned. Nonetheless, the incident and the NFL's tepid reaction before the video was released sparked a national debate about domestic abuse and the league's erratic responses to the issue throughout the years.

"An institution that rewards the reckless will act as a spawning ground for recklessness," writes Hayes. In another era, it would have been unthinkable to see photos of boxer Oscar De La Hoya dressed in women's clothing or listen to vivid details about the sexcapades of golfer Tiger Woods. But now the digital world brings the less heroic actions of star athletes to their fans at an instantaneous pace. The seemingly constant stream of the rogues' gallery in sports, including those who commit mayhem, rape, and even murder, is global in its reach.

SELF-ESTEEM = SELF-ABSORPTION

In trying to understand a culture of bad behavior, I turned toward the self-esteem movement for an explanation. Self-esteem became a go-to topic in the late 1960s as a way to predict success in life. A healthy dose of self-esteem means feeling good about yourself, no matter how you act or what you've done. *Saturday Night Live*'s Al Franken poked fun at the movement with his character Stuart Smalley and the dead-on mantra, "I'm good enough. I'm smart enough. And doggone it, people like me!"

For 35 years, psychologists have suggested that a strong belief in the concept of self-esteem is a predictor of happiness. If you believe in yourself, you can be anything you want to be. Success, prosperity, and health can be improved with a helping of self-esteem. In response, well-meaning parents and leaders have tried to make changes to develop healthy self-esteem in our kids. Schools reward students for showing up to class rather than actual achievement. Coaches hand out trophies to all participants, not just the winners, and don't keep score. Parents eschew traditional discipline and allow children to be the masters of their own destiny. California even created a self-esteem task force during the mid-1980s to figure out how to save money based on happier citizens. (Only in California!) I once had a friend tell me she suffered from "low self-esteem," like it was a bad allergy.

But in the past decade, the hold of self-esteem as a cure-all has begun to erode. An entire genre of literature—*The Myth of Self Esteem*, *Nurture Shock*, and *Generation Me: Why Today's Young Americans Are More Confident, Assertive, Entitled—and More Miserable Than Ever Before*—has set out to debunk self-esteem as a panacea. As for that California task force, it couldn't even confirm its basic premise that boosting self-esteem leads to more positive outcomes.

This discussion left me wondering if the self-esteem movement had helped create a generation of entitled and obnoxious sports fans. I relied on Jean Twenge, psychologist, generational consultant, and author of the aforementioned *Generation Me*, for answers. According to her research, in the early 1950s, only 12 percent of teens aged 14 to 16 agreed with the statement, "I am an important person." By the late 1980s, 80 percent—almost seven times as many—were claiming they were important. Twenge calls those born after 1970 "Generation Me" and says this group displays an unrealistic sense of entitlement. Twenge, who teaches "Generation Me"-age students as a psychology professor at San Diego State, quoted the character Tyler Durden in the movie *Fight Club*: "We've all been raised on television to believe that one day we'd all be millionaires, and movie gods, and rock stars. But we won't. And we're slowly learning that fact. And we're very, very pissed off."

Durden, Brad Pitt's character in the movie, links high self-esteem to aggression—he's ticked off—and so does psychology. According to Twenge, aggressive people score high in narcissism, which is sort of like self-esteem on steroids. This is the topic of Twenge's next book, fittingly called *The Narcissism Epidemic: Living in the Age of Entitlement*, written with W. Keith Campbell. Narcissism is a psychological affliction with a clinical diagnosis, although the normal population has plenty of narcissistic personality traits that are becoming all too common. The word comes from Greek mythology: Narcissus fell in love with his own image, couldn't stop staring at his own reflection, and ultimately died from this obsession.

Not all people who think highly of themselves are predisposed to violence, but once questioned, threatened, or undermined, narcissists may become aggressive and respond with an oversized action. Narcissists exhibit aggressive behavior when someone tries to impinge on their freedom, asking: "Who are you to tell me what I can or cannot do?"

Roy Baumeister, the evil expert from Florida State University, takes on this connection in his theories on violence and cruelty. He writes, "People whose self-esteem is high but lack a firm basis in genuine accomplishment are especially prone to be violent because they are more prone to get their narcissistic bubble burst."

In *The Narcissism Epidemic*, Twenge and Campbell write that, "America has overdosed on self-admiration . . . and the result is a fundamentally imbalanced self—a grandiose, inflated self-image and a lack of deep connections to others." Twenge and Campbell propose that narcissism and high self-esteem have exploded for a variety of reasons: In the first half of the 20th century, the country was focused on overcoming war and depression. Community was a priority. The emphasis on the needs of the individual rather than the needs of society probably started with the human potential movement and self-love of the 1960s and 1970s. These days, many parents raise kids to be "special." Meanwhile, the media sets the example of the self-obsessed celebrity, while the Internet promotes personal branding and celebrates the loudest opinion.

Narcissism helps explain why Americans are five times more likely to opt for plastic surgery than ten years ago or why teachers report that students and parents refuse to accept mediocre grades, often complaining to the administration. It's the reason why some people spend hours on Facebook and others accrue massive debt to pretend they are wealthier than they really are. "We found so many examples of narcissism in American culture that we had to stop collecting them," add Twenge and Campbell.

Antisocial behavior personifies the epidemic and perhaps explains the culture of rudeness and violence we see in sports. Poor manners can be the norm. There is no need to be nice to others. If this lack of empathy can bring fame, even better. Fights and bullying get posted on YouTube.

There's a saying in baseball that gets thrown around when talking about narcissism in the modern athlete: "The difference between the old ballplayer and the new ballplayer is the jersey. The old ballplayer cared about the name on the front. The new ballplayer cares about the name on the back." Twenge and Campbell hone in on the sports world, labeling some stars "super spreaders" of narcissism. "Americans are obsessed with people who are obsessed with themselves," they write. They cite examples, for instance, baseball slugger Barry Bonds, who was known to skip team activities like official photos and stretching sessions and who showed arrogance and indifference toward his teammates. They also point to skier Bode Miller, who competed at the 2006 Olympics in Turin, Italy. While Miller arrived at the Games with a frontrunner's swagger, he left town with little more than a hangover. Failing to medal, much less finish more than two of his five events, Miller boasted how much he partied during the event. "I just did it my way. I'm not a martyr, and I'm not a do-gooder. I just want to go out and rock. And man, I rocked here." My personal favorite is NFL player and reality television star Terrell Owens, who trademarked one of his favorite catchphrases, "I love me some me."

I understand Twenge's theory when it comes to narcissistic athletes, but I wondered how it translates to sports fans, since so much of fan psychology is about losing yourself to a group and the need to belong. Yet, here we are talking about shameless individualism, self-promotion, and a lack of a connection to others. Twenge told me yes, the two can coexist. "Being part of a group can meet one's narcissistic needs," she said. Her ideas absolutely relate to fandom.

Entitlement, a component of high self-esteem and narcissism, reveals itself in the behavior of both athletes and fans. Professional athletes are some of the most entitled people out there. By virtue of their fame and wealth, this rarified group enjoys a reality where others cater to their every demand. People rarely tell them "no." From a young age, their talent gives them entree into a world of favoritism and privilege. Coaches and teachers treat them differently. This behavior snowballs as the stakes get higher. When Tiger Woods held a press conference to apologize to the nation in the winter of 2010 for his sordid infidelities, he encapsulated this idea perfectly. "I convinced myself that normal rules didn't apply," Woods said. "I never thought about who I was hurting. Instead, I thought only about myself."

Entourages and bodyguards have long helped create a "bubble" that fences off high-profile athletes from the regular world. In 2010, Pittsburgh Steelers quarterback Ben Roethlisberger was accused of sexually assaulting a college student, but no charges were ever filed. It was later reported that one of the quarterback's bodyguards, a police officer, had led the woman to Roethlisberger, and another bodyguard, a state trooper, stood in front of the bathroom that the two had entered and ignored a friend who was trying to intervene. This was not the first time Roethlisberger had been accused of rape; he had previously settled a civil suit after a casino hostess accused him of sexual assault during a celebrity golf weekend at Lake Tahoe in 2008.

Major League Baseball slugger Alex Rodriguez, nicknamed A-Rod, is known for an oversized contract, big ego, and relentless fight with MLB regarding a season-long suspension for drug use. In 2009, in a seemingly tongue-in-cheek reference to his reputation, Rodriguez posed in a *Details* magazine photo shoot that showed him kissing his own reflection in a mirror.

The shine of the sports stars may be getting dull for some fans. In 2011, consumer advocate Ralph Nader relaunched an organization called the League of Fans, to reform sports and promote better citizenship. Nader blames the athletes for some of the ugly fan behavior. "There is a symbiotic relationship," Nader told the *Washington Post* at the time. "The more coarse the players who play are, it feeds the fans."

Other examples of entitlement abound. When fans complain that they deserve better from their team after a poor performance, that's entitlement. So is demanding an autograph from an athlete or coach without respect for time and place. Or booing the national anthem. Have you ever heard someone yell at a professional athlete that he "sucks," even though he's doing something a fan could never come close to doing? Then there's the quest for viral superstardom, where fans publicly plot how to call attention to themselves during a game. During the 2013 MLB All-Star Game, one fan tweeted that he was ready to hop the fence and run onto the field if 1,000 people retweeted his message. After getting his requisite encouragement, he made it onto the field and dashed toward second base. He was eventually violently tackled and arrested. Sometimes entitled is just another word for asinine. My personal favorite is when fans shove one another out of the way to catch a historic home run ball, hold a press conference about the experience, and then sell it to the highest bidder.

Fighting over a ball is exactly what happened in 2001, when controversy erupted regarding Barry Bonds's record-setting 73rd home run ball, when one fan sued another in an ownership dispute. A Bay Area restaurateur named Alex Popov said he had caught the ball from his seat in the right field stands and claimed that student Patrick Hayashi attacked him in the crazy scrum and grabbed the ball. No assault was proven, and a judge ruled that the proceeds from the ball should be split between the two litigants.

Estimates had predicted that the Bonds ball would sell for $1 million, but by the time an auction was held, its value had declined and it fetched just $225,000 for each man. Popov's attorney never saw a dime of the proceeds and wound up suing his client for unpaid legal fees. Was this love of the game or a tale of misplaced priorities and love of the greenback? In the 2004 documentary *Up For Grabs*, filmmakers went behind the scenes of this madness and concluded it was probably the latter. Rather than being regarded as a fan of "America's pastime," Alex Popov garnered the reputation of a fan of the spotlight.

A few years later, when Bonds was on the brink of blasting home run 755 in his chase for the all-time career mark, he too acknowledged the financial implications of catching the ball. "I had a little kid come up to me and say he would give it back to me," Bonds told reporters. "I said, 'Are you stupid? You'd have more money than your parents.'"

FOR BETTER OR WORSE?

Rooting for individuals regardless of their team is the hallmark of fantasy sports, where team "owners" draft professional players to their personalized teams to compete in leagues based on the players' stats. According to the Fantasy Sports Trade Association, more than 41 million people play fantasy sports in the United States and Canada. It's a $3.3 billion industry, and it's damn fun. While fantasy can enhance fan engagement—these people are some of the most hardcore, obsessive fans out there—playing fantasy may also change the nature of fandom when fantasy team owners buy and sell players like a commodity and, in effect, dehumanize the player.

"All of a sudden everybody knows who third- or fourth-string guys are, and people are picking defenses and favorite players," retired NFL linebacker Brendon Ayanbadejo told me. He doesn't see this shift as necessarily good for the game because fans feel a false sense of power. "They feel like they can do more, and they feel like they can go farther."

In a 2006 television interview, former NFL quarterback Jake Plummer told ESPN's Greg Garber that he thinks fantasy football "has ruined the game" and that "there are no true fans anymore." Fans have already expressed how they don't want to be treated as a commodity, yet here they are doing the same thing to athletes.

In rooting for individual players rather than a favorite team, fans may be damaging long-standing team loyalties. Fantasy players will tell you they support both their fantasy team and their hometown team, but sometimes the two allegiances turn out to be at odds.

As mentioned earlier, New York Giants running back Brandon Jacobs received a death threat from a disgruntled fantasy owner after missing a game because of injury. "We recommend that people do not interact with their real-life Fantasy team players," said Paul Charchian, president of the Fantasy Sports Trade Association, adding,

> If you see Colin Kaepernick down the street and you want to give him a slap on the back and say, "You're on my Fantasy team," that's great. There's no business to be razzing them for their performance when you know they're trying everything they can do to be successful. Also, they have team goals that don't necessarily match your Fantasy goals.

Case in point about team goals conflicting with fantasy goals: In 2009, with the New York Jets leading the Jacksonville Jaguars by two points, Maurice Jones-Drew ran unobstructed toward the end zone, poised to score. But at the last second, instead of taking the ball in for a touchdown, he followed his coach's orders and fell to one knee to run out the clock and give the Jags a better chance of winning. Since the Jets were out of time-outs, the Jags were able to kick a game-winning field goal right before the final whistle. As a fantasy team owner himself, Jones-Drew realized the conflict and apologized to other fantasy owners because he knew his coaches' strategy had cost them. He had chosen not to disobey orders in the name of fantasy.

Don't look for fantasy to fade into the woodwork anytime soon. It's only getting more intense. The latest trend in fantasy speeds up the entire equation. While traditional fantasy unfolds during the course of an entire season, daily fantasy is fantasy sports on uppers. Sort of like Wall Street's day trading, teams get picked daily, and the payout is divvied up at the end of the night. Charchian called daily fantasy players "hyperanalytical superfans." While just 1 percent of fantasy sports players go daily, investors are bullish on this new option. Daily fantasy has garnered more investment in the past two years than the entire fantasy industry—and the fans who embrace it spend big. Daily fantasy accounts for about a quarter of all money played in the entire fantasy sports industry and is expected to grow. At the start of the 2014 season, within days of one another, the NBA and NHL inked exclusive deals with competing daily fantasy leagues, further signaling the legitimacy of this fast-growing sector.

There is no question that fantasy brings a new level of fun to sports, but it may add a dangerous narcissistic tendency to the process. It's this narcissism and entitlement that leaves me with a feeling of foreboding. And I'm not the only one. According to Twenge and Campbell, the prognosis for the future is not inspiring. They write, "If the narcissism epidemic continues, there will be more entitlement, materialism, vanity, antisocial behaviors, and relationship troubles." And that can't be a good thing for the sports world.

CONCLUSION

Moving the Chains

You can't hold a whole fraternity responsible for the behavior of a few sick, twisted individuals .—"Otter," from the movie *Animal House*

Fans at the Scottsdale Ferrari Maserati Polo Championships, the largest polo event in the United States, began arriving at the entrance gate. Mostly men in sport coats and women in cocktail dresses, the crowd had no idea that they were attending a sporting event like no other. It wasn't that the top polo players in the world were in town or that the fancy cars on display were worth millions of dollars, thanks to the sponsors. Most people didn't see the small black-and-white sign hanging at the entrance that read, "Security Systems in Use." They didn't know they were being spied on in the name of security.

A police car was parked in a dirt patch along the road with a camera mounted on its roof, which was taking a photo of each car's license plate and running the number through a database to check for warrants or other red flags. Once the patron parked, his or her face was being photographed by six different hidden cameras placed in several strategic positions as they entered the venue. This data was then transmitted at high speed to a security control room, otherwise known as a fusion center. Biometric information like distance between the eyes, width of the nose, depth of the eye sockets, shape of the cheekbones, and length of the jaw line was cross-referenced with driver license photos, mug shots, and other types of images. The license plate readers, coupled with the facial recognition software, was being used by law enforcement to gather information for hunting down wanted criminals, individuals previously associated with sports fan violence, and those currently on a terrorist watch or no-fly list.

At the entrance to the polo grounds, a dozen people were listening to Stan Kephart delineate how this system, known as IBIS2, which stands for Intelligence-Based Integrated Security Systems, works and what the beta test of the system hoped to accomplish. Kephart's audience, which included law enforcement and tech company executives, listened intently to his explanation of the need for such a high-tech approach. "When you go to a NFL game, you walk through, put all of your belongings and everything you have in a plastic bag, stand there and you empty your pockets, you're wanded with a metal detector system or walk through a metal detection system," he said. "Which is more intrusive, a picture of your face or that process?" It's a valid question.

As he was pointing to where his cameras were installed, a chauffeured SUV pulled up to the entrance. The door opened, and a wine glass fell out and shattered. A group of women piled out of the vehicle, dressed like fashionistas, unstable in high heels, perhaps thanks to their pregame polo activities, which, in all likelihood, involved drinking wine from that now-broken glass.

Kephart glanced at the new arrivals and returned to his explanation of how IBIS2 utilizes state-of-the-art, highly mobile, integrated security technology for instant data retrieval. Information gleaned from the blending of the license plate reader and the facial recognition software can result in preemptive action by law enforcement or security to prevent sports fan violence. The organizers of the event had given him the green light to test the system there. Polo hooliganism is probably a minor concern, but excessive drinking may be more problematic.

A FESTIVAL OF SPORT

As a police chief in Arizona and head of security for the 1984 Olympics, held in Los Angeles, Kephart has been working to keep people safe for more than 40 years. Hired by Peter Ueberroth, president of the organizing committee for the Los Angeles Games, to oversee 21,000 security personnel, Kephart recounted the charge Ueberroth gave him. Ueberroth told him, "I don't want this to be a festival of security. I want it to be a festival of sport." To Kephart it was clear, both then and now, that people like their security to be as peripheral as possible.

"Many of the venue contract operators do not want harsh treatment of their patrons, and they will tolerate a certain amount of drunkenness and ridiculous behavior," said Kephart. He sees modern-day sports security as too tangled up in budgets. Should teams be hiring more expensive police officers or paying less to private security? This is way too reactive for his taste. "I want to fix the damn system that's broken," he continued. In his eyes, IBIS2 would cut costs at venues by a third by slicing the need to hire as many security workers. This patented technology would keep bad guys out of stadiums and event grounds, preventing trouble from erupting. "If you're wanted for anything, you're going to jail. Probation violation, parole violation, or a wanted criminal, you're all going to jail," he said. Fewer criminals inside the stadium means less criminal behavior.

IBIS2 scanned more than 1,500 plates during the first two days of the polo tournament and didn't turn up any red flags. As a test of the facial recognition component, a police officer was assigned to identify IBIS' director of operations—and succeeded. At the close of the tournament, Kephart turned off his cameras, but according to him, 15 minutes later, two vandals drove their car onto the field, pulling donuts and grazing a person who was running out to stop them. While Kephart said police on the scene attended to the issue, Scottsdale police have no record of such an incident. As for high-tech security solutions, this situation demonstrated that it still takes a human to flip the switch.

Facial recognition has been used before at sporting events. In 2001, at Super Bowl XXXV, or the "Snooper Bowl," as some nicknamed it, law enforcement in Tampa, Florida, used facial recognition technology to try to identify people arriving at the stadium with ties to illegal activities. No arrests were made using this tool. I was there that day with my dad. What I remember most were the massive lines to get inside, since this was the first Super Bowl post–9/11, and security was maxxed out. That and the painful fact that the New York Giants got trounced by the Baltimore Ravens, 34–7. We had no idea our faces were being scanned, although apparently there were signs advising patrons of the practice.

Thus far, the use of facial recognition as a security tool at the Super Bowl has been a one-and-done phenomenon, according to the NFL, but this experimentation seems to predict the future. "I look at access control at the stadiums changing over the next five years," said Lou Marciani, head of the National Center for Spectator Sports Safety and Security. I think the less human influence and the more we can apply technology, the better off we're going to be, period, in the industry."

Critics are quick to attack the use of high-tech surveillance, citing violations of privacy when fans are unaware of its presence. Alameda County sheriff Greg Ahern expressed interest in IBIS2 and met with Kephart and his company several times to learn about testing the system at an Oakland Raiders game, igniting privacy concerns. "It's a sensitive issue in regards to the American Civil Liberties Union and the privacy people," said Ahern, continuing,

> One legal opinion says that once you purchase a ticket with the intent to come in, you're surrendering some of those privacy issues. Others say no, the ticket itself allows access to the game and shouldn't give access to all of your information. But technology is going to get pretty advanced rather quickly, and those legal issues are going to have to be addressed by both sides.

TOWARD REFORM

Whether it's facial recognition software or more police officers, the solution to the problem of unruly crowds always seems slightly out of reach, be it too expensive or too invasive. People have been trying to figure out how to control crowds for centuries. According to historian Allen Guttmann, during early Olympic Games, *mastigophoroi* and *rabdouchoi*, Greek for "whip-bearers" and "truncheon-bearers," respectively, roamed the fields, keeping both the athletes and spectators in line. During the Greek Pythian Games, a competition similar to the Olympics but held in the town of Delphi, wine was banned in the stands in an effort to prevent fans from acting too rowdy.

These days, every entrepreneur thinks they have invented the next must-have item or killer app. Ray DiNunzio, the NFL's director of strategic security programs, sees technology as a great way to improve reporting options for fans with security concerns. He explained,

> We're looking at a number of technologies that will provide apps to fans that have smart devices that will geo-locate them, regardless of what stadium they're in or where they're at in that stadium or around

that stadium. They won't have to text, they can send real-time video of what's occurring, we'll know exactly where they are, and we can see in real time what's happening.

DiNunzio said this information will flow directly to the command center.

Technology often comes with unintended consequences. At Super Bowl XLVIII, held in New Jersey's MetLife Stadium in February 2014, the weather was a big concern for the outside game. "We had a company that wanted to sell jackets that would be wired with heating elements and battery components," recalled the NFL's Jeff Miller. These jackets happen to bear a striking similarity to suicide vests, which posed problems for law enforcement. Miller quickly nixed that idea. "The last thing I want to do is desensitize screeners. Holy crap!" he added.

The NFL strongly recommended a nontech security measure for the 2014–2015 season: deploying undercover officers dressed in visiting team jerseys at every game. It's a practice that has worked, according to Miller and DiNunzio, during playoffs and other tense matchups. The logic is that it can be tough to sort out exactly what occurs in the middle of a large crowd, but if an undercover cop observes an incident, it's easier to grasp what happened and understand who is to blame. The Raiders' Tom Blanda told me teams are now responsible for bringing jerseys on the road with them to outfit these undercover officers.

Sometimes less security, or less obvious security, can be more effective than a blatant show of force. In 2002, the Ohio State Buckeyes beat archrival Michigan in football, clinching a trip to the BCS National Championship Game. To celebrate this huge win, football fans stormed the field and then rioted throughout the night. Thousands of people, both students and locals, gathered downtown. The crowd set more than 100 fires, and police donned riot gear and used tear gas to quell the disturbance. Police arrested approximately 50 people.

After the uprising, Ohio State convened a task force to figure out how to avoid similar destruction in the future. They concluded that trying to minimize an "us versus them" mentality between law enforcement and revelers was a winning strategy. According to Richard Morman, Ohio State's deputy chief of police, the Columbus police who patrol the off-campus areas had showed up in riot gear, which inevitably invited trouble. "We asked them several years ago to change that tactic, and they did," he pointed out.

Another step Ohio State took to break down this "us versus them" mindset was to promote better sportsmanship. The school resurrected a long-dormant OSU Sportsmanship Council run by students, which backed a campaign to engage with visiting fans. As part of the program, students and police handed out "Best Fans in the Land" badges. Said Morman, "The concept was if you see somebody wearing the opposing school's shirt, you go up and say, 'Hey, welcome to Ohio State. Here's the Best Fans in the Land badge.' It was kind of an icebreaker." He was surprised at how easily police officers embraced the badge plan.

Morman said these steps have helped decrease the violence and that Columbus hasn't seen such bad postgame mayhem at the stadium or downtown since the infamous riot of 2002, when students rushed the field and tried to tear down the goalposts. Police unleashed pepper spray on them. In 2004 and 2006, while students rushed the field after the Michigan game, it was less confrontational, according to Morman. In 2006, he said most students just wanted to take selfies with police.

Kathy Samoun, of Fans against Violence, agrees with taking a more personal approach. "The best way to really resolve conflict is for two people to get to know each other," she said. That's how the "Fan Shake" was born. In a short video spot shown on the Jumbotron at Raiders home games, two fans, one from the home team and one from the visiting team, shake hands. Samoun came up with this idea, and three days later, the practice was put into place for a *Monday Night Football* game. Now the Fan Shake gets two airings per game. "When we first started Fans against Violence, it was a blog where people could share their stories," related Samoun. "We realized we needed to be about the solutions." She posted legendary coach Knute Rockne's quote on the website: "One man practicing sportsmanship is far better than a hundred teaching it."

When I visited with Filip Van Doorslaer, marketing director for the Belgian national football team, after the World Cup qualifying match, he explained similar efforts: "We organize a fan game the day of the match, so yesterday in the afternoon we had a delegation of Welsh fans playing Belgian fans. We won. And then we do a barbecue, and we exchange jerseys or scarves."

BEHIND IN THE COUNT

Is shaking hands, passing out pins, and playing ball enough to solve an enduring problem? What about the actual law? After the Stow beating, Mike Gatto, a Democratic assemblyman from Los Angeles, decided that California needed stricter laws when it came to out-of-control fans.

If anyone knows Dodger Stadium, it's Gatto. He grew up around the corner, and his late father sold peanuts there. His father would often take him along to work and let him sit in the stands while he worked. "I don't think anybody could do that nowadays," he reflected.

Taking a page from antihooliganism legislation in England and other countries, in 2012, Gatto crafted AB 2464, a bill that called for stricter punishments for fan violence. His proposed legislation would require teams to publicize text-messaging services that directly link spectators to security. The bill also called for a reward fund that would pay for tips on violent incidents, to be bankrolled by the pro teams, and for the creation of a list of repeat offenders that would prohibit the worst fans from attending games. "For people who are brawlers and this is a regular occurrence in their life, what really matters to them is not being able to go to sporting events," Gatto explained.

But a banned list scared civil rights advocates. Others didn't like the mandated annual $10,000 fee earmarked for police to offer as a reward in fan violence cases.

A watered down version of Gatto's bill took effect in 2013. It required stadiums to post emergency numbers for fans to text in case of problems. The idea was hardly revolutionary. Remember the NFL Code of Conduct? It had been around since 2008, and from the onset encouraged texting security, which by 2013 was standard at NFL stadiums. By then, only three professional sports franchises in the state lacked such a system. Change is not simple.

At Ohio State, where administrators were touting improvement on the fan behavior front after the 2002 riots, the university was still facing problems. In 2005, Ohio State took on the University of Texas at home in one of the most anticipated games of the season. After Texas beat OSU, Texas fans bore the brunt of Ohioans' frustrations. Both the school's president and athletic director ended up sending apologies in response to e-mail complaints from Texas fans for their rough treatment in the stands. In 2006, after the Michigan game, while students didn't tear down the goalposts because they were too busy taking selfies with police officers, rioting still erupted. Approximately 40 people were arrested, and dozens of fires burned.

NATURE OR NURTURE?

As I was conducting research for this book, some potential fixes for fan misbehavior came across my desk. Some ideas had to do with money. What if an athletic booster of a university donated funds earmarked for security? Wealthy patrons already endow academic positions, and top boosters are honored with stadiums and have arenas named for them. Some subsidize a coach's salary. Why not add security to the fund-raising wish list?

Other suggestions deal with changes on the Internet. Could Internet trolls who dominate the sports conversation with their hostility be curbed by changing the standards for anonymous posting? Of course, anonymity is essential to some Internet communication. "You'll say and do things you wouldn't ordinarily say because you have this protection, and some of what you're saying and doing is really important," said cyber privacy and civil rights expert Danielle Citron. Citron suggested that anonymity be treated as a privilege and, if abused, be taken away. "Look, you've done this. This speech has been reported. You can continue to post, but you'd have to do it in some identifiable form so as to stand behind your words," she continued. While the obligation to protect free speech must be met by the government, Facebook and Twitter are private services that choose their own approach to derogatory speech.

Then there is the legal angle. Are the legal remedies for fighting harsh enough? Australia recently passed a law strengthening jail terms for what are known as one-punch homicides, when someone gets knocked out by a sucker punch and dies. More than 90 people have been killed there since 2000, often in boozy assaults where death is caused by a knockout punch to the head. Researchers say these attacks are mostly fueled by alcohol. Advocates believe there needs to be more awareness that one punch can kill. For prosecutors, punishment in these cases can be a challenge, as a one-punch homicide can fall between accepted legal definitions of murder and manslaughter.

These are interesting ideas, But I am not convinced that any reforms along these lines will make a difference. I've come to believe that bad fan behavior is part of human nature. History documents the enduring nature of violent fans. Science tells us that's because our brain is primed for aggression and easily influenced by other examples of violence.

When I first started this inquiry, I felt it was important to qualitatively address whether fan behavior is getting better or worse, but metrics were disparate and subjective. Do more arrests indicate a stronger police presence and less tolerance for bad behavior or more drunken brawls and more fans trying to go viral with their outrageousness? I eventually came to believe that it ultimately didn't matter. Difficult-to-synthesize statistics don't change the reality that people die at the hands of other fans and suffer damaging harassment on the Internet, not to mention that any given downtown or college campus can face significant physical damage because of a single win or loss.

"Fan behavior is directly correlated with how much one fan drinks," John Skinner, MLB's security chief told me. Yet, there has been no effort to remove alcohol from the equation. Would fans still show up if booze was taken away? No one knows for sure, and no one wants to find out. Big business certainly doesn't want to reconfigure the bottom line in a world without beer sales.

Daniel Wann, the leading social psychologist in the area of sports fandom, advises that if the sports world *really* wanted to improve fan behavior, they should get rid of tailgating and other drinking opportunities, but he knows that is as likely as Apple discontinuing texting on the iPhone. "What are you going to do? You're going to eliminate alcohol at Colorado Rockies games at Coors Field, Cardinals games at Busch Stadium, Brewers games at Miller Park?" asked Wann.

If the system refuses to change, how can you expect the individual to change? Calling fans "overserved," a popular euphemism for blotto, shifts responsibility and blames the server instead of the drinker for getting drunk. Cutting off beer sales during the seventh inning or third quarter is not asking a fan to take responsibility for their alcohol management, it's just dictating accessibility. What's more, these cutoffs are really only standard in the proverbial cheap seats. In the club and suite levels for both MLB and the NFL, booze flows longer, as long as an hour after the game ends.

Even if fans were to take more personal responsibility for their drinking, the deck may be stacked against them. Scientific studies say that the mere suggestion of alcohol in ads and sponsorship logos fans see at an arena can increase aggression—no imbibing necessary. In 2014, in a study entitled "Are You Insulting Me?" researchers in the United States and United Kingdom determined that participants exhibited aggression following the simple act of being exposed to words related to alcohol. Upon release of the study, Dr. Eduardo Vasquez, from the University of Kent in the United Kingdom and lead writer on the research, concluded, "We've shown that people attending events where alcohol is typically present do not have to drink to experience, or be subject to, the aggression-enhancing effects of alcohol, a fact that would seem to suggest caution in all such environments."

WILLING TO GO THERE?

At our breakfast in Albuquerque, Daniel Wann told me about a talk he gave at a NCAA convention on sportsmanship more than a decade ago. The NCAA president at the time, the late Myles Brand, asked Wann what could be done about the bad sportsmanship and ugly fan behavior in college sports.

Wann's answer made the audience laugh. "Here are some suggestions: Get your students to care less about their football team." He said they got the point. "I think there are things you can do, but I don't know if there are things that people would be *willing* to do."

For Wann, one thing makes him think lasting change is possible. "There are enough fans out there that want to see it cleaned up," he said. "There are enough fans out there that are going to stop going to games because they don't feel safe. There are going to be enough lawsuits out there that are going to cost people a *ton* of money, and money talks. It really does."

As I explored fandom during a span of several years to write this book, I discovered that many schools, philosophies, and theories help explain fandom: Crowd psychology, sociology, neuroscience, anthropology, the science of evil, tribalism, hormones, self-esteem, schadenfreude, competition, and demographics. Fandom touches on controversial issues far outside the sports world, for example, surveillance, privacy, and free speech. What this shows is how deeply embedded fandom is in our basic identity.

I'd like to think greater analysis and understanding of the history of fan mayhem will enhance our understanding and tolerance of one another. From integration to free agency to Title IX, the sports world has proven that it can adapt to a shifting cultural landscape. As for the dark side of fandom, there is hope.

The Ohio State fans on Twitter forgot about me. That nasty @OSU-Blacklist Twitter account no longer exists, at least not under its original handle. The NFL scheduled the Raiders and 49ers to play one another again in 2014, since putting that matchup on hold after the preseason beat-down game. The radio show host who initiated the fan hostility toward me was fired from the top-rated station in Columbus for derogatory comments about another ESPN employee. On the other hand, he was hired at a different station a year later.

ACKNOWLEDGMENTS

Several years ago, I came up with the littlest kernel of an idea. With the guidance and wisdom of many others, my idea eventually grew into this book.

Nora Isaacs held my hand throughout the process and provided deft editing and soulful counseling. And although she claims not to be a sports fan, she revealed to me that as a child, she attended the Pine Tar Game, which gives her true sports cred, long before I came along. This book would not have been completed without her help.

Steve Delsohn, Edward Gubar, Deaton Bell, Shelley Smith, Rachel Alberts, and Elida Witthoeft, my favorite long-suffering Cubs fan, provided inspiration and support from the very beginning and found time in their busy lives to read my manuscript and deliver invaluable feedback.

Thanks to Husam and the H Café crowd, the San Francisco Writers' Grotto, and the divine Hedgebrook Writers Residency, who gave me a quiet respite to finish my first draft when I wasn't sure I could.

I am indebted to numerous colleagues at ESPN and many other friends and family members who shared knowledge and provided guidance, including my Microsoft expert Doug Kim, my water glass compatriot Kale Kim, Bryan Spillane, Scott Winters, Kathleen McCoy, Christine Champe, Andy Gustin, Nancy Rommelmann, Lisa Olson, Steve Peresman, Wright Thompson, Jed Henry, and James Young. Jos Verschueren showed me around Belgium, Christianne Gonzalez never flinched when I queried her for contact after contact in Brazil, Fred Marconi selflessly connected me with passionate fans in Tuscany, and Kieran Sietya consulted with me on various matters of philosophy. Deepest thanks to Susan Gubar, Robin Goffman, Melanie Goffman, Gwen Knapp, and Sam Marchiano for their continuous support.

I am also grateful for the financial support of the Fund for Investigative Journalism and research assistance from the National Baseball Hall of Fame and Museum, the Mechanics Institute Library, and Suhail Shaikh. In addition, I am thankful for the work of my translator in Italy, Paola Pesares, and fact checker Kevin Fixler.

In nonfiction books, interviews sometimes get left on the "cutting room floor" due to a host of factors, for instance, space and editorial decisions. I want to thank my sources that didn't make it into the book but generously gave their time to me.

Thanks to my exceptional agent, Jennifer Unter; phenomenal publicist, Gretchen Koss; and editor, Christen Karniski, a fellow sports fan; as well as production editor Jessica McCleary, designer Dustin Watson, copy editor Nicole McCullough, and the other hardworking staff, including Jacqline Barnes, at Rowman & Littlefield.

Finally, my deepest gratitude is reserved for Sandy and Leonard Gubar, who unconditionally support everything I do.

NOTES

INTRODUCTION

xiv   **According to the late John Paul II:**
Message of the Holy Father. To the Managers, Players, and
Supporters of the Roma Sports Association. Speeches 2000, 30
November 2000, http://www.clerus.org/bibliaclerusonline/en/
e3l.htm#bbj (accessed 11 October 2014).

xiv   **Sport has been increasingly recognized and used as a low-
cost and high-impact tool in humanitarian, development,
and peace-building efforts:** United Nations Office on Sport for
Development and Peace, "Sport for Development and Peace,"
United Nations, http://www.un.org/wcm/content/site/sport/
home/sport (accessed 14 October 2014).

xiv   **More than half of Americans consider themselves sports
fans:** Public Religion Research Institute, "January Religion and
Politics Tracking Survey, 2014," *Public Religion Research
Institute*, 16 January 2014, http://publicreligion.org/research/
2014/01/jan-2014-sports-poll (accessed 11 October 2014).

xv   **In Philadelphia, a man was arrested trying to spread the
ashes of his mother:** Associated Press, "Man Unapologetic for
Spreading Ashes at Linc," *ESPN*, 30 November 2005, http://
sports.espn.go.com/nfl/news/story?id=2241909 (accessed 18
October 2014).

xv   **Argentina and Germany have opened adjoining cemeteries:** "Preparing for the Final Whistle," *Der Spiegel*, 17 September 2007, http://www.spiegel.de/international/zeitgeist/preparing-for-the-final-whistle-german-soccer-club-builds-cemetery-for-its-fans-a-506164.html (accessed 14 October 2014).

xv   **"Please, be tolerant of those who describe a sporting moment as their best ever":** Nick Hornby, *Fever Pitch* (New York: Riverhead Books, 1992). Kindle Edition.

xvi   **In Latin, fanaticus indicated a religious devotee :** P. G. W. Glare, ed., *Oxford Latin Dictionary* (New York: Oxford University Press, 1982), 676.

xvi   *Tifosi* **, which originates from the Greek word for the disease typhoid and its associated states of contagion and confusion:** John Foot, *Winning at All Costs: A Scandalous History of Italian Football* (New York: Nation Books, 2006). Kindle Edition.

xvii   **Police eventually fired a crowd control weapon at the revelers:** Pam Belluck and Katie Zezima, "Death of Red Sox Fan Leads to Stricter Rules," *New York Times*, 23 October 2004, http://www.nytimes.com/2004/10/23/sports/baseball/23boston.html?_r=0.Assessed (accessed 11 October 2014).

xvii   **Huish spent several months in a psych ward:** "Rugby Fan Can't Explain Self-Mutilation," *Sydney Morning Herald*, 16 November 2005, http://www.smh.com.au/articles/2005/11/16/1132016820398.html (accessed 11 October 2014).

xviii   **Fans bought tickets to support their team despite the fact that they wouldn't be let in to what became known as the "ghost game":** Associated Press, "German Club Sells Out 'Ghost Game,'" *ESPN*, 11 March 2012, http://espn.go.com/sports/soccer/story/_/id/7672386/german-club-dynamo-dresden-sells-stadium-ban (accessed 11 October 2014).

xix   **Die-hard Egyptian football fans had played a vital role in Egypt's Arab Spring:** David D. Kilpatrick, "Egyptian Soccer Riot Kills More Than 70," *New York Times*, 1 February 2012, http://www.nytimes.com/2012/02/02/world/middleeast/scores-killed-in-egyptian-soccer-mayhem.html (accessed 11 October 2014).

xix **This match was believed to be the deadliest soccer match anywhere since 1996, when 84 people died in a stampede:** "Recent Soccer Stadium Disasters," *USA Today*, 19 June 2001, http://usatoday30.usatoday.com/news/world/2001-05-10-soccer-side.htm (accessed 18 October 2014).

xix **Eight deaths were directly linked to matches between the Celtics and Rangers:** Michael Gerrard and Richard Giulianotti, "Cruel Britannia? Glasgow Rangers, Scotland, and 'Hot' Football Rivalries," in *Fear and Loathing in World Football*, ed. Gary Armstrong and Richard Giulianotti (New York: Berg, 2001), 23–43.

xix **A Romanian fan charged onto the field and attacked a player:** Associated Press, "Romanian Soccer Fan Charged in Attack on Player," *ESPN*, 31 October 2011, http://sports.espn.go.com/espn/wire?section=soccer&id=7173201 (accessed 11 October 2014).

CHAPTER 1: AND THEN WE BURN A COUCH

3 **It was later estimated that about 1,500 people had assembled:** Brian Canova, "Riot Police Disperse 1,500 Students at UMass-Amherst Following Super Bowl," *MassLive.com*, 5 February 2012, http://www.masslive.com/news/index.ssf/2012/02/riot_erupts_at_umass_amherst_f_1.html (accessed 11 October 2014).

4 **He had been one of 14 people, 13 of them UMass students, arrested:** Taylor C. Snow, "UMass Crime Log: Super Bowl Edition," *Daily Collegian*, 8 February 2012, http://dailycollegian.com/2012/02/08/umass-crime-log (accessed 11 October 2014).

5 **With the unruly spirit of townsfolk, they began with abusive language:** Tacitus. *The Annals*. Oxford, U.K.: Acheron Press, 2012. Kindle Edition.

5   **Authorities in Rome told the people in Pompeii there would be no more sports events for the foreseeable future:** Allen Guttmann, *Sports Spectators* (New York: Columbia University Press, 1986). Kindle Edition.

5   **"We are not gladiators, and this is not the Roman Coliseum":** Joel Thorman, "Eric Winston: Fans Cheering Matt Cassel's Injury Are 'Sickening,'" *Arrowhead Pride*, 7 October 2012, http://www.arrowheadpride.com/2012/10/7/3470224/eric-winston-quotes-matt-cassel-injury-fans-cheering (accessed 11 October 2014).

6   **"The circus factions rioted at a level that makes modern mobs seem almost nonviolent":** Guttmann, *Sports Spectators*.

6   **"They forget themselves completely and shamelessly say and do the first thing that occurs to them":** Guttmann, *Sports Spectators*.

6   **The Blues and Greens shouted the word during the races to mark their displeasure with the emperor's rule:** Geoffrey Greatrex, "The Nika Riot: A Reappraisal," *Journal of Hellenic Studies* 117 (1997): 60–86.

6   **The final toll was staggering, with more than 300 fatalities and more than 500 injured :** "Hundreds Dead in Stampede at Football Match," *Guardian*, 26 May 1964, http://www.theguardian.com/football/2014/may/26/stadium-disaster-lima-peru-1964-archive (accessed 11 October 2014).

6   **The resulting stampede led to the deaths of more than 125 fans:** Kwaku Sakyi-Addo, "At Least 12 Die in Ghana Football Stadium Stampede," *Guardian*, 10 May 2001, http://www.theguardian.com/world/2001/may/11/football (accessed 11 October 2014).

7   **One longstanding practice to control hooligan violence is to escort visiting fans to and from the train and stadium:** "Football Policing," *British Transport Police*, http://www.btp.police.uk/advice_and_info/how_we_tackle_crime/football_policing.aspx. (accessed 11 October 2014).

7   **More than 25 people were arrested for smashing shop windows and overturning cars:** Alan Snel, "Police Disperse Rowdy Fans, Cars Overturned in LoDo Revelry," *Denver Post*, 26 January 1998, p. A1.

7   **Phillies fans lost control after their 2008 World Series triumph:** Regina Medina, "After Phils Rally, Fire Volunteer Finds Himself in Hot Seat," *Philadelphia Daily News*, 11 November 2008, p. 12.

7   **At the ballpark, fans broke windows at the stadium store:** "Six Arrested, Police Officer among Injured during Giants Celebrations in San Francisco," *San Jose Mercury News*, 2 November 2010, http://www.mercurynews.com/giants/ci_16500838?source=rss (accessed 11 October 2014).

7   **More than 20 people were arrested for rioting after the U.S. Open of Surfing:** Anthony Clark Carpio, "After Huntington Beach Riot, Music and Alcohol Out for Surfing Contest," *Los Angeles Times*, 4 April 2014, http://www.latimes.com/local/lanow/la-me-ln-in-huntington-beach-riots-20140404-story.html (accessed 11 October 2014).

7   **About 1,000 revelers at Purdue University gathered after the women's basketball team lost the national title game:** Adam Kovac and Matt Holsapple, "Purdue Students Stir Pandemonium," *USA Today*, 2 April 2001, http://usatoday30.usatoday.com/sports/basketba/marchmania/2001womens/championship/2001-04-01-aftermath.htm (accessed 11 October 2014).

7   **In 2007, 300 Greek fans brawled prior to a women's volleyball match:** Associated Press, "Greece Suspends All Team Sports after Volleyball Fan Killed," *USA Today*, 30 March 2007, http://usatoday30.usatoday.com/sports/2007-03-30-greece-ban_N.htm (accessed 11 October 2014).

8   **During the 1909 Scottish Cup riots, rival football fans united to protest a match that had ended in a tie :** Wray Vamplew, "Sports Crowd Disorder in Britain, 1870–1914: Causes and Controls," *Journal of Sport History* 7, no. 1 (Spring 1980): 6.

8   **More than 60 rioters were arrested:** Thomas Neumann,
         "Vancouver Evokes Infamous Sports Riots," *ESPN.com*, June
         24, 2012, http://m.espn.go.com/wireless/story?storyPage=
         neumann-110617_vancouver_canucks_riot&wjb (accessed 22
         November 2014).

8   **Officials called the match and awarded the victory to Sri
         Lanka:** "Riot Ends India's Cricket Dream," *South China
         Morning Post*, 14 March 1996, http/
         :www.scmp.com:article:152791:riot-ends-indias-cricket-dream
         (accessed 11 October 2014).

8   **Penn State University students rioted when legendary coach
         Joe Paterno was fired:** Associated Press, "Police: PSU Rioters
         Caused $190K in Damages," *WDEL*, 21 December 2011, http://
         www.wdel.com/story.php?id=39677 (accessed 9 January 2015).

8   **Tennessee students rioted when head coach Lane Kiffin
         resigned:** Tom Weir, "Kiffin Haters Riot, but Haiti Might
         Benefit," *USA Today*, 14 January 2010, http://content.usatoday.
         com/communities/gameon/post/2010/01/620006197/1 (accessed
         11 October 2014).

9   **Studies confirm that fans get a vicarious endocrinological
         lift:** P. C. Bernhardt, J. M. Dabbs, J. A. Fielden, and C. D.
         Lutter, "Testosterone Changes during Vicarious Experiences of
         Winning and Losing among Fans at Sporting Events,"
         Physiology and Behavior 65, no. 1 (1998): 59–62.

9   **When the Tigers won the World Series in 1984, another
         Detroit fan was killed:** Mike Klingaman, "Detroit Fans Have
         History of Combustible Behavior," *Baltimore Sun*, 25
         November 2004, http://articles.baltimoresun.com/2004-11-25/
         sports/0411250093_1_pistons-detroit-tigers (accessed 11
         October 2014).

9   **In Boston, a fan died after being hit by a drunk driver
         during the celebrations:** Andrea Estes, "The Mother of
         Postgame Victim Rips City Officials," *Boston Globe*, 9 February
         2004, http://www.boston.com/news/local/massachusetts/
         articles/2004/02/09/riot_victims_mother_rips_menino_and_
         hussey (accessed 11 October 2014).

9   **Snelgrove, who according to police was acting lawfully, was rushed to the hospital:** Franci Richardson, "Tragedy at Fenway: At Funeral Mass, Grief, Faith, and Outrage at Riot," *Boston Herald*, 27 October 2004, p. 6.

10   **He stopped breathing while in custody:** Kevin Cullen, "Asking for Trouble," *Boston Globe*, 21 July 2008, http://www. boston.com/news/local/articles/2008/07/21/asking_for_trouble/ (accessed 11 October 2014).

11   **Dozens were arrested:** Chris Kenning and Mike Wynn, "Lexington Arrests, Fires Follow Victory," *Courier-Journal* (Louisville), 3 April 2012, p. A6.

11   **Listeners heard the local dispatcher report people shooting fireworks out of a moving car:** Timothy Burke, "Two Hours of the Lexington Police Scanner after UK Wins, Set to Music," *Deadspin*, 6 April 2014, http://deadspin.com/5898759/heres-what-kentuckys-championship-celebration-sounded-like-over-the-lexington-police-scanner (accessed 10 April 2014).

11   **Algerian football fans rioted in the South of France to celebrate:** "Fans Celebrate across France as Algeria Makes World Cup History," *France 24*, 27 June 2014, http://www. france24.com/en/20140627-algeria-world-cup-france-celebration-history (accessed 12 October 2014).

11   **French football fans of the Paris Saint-Germain team rioted to celebrate:** Jerome Pugmire, Associated Press, "PSG Riot: Paris Saint-Germain Title Celebrations Marred by Fan Violence," *Huffington Post*, 13 May 2013, http://www. huffingtonpost.com/2013/05/13/psgs-fan-violence-paris-parade_ n_3268973.html (accessed 9 January 2015).

12   **Ten students, including Lagodinski, were arrested, all but one for disorderly conduct:** Bridget Bennett, "Officials Warn 'Zero Tolerance' after Rowdy Dinkytown Crowd," *Minnesota Daily*, 11 April 2014, http://www.mndaily.com/news/campus/ 2014/04/11/hundreds-swarm-dinkytown (accessed 12 October 2014).

14   **Two years later, fans, many of whom wore "Riotville" T-shirts to commemorate the previous victory, rioted again:**

"Justinian Didn't Understand Fans," *Wichita Eagle*, 2 November 2008, p. 2(D).

14   **After the Grey Cup, the Canadian Football League championship, riots broke out:** Jenny Uechi, "Vancouver No Stranger to Grey Cup Riots," *Vancouver Observer*, 27 November 2011, http://www.vancouverobserver.com/sports/2011/11/27/vancouver-no-stranger-grey-cup-riots (accessed 12 October 2014).

15   **Damage was estimated at almost $4 million (Canadian):** "Canada 2012 Crime and Safety Report: Vancouver," *Bureau of Diplomatic Security*, 3 April 2012, https://www.osac.gov/pages/contentreportdetails.aspx?cid=12304 2013 (accessed 12 October 2014).

15   **While alcohol sales had been cut off at 4:00 p.m., fans had known about this stipulation and were able to plan accordingly:** John Furlong and Douglas J. Keefe, *The Night the City Became a Stadium: Independent Review of the 2011 Vancouver Stanley Cup Playoffs Riot*, 31 August 2011, p. 10, http://www.ag.gov.bc.ca/public_inquiries/docs/vancouverriotreview/report.pdf (accessed 10 October 2014).

16   **More than 2,000 calls were made to 911 that evening:** Furlong and Keefe, *The Night the City Became a Stadium*, 19.

17   **As of July 2014, 298 rioters have been charged and 267 convicted:** "Can You Identify Any of These Suspects?" *Vancouver Police Department*, https://riot2011.vpd.ca (accessed 11 October 2014).

17   **One lesson learned was that "there were too many people":** John Furlong and Douglas J. Keefe, *The Night the City Became a Stadium: Independent Review of the 2011 Vancouver Stanley Cup Playoffs Riot*, 31 August 2011, p. 10, http://www.ag.gov.bc.ca/public_inquiries/docs/vancouverriotreview/report.pdf (accessed 10 October 2014).

18   **"I know what I did was wrong and there is no excuse":** For more of the apology, see Lise Broadley, "Comox Valley Man Apologizes for Role in Vancouver Riot," *Comox Valley Echo*, 4 October 2012, http://www.comoxvalleyecho.com/news/local/

comox-valley-man-apologizes-for-role-in-vancouver-riot-1.
970666 (accessed 11 October 2014).

18   **Sean Burkett, a high school student who was caught on tape
      slamming a police barricade through the window of a
      Hummer:** *R. v. Burkett*, BCPC 315 (2012), http://caselaw.
      canada.globe24h.com/0/0/british-columbia/provincial-court-of-
      british-columbia/2012/09/07/r-v-burkett-2012-bcpc-315.shtml
      (accessed 11 October 2014).

19   **"What difference does it make if I take a couple things?":**
      Camille Cacnio, "Dear Vancouver, I Am Sorry," *Real Camille*,
      20 June 2011, http://therealcamille.wordpress.com/2011/06/20/
      dear-vancouver-i-am-sorry (accessed 11 October 2014).

19   **He describes a person in a crowd as a "grain of sand amid
      other grains of sand, which the wind stirs up at will":**
      Gustave Le Bon, *The Crowd: A Study of the Popular Mind*
      (Mineola, N.Y.: Dover Books, 1895). Kindle Edition.

19   **Both Hitler and Mussolini supposedly studied his work:** Greg
      A. Annussek, *Hitler's Raid to Save Mussolini: The Most
      Infamous Commando Operation of World War II* (Cambridge,
      Mass.: Da Capo, 2005), 49. Google Books download.

20   **Basketball fans at a high school state championship focused
      their gaze in the same direction only 3 percent of the time:**
      Clark McPhail, *The Myth of the Madding Crowd* (New York:
      Walter de Gruyter, 1991). Google Books download.

20   **"Riots are patchworks and kaleidoscopes of individual and
      collective, nonviolent and violent, alternating and varied
      action":** Clark McPhail, "Presidential Address: The Dark Side
      of Purpose: Individual and Collective Violence in Riots,"
      Sociological Quarterly 35, no. 1 (1994): 12.

20   **"Most participants are neither alone nor anonymous":**
      McPhail, *Myth of the Madding Crowd*, 72.

22   **A thrill seeker's quest for new experience can make him or
      her vulnerable to reckless behavior:** For an overview of
      sensation-seeking studies, read Christopher Munsey, "Frisky,
      but More Risky," *American Psychological Association* 30, no. 7

(July/August 2006): 40, http://www.apa.org/monitor/julaug06/frisky.aspx (accessed 10 October 2014).

22   **After Paris rioted in 2013, authorities claimed that the "party was spoiled by a few hundred troublemakers who have nothing to do with football":** "David Beckham's Big Night Is Ruined as PSG Ligue 1 Trophy Celebrations Descend into Chaos and Rioting," *Independent*, 14 May 2013, http://www.independent.co.uk/sport/football/european/david-beckhams-big-night-is-ruined-as-psg-ligue-1-trophy-celebrations-descend-into-chaos-and-rioting-8614731.html (accessed 10 October 2014).

CHAPTER 2: FANDEMONIUM: UNFORGETTABLE MOMENTS IN FAN VIOLENCE

26   **"Nobody could have been prepared for what happened":** Joe Coté and Jaxon Van Derbeken, "Crackdown at Candlestick: Raider Rivalry on Hold," *San Francisco Chronicle*, 22 August 2011, http://www.sfgate.com/49ers/article/Crackdown-at-Candlestick-Raider-rivalry-on-hold-2334044.php (accessed 18 October 2014).

26   **One fan was cited for misdemeanor battery:** Vivian Ho and Kevin Fagan, "Fan Says He Was Attacked by 3 Men at 49ers Game," *San Francisco Chronicle*, 23 December 2011, http://www.sfgate.com/bayarea/article/Fan-says-he-was-attacked-by-3-men-at-49ers-game-2423742.php (accessed 18 October 2014).

27   **Arrests were slightly higher as well:** "110 Kicked Out of Candlestick Park during NFC Championship Game," *Los Angeles Times*, 24 January 2010, http://latimesblogs.latimes.com/lanow/2012/01/nfc-championship-candlestick-park-arrests.html (accessed 12 October 2014).

27   **Several months after the game, the *Sports Business Journal* surveyed fans and found that 40 percent of those polled didn't feel comfortable bringing children to NFL games:** "SBD/SBJ Reader Survey: Thoughts on Teams, Leagues,

Motorsports, and Colleges," *Sports Business Journal*, 29 November 2012, http://www.sportsbusinessdaily.com/Daily/Issues/2012/11/29/Reader-Survey/Reader-Survey.aspx?hl=nfl%20games%20comfortable%20children&sc=0 (accessed 26 January 2015).

28 **"We want everyone to be able to come to our stadiums":** "NFL Teams Implement Fan Code of Conduct," *NFL.com*, 5 August 2008, http://www.nfl.com/news/story/09000d5d809c28f9/printable/nfl-teams-implement-fan-code-of-conduct (accessed 13 October 2014).

28 **A fan Tasered other fans during a dispute about the national anthem:** Gary Myers, Frank DiGiacomo, and Bill Hutchinson, "Cowboys Fan Uses Taser Gun on Jets Crowd at MetLife Stadium Despite Security on 9/11 Anniversary," *New York Daily News*, 13 September 2011, http://www.nydailynews.com/sports/football/jets/cowboys-fan-taser-gun-jets-crowd-metlife-stadium-security-9-11-anniversary-article-1.957926 (accessed 18 October 2014).

28 **A fan was beaten to death in the parking lot at Arrowhead Stadium in Kansas City:** Christine Vendel, "Man Who Died Outside Arrowhead Stadium Was Punched Repeatedly, Authorities Say," *Kansas City Star*, 4 December 2013, http://www.kansascity.com/news/local/article333159/Man-who-died-outside-Arrowhead-Stadium-was-punched-repeatedly-authorities-say.html (accessed 18 October 2014).

28 **Security personnel confiscated approximately 30 knives per game:** According to a PowerPoint presentation provided by the NFL, 7,952 knives were intercepted in 2013, a 29 percent decline from 2012, when 11,194 knives were confiscated. "Stadium Security and Fan Conduct Committee Report," *NFL Security Department*, March 2014.

29 **The Giants fan was required to undergo anger-management counseling:** Larry McShane, "Jets Fan Fireman Ed Cleared of Assault as Giants Fan Christopher Black Drops Charges," 28 October 2010, http://www.nydailynews.com/news/crime/jets-fan-fireman-ed-cleared-assault-giants-fan-christopher-black-drops-charges-article-1.192581 (accessed 18 October 2014).

30   **"Who else wants to fight?":** "Court Docs Detail Bryan Stow's
      Beating," *ESPN*, 2 August 2011, http://espn.go.com/los-angeles/
      mlb/story/_/id/6824307/court-docs-detail-beating-san-francisco-
      giants-fan-bryan-stow (accessed 18 October 2014).

31   **Barry Bonds previously pledged to pay for Stow's two
      children to attend college:** "Bonds's Gift to Stow's Children:
      College Education," *ESPN.com*, 26 May 2011, http://sports.
      espn.go.com/mlb/news/story?id=6590118 (accessed 22 October
      2014).

32   **"You are the biggest nightmare for people who attend public
      events":** Associated Press, "Two Admit Guilt in Bryan Stow
      Attack," *ESPN*, 20 February 2014, http://espn.go.com/los-
      angeles/mlb/story/_/id/10489372/two-men-admit-guilt-dodger-
      stadium-attack-bryan-stow (accessed 18 October 2014).

32   **The family will need between $34 and $50 million to care for
      him for the rest of his life:** Ramona Shelburne, "Bryan Stow
      Lawyer Approached MLB," *ESPN*, 3 November 2011, http://
      espn.go.com/los-angeles/mlb/story/_/id/7187358/bryan-stow-
      lawyer-eyes-reasonable-deal-mlb (accessed 18 October 2014).

33   **When some tossed their coats on a player's head after he
      caught a fly ball to prevent him from throwing it back and
      making a play, the umpire called a do-over:** The incident is
      described in Cook's chapter on postseason fan rowdiness.
      William A. Cook, *Diamond Madness: Classic Episodes of
      Rowdyism, Racism, and Violence in Major League Baseball*
      (Mechanicsburg, Pa.: Sunbury Press, 2013). Kindle Edition.

33   **Baseball officials offered rewards for the identities of rowdy
      fans who threw projectiles onto the field:** Bob Gorman and
      David Weeks, "Foul Play: Fan Fatalities in Twentieth-Century
      Organized Baseball," *Nine* 12, no. 1 (2003): 115–32.

34   **Fans shot guns:** Bruce Nash and Allan Zullo, *The Baseball Hall
      of Shame: The Best of Blooperstown* (Guilford, Conn.: Lyons
      Press, 2012). Kindle Edition.

34   **"Any man who will throw a bottle or any other life-
      endangering object from the midst of a crowd at any official
      or player is the rankest type of coward":** Sam Otis, "Wake Up

Cleveland! Let's Have No More Pop Bottle Throwing or Other Forms of Unsportsmanlike Outbursts," *Cleveland Plain Dealer*, 13 May 1929.

36   **Authorities also banned him from attending other events at the Palace:** "Brief in Support of Defendant Indiana Pacers' Response to Motion in Limine Re: Testimony of Timothy R. Smith," *Haddad v. O'Neal, Johnson, Pacers* (United States District Court Eastern District of Michigan Southern Division), 17 July 2006.

26   **Artest was banned for the rest of the season, the longest suspension ever meted out by the NBA for an on-the-court incident:** Jonathan Abrams, "The Malice at the Palace," *Grantland*, 20 March 2012, http://grantland.com/features/an-oral-history-malice-palace (accessed 18 October 2014).

37   **"I honestly believe this is mob mentality":** Associated Press, "Man Who Threw Chair during Pacers–Pistons Brawl Gets Probation," *USA Today*, 3 May 2005, http://usatoday30.usatoday.com/sports/basketball/nba/2005-05-03-fan-probation_x.htm (accessed 18 October 2014).

37   **"I wanted to win way too bad. I had to calm down":** Jack McCallum, "Sir Charles Speaks—as Usual," *SportsIllustrated.CNN.com*, 5 March 2002, http://sportsillustrated.cnn.com/inside_game/jack_mccallum/news/2002/03/05/nba_insider (accessed 27 January 2015).

CHAPTER 3: FANS THROUGHOUT THE WORLD

40   **Officials suspended league play, and a violent sport culture in this African nation came to the fore:** Ian Hughes, "Albert Ebosse: Player's Death Leads to League Suspension," *BBC*, 25 August 2014, http://www.bbc.com/sport/0/football/28902441 (accessed 18 October 2014).

40   **Even in Japan, where there is a cultural premium on good manners, racist fans have, for decades, displayed ugliness:** Debito Arudou, "J. League and Media Mush Show Red Card to

Racism," *Japan Times*, 12 March 2014, http://www.japantimes.
co.jp/community/2014/03/12/issues/j-league-and-media-must-
show-red-card-to-racism/#.VCH3PvaB_rY (accessed 18
October 2014).

40 **Two top football teams were forced to play a match in an
empty stadium as punishment for raising a "Japanese Only"
banner:** Andrew McKirdy, "Players Push for More Action
against Racism Scourge," *Japan Times*, 24 March 2014, http://
www.japantimes.co.jp/sports/2014/03/24/soccer/j-league/
players-push-for-more-action-against-racism-scourge/#.VCH1-_
aB_rY (accessed 18 October 2014).

43 **Thirty-nine fans died in the chaos, and several hundred were
injured:** Jerry M. Lewis, *Sports Fan Violence in North America*
(Lanham, Md.: Rowman & Littlefield, 2007), appendix C.

44 **For five years, English teams were banned from competing
anywhere in Europe:** Paul Coslett, "Heysel Disaster," *BBC*, 4
December 2008, http://www.bbc.co.uk/liverpool/content/
articles/2006/12/04/local_history_heysel_feature.shtml
(accessed 18 October 2014). This event is also detailed in Lewis,
Sports Fan Violence in North America, appendix C.

44 **Several officials were convicted of criminal negligence:** Jon
Carter, "Rewind: The Heysel Aftermath," *ESPN*, 2 June 2011,
http://www.espnfc.com/story/925085/rewind-the-heysel-
aftermath-in-1985 (accessed 18 October 2014). Also detailed in
Lewis, *Sports Fan Violence in North America*, appendix C.

45 **Statements of more than 100 officers were doctored to
obscure the multiple failures that contributed to the death
count:** Sheila Coleman, Ann Jemphrey, Phil, Scraton, and Paula
Skidmore, "The Liverpool Experience," *Hillsborough
Independent Panel*, April 1990, http://
hillsborough.independent.gov.uk/repository/
SYP000119160001.html (accessed 18 October 2014).

45 **Belgium passed sweeping antihooligan legislation that
created a national "football unit" to oversee law enforcement
and mete out harsher sanctions for misbehavior:** "Country
Profile: Belgium," *Council of Europe*, 11 March 2011, http://

www.coe.int/t/dg4/sport/Source/T-RV/Country_profiles/
Belgium_EN.pdf (accessed 18 October 2014).

45   **The stadium has been renovated and renamed King
     Baudouin Stadium, after the introverted fifth king of
     Belgium:** Richard D. Lyons, "Baudouin I, King of Belgium,
     Dies at 62," *New York Times*, 1 August 1993, http://www.
     nytimes.com/1993/08/01/obituaries/baudouin-i-king-of-
     belgium-dies-at-62.html (accessed 18 October 2014).

47   **Rimoux had said the sculpture was meant "to commemorate
     the tragedy and to say 'don't forget'":** Duncan White,
     "Anniversary Monument Honours Heysel Dead," *Telegraph*, 30
     May 2005, http://www.telegraph.co.uk/sport/football/2360360/
     Anniversary-monument-honours-Heysel-dead.html (accessed 18
     October 2014).

49   **Pape Diop, a Senegalese midfielder playing for the Spanish
     team Levante, danced like a monkey when he heard fans
     making the racist noises:** "Levante's Papakouli Diop Dances to
     Defy Racist Supporters," *Guardian*, 4 May 2014, http://www.
     theguardian.com/football/2014/may/04/papakouli-diop-racism-
     atletico-levante (accessed 18 October 2014).

49   **The hashtag #somostodosmacacos, translated as "We are all
     monkeys." was born and tweeted by Brazilian star forward
     Neymar:** Nick Schwartz, "Barcelona's Dani Alves Eats Banana
     That Was Thrown at Him by a Fan," *USA Today*, 27 April 2014,
     http://ftw.usatoday.com/2014/04/barcelona-dani-alves-banana
     (accessed 18 October 2014).

50   **Croatian fans stood in the stands, shoulder to shoulder, in
     the shape of a cross to form a human swastika:** Kirsten
     Sparre, "FIFA Takes Action against Croatian Fans Forming
     Human Swastika," *Play the Game*, 24 August 2006, http://www.
     playthegame.org/news/news-articles/2006/fifa-takes-action-
     against-croatian-fans-forming-human-swastika (accessed 18
     October 2014).

50   **A Nazi flag was displayed at a Russian league match:** "Fan
     Ordered to Compensate Spartak Moscow for Swastika Display,"
     RiaNovosti, 25 February 2014, http://en.ria.ru/russia/20140225/

187881368/Fan-Ordered-to-Compensate-Spartak-Moscow-for-Swastika-Display.html (accessed 18 October 2014).

50   **Supporters of the German team Bayern Munich raised a banner with the phrase "Gay Gunners":** Ben Rumsby, "Bayern Munich Facing £50,000 Fine for Fans' Homophobic 'Gay Gunners' Banner during Clash against Arsenal," *Telegraph*, 12 March 2014, http://www.telegraph.co.uk/sport/ football/teams/arsenal/10692228/Bayern-Munich-facing-50000- fine-for-fans-homophobic-Gay-Gunners-banner-during-clash- against-Arsenal.html (accessed 18 October 2014).

51   **Play resumed once the offending chants died down:** Press Association, "Roma Fined €50,000 over Racial Abuse Aimed at Milan Players," *Guardian*, 13 May 2013, http://www. theguardian.com/football/2013/may/13/roma-fined-racial-abuse- milan (accessed 24 August 2014).

52   **The newly elected leader of the Italian Football Association, which oversees amateur football in Italy, is being investigated for referring to African players as banana eaters:** Associated Press, "UEFA Investigates Italian Soccer Head over Racism," *USA Today*, 20 August 2014, http://www. usatoday.com/story/sports/soccer/2014/08/20/uefa-investigates- italian-soccer-head-over-racism/1432617 (accessed 18 October 2014).

52   **Brazilian authorities did arrest two fans for hate speech after they chanted racist insults, violating Brazilian hate speech law:** Angelina Theodorou, "As FIFA Attempts to Curb Racism at the World Cup, a Look at Hate Speech Laws Worldwide," *Pew Research Center*, 20 June 2014, http://www. pewresearch.org/fact-tank/2014/06/20/as-fifa-attempts-to-curb- racism-at-the-world-cup-a-look-at-hate-speech-laws-worldwide (accessed 1 September 2014).

53   **Boston Bruins fans sent, by one measure, more than 200 racist tweets voicing their displeasure with the outcome:** "The Real Numbers behind Those 'Racist Tweets from Bruins Fans,'" *Boston.com*, http://www.boston.com/sports/blogs/ obnoxiousbostonfan/2014/05/exclusive_the_real_numbers_beh. html (accessed 1 September 2014).

53   **"Football victories shape a nation's identity as much as wars do"**: Dario Brentin, "'A Lofty Battle for the Nation': The Social Roles of Sport in Tudjman's Croatia," *Sport in Society: Cultures, Commerce, Media, Politics* 16, no. 8 (2013): 993.

54   **Police unleashed tear gas on the crowd, and more than 60 people were injured:** "Yugoslavia's Soccer Riot Leaves 138 Injured," *United Press International*, 14 May 1990, International Section.

55   **The bank pulled their sponsorship of the football team, and the team has since teetered on the edge of collapse:** Nick Squires, "Decline of Monte dei Paschi di Siena, World's Oldest Bank, Leaves City Paying the Price," *Telegraph*, 8 September 2012, http://www.telegraph.co.uk/news/worldnews/europe/italy/9530852/Decline-of-Monte-dei-Paschi-di-Siena-worlds-oldest-bank-leaves-city-paying-the-price.html (accessed 30 May 2014).

57   **A fan was killed by a toilet bowl that had been ripped from a stadium bathroom and thrown at him by rival fans:** Associated Press, "Brazilian Fan Killed by Thrown Toilet Bowl," *ESPN*, 3 May 2014, http://www.espnfc.com/futebol-brasileiro/story/1807916/brazilian-fan-killed-by-thrown-toilet-bowl-in-recife (accessed 18 October 2014).

57   **Upset with the team's performance, fans went after several players with weapons:** Jonathan Watts, "Angry Brazilian Fans Break into World Cup Centre and Attack Players and Staff," *Guardian*, 2 February 2014, http://www.theguardian.com/football/2014/feb/03/brazilian-football-fans-assault-team-players (accessed 18 October 2014).

58   **In retaliation, the official was stoned by the crowd and then beheaded:** "Brazil Referee Decapitated after Stabbing Player," *BBC*, 7 July 2013, http://www.bbc.com/news/world-latin-america-23215676 (accessed 18 October 2014).

58   **In the 25-year period between 1988 and 2013, 234 people have died:** James Young, "World Cup 2014: Another Supporter's Death Fuels Brazil Security Concerns," *Independent*, 4 May 2014, http://www.independent.co.uk/sport/football/worldcup/world-cup-2014-another-supporters-death-

fuels-brazil-security-fears-9321432.html (accessed 18 October 2014).

58   **The largest country in Latin America actually passed Europe's leader, Italy, in the lethal fan category almost two decades ago:** Mauricio Murad, *A violência no futebol* (São Paulo, Brazil: Saraiva, 2012), 37.

58   **"The flags that fluttered in the stands before have been tuned into knives in the hands of these bandits":** "Fred critica as organizadas e teme por tragédia após jogo contra o Horizonte," *Globo Esporte*, 4 August 2014, http://globoesporte. globo.com/futebol/times/fluminense/noticia/2014/04/fred-ataca-torcidas-organizadas.html (accessed 18 October 2014).

59   **In that country's top league, known as Primera División, there were 15 football-related deaths in 2013:** "List of Victims," *Salvemos Al Futbol*, http://salvemosalfutbol.org/lista-de-victimas-de-incidentes-de-violencia-en-el-futbol (accessed 25 October 2014).

59   **More than 70 fans died in a stampede at the exit, and some 500 were injured:** Jerrad Peters, "El Superclásico: The Immigrant Story of River and Boca," *Sportsnet*, 4 October 2013, http://www.sportsnet.ca/soccer/el-superclasico-the-immigrant-story-of-river-and-boca (accessed 18 October 2014).

59   **Some say stadiums in Argentina have barely changed:** Marc Rogers, "La Puerta 12: Interview with Pablo Tesoriere," *Argentina Independent*, 27 June 2008, http://www. argentinaindependent.com/socialissues/humanrights/la-puerta-12-interview-with-pablo-tesoriere (accessed 18 October 2014).

59   **Argentine football fans who were identified as potential troublemakers were prohibited from traveling to Brazil for the 2014 World Cup:** Hannah Karp, "Brazil's Biggest Fear: Argentina Fans," *Wall Street Journal*, 15 June 2014, http:// blogs.wsj.com/dailyfix/2014/06/15/argentinafans (accessed 25 July 2014).

59   **Visiting fans were banned from attending games by the country's football association because of fears of violence:** Gustavo Yarroch, "Berni confirmó que tampoco habrá visitants

en el próximo torneo," *Clarin*, 29 July 2014, http://www.clarin.
com/deportes/Berni-confirmo-visitantes-proximo-torneo_0_
1183681975.html (accessed 18 October 2014).

60 **"Football is popular because stupidity is popular":** Quoted in
Mario Paoletti and Pilar Bravo, *Borges Verbal* (Buenos Aires,
Argentina: Emecé, 1999), 90.

CHAPTER 4: YOUR BRAIN ON SPORTS

61 **An official from Guinness described the racket as a "far
louder, tribal kind of passion":** Mike Lindblom, "136.6
decibels! Hawks Fans Break Guinness Mark for Loudest
Stadium," *Seattle Times*, 16 September 2013, http://seattletimes.
com/html/seahawks/2021833455_seahawksscene16xml.html
(accessed 18 October 2014).

62 **"Sportsmen and their followers are the closest analogue we
have today to the age-old human tribal hunters":** Desmond
Morris and Peter Marsh, *Tribes* (Salt Lake City, Utah: Peregrine
Smith, 1988), 7.

62 **"We hate those who oppose us and praise those who support
us":** Morris and Marsh, *Tribes*, 8.

63 **According to Brill, "no fight fan could be a criminal":** A. A.
Brill, "The Why of the Fan," *North American Review* 228
(1929): 433.

64 **The violent programming primed people for aggression:**
Leonard Berkowitz, "The Effects of Observing Violence,"
Scientific American 210, no. 2 (1964): 35–41.

65 **The first Vancouver Stanley Cup rioter to be sentenced to
jail time claimed he got "caught up in the moment":** Sunny
Dhillon, "Young Man Sentenced to 17 Months in First Stanley
Cup Riot Conviction," *Globe and Mail*, 16 February 2012, http:/
/www.theglobeandmail.com/news/british-columbia/young-man-
sentenced-to-17-months-in-first-stanley-cup-riot-conviction/
article546842 (accessed 10 October 2014).

66   **"If you want to change the situation, you've got to know where the power is, in the system":** Philip Zimbardo, "The Psychology of Evil," *TED Talk*, February 2008, https://www. ted.com/talks/philip_zimbardo_on_the_psychology_of_evil (accessed 11 October 2014).

66   **Baumeister lists "frustration, violent movies, poverty, hot weather, alcohol, and unfair treatment" as potential triggers:** Roy Baumeister, *Evil: Inside Human Violence and Cruelty* (New York: Holt Paperbacks, 1999), 13.

67   **"Regardless of the root causes of violence, the immediate cause is often a breakdown of self-control":** Baumeister, *Evil*, 14.

67   **"To understand evil, we must set aside the comfortable belief that we would never do anything wrong":** Baumeister, *Evil*, 5.

70   **"These individuals appear to make a career out of engaging in confrontational behaviors extending well beyond the arena or stadium walls on game days":** Kirk Wakefield and Daniel. L. Wann, "An Examination of Dysfunctional Sport Fans: Method of Classification and Relationships with Problem Behaviors," *Journal of Leisure Research* 38 (2006): 170.

70   **"The sporting event context gives rise to circumstances where the true nature of the individual quickly rises to the surface":** Wakefield and Wann, "An Examination of Dysfunctional Sport Fans," 182.

72   **Officials who oversaw high school sports in Kentucky issued a directive that postgame handshakes must be better supervised:** "Commissioner's Directive on Postgame Activity," *Kentucky High School Athletic Association*, 8 October 2013, http://khsaa.org/10082013-commissioners-directive-on-postgame-activity (accessed 18 October 2014).

72   **In the mid-1990s, some schools in Ventura County, California, banned the practice for a month:** L.A. Times News Service, "High School League Rescinds Postgame Handshake Ban," *Wilmington Star-News*, 21 April 1994, http:// news.google.com/newspapers?nid=1454&dat=19940421&id=

i2NSAAAAIBAJ&sjid=AxUEAAAAIBAJ&pg=3664,2296843 (accessed 18 October 2014).

72   **A dad tried to temporarily blind an opposing goalie by pointing a laser at her:** Zachary T. Sampson, "Winthrop Man Charged with Disturbing the Peace for Pointing Laser at Players during High School Hockey Game," *Boston Globe*, 7 March 2012, http://www.bostonglobe.com/metro/2012/03/07/winthrop-man-charged-with-disturbing-peace-for-pointing-laser-players-during-high-school-hockey-game/5qc2VLdywUNQidekomrGvM/story.html (accessed 18 October 2014).

72   **A father issued death threats and threatened to rape a coach's family:** Clifford Ward, "Lisle Man Accused of Death, Rape Threats over Volleyball Game Substitution," *Chicago Tribune*, 30 October 2012, http://articles.chicagotribune.com/2012-10-30/news/chi-lisle-father-volleyball-arrest-20121030_1_kasik-lisle-man-berlin (accessed 18 October 2014).

72   **Some have banned parents from attending:** Associated Press, "Massachusetts YMCA Bans Parents from Youth Basketball Games," *MassLive.com*, 25 February 2010, http://www.masslive.com/news/index.ssf/2010/02/massachusetts_ymca_bans_parent.html (accessed 18 October 2014).

72   **Thomas Junta beat fellow hockey dad Michael Costin to death:** Fox Butterfield, "Man Convicted in Fatal Beating in Dispute at Son's Hockey Game," *New York Times*, 12 January 2002, http://www.nytimes.com/2002/01/12/us/man-convicted-in-fatal-beating-in-dispute-at-son-s-hockey-game.html (accessed 18 October 2014).

73   **"We know why we're here, and we search for explanations":** Joe Fitzgerald, "A Death Revives Memories of Tragedy," *Boston Herald*, 26 October 2011, http://www.bostonherald.com/news_opinion/columnists/2011/10/death_revives_memories_tragedy (accessed 26 February 2015).

74   **A 2014 survey undertaken by Liberty Mutual Insurance revealed:**

"2014 Sportsmanship Survey," *Liberty Mutual Insurance Play Positive*, 3 June 2014, https:// play-positive.libertymutual.com/ 2014-sportsmanship-survey?src=cm-dtxt-brd-ssnrs1406101057&utm_source=ussnow&utm_medium=a& utm_term=june2014&utm_ (accessed 16 October 2014).

74 **One widely quoted survey from 2003:** "2003 Survey: Parents Believe Rash of Adult Violence at Youth Sporting Events Requires Nationwide Solution. Sporting Kid Magazine." *Free Library*, 19 March 2003, http:// www.thefreelibrary.com/Survey: Parents Believe Rash of Adult Violence at Youth Sporting...-a098929366 (accessed 16 October 2014).

75 **When Jack Dempsey faced French fighter Georges Carpentier in 1921's heavily promoted "Fight of the Century," held in Jersey City, New Jersey, 2,000 women were on hand:** For more on the "Fight of the Century," see Allen Guttmann, *Sports Spectators* (New York: Columbia University Press, 1986), chapter 4.

77 **"To reduce opportunities for such aggression is to tamper with an ancient and central pattern of human behavior":** Lionel Tiger, *Men in Groups* (New Brunswick, N.J.: Transaction, 2005), 190. Google Books download.

78 **"Men use sports to both hide their feelings and to express their feelings":** Michael Kimmel, *Guyland: The Perilous World Where Boys Become Men* (New York: HarperCollins E-books, 2009). Kindle Edition.

78 **"The boys they still are struggle heroically to prove that they are real men despite all evidence to the contrary":** Kimmel, *Guyland*.

78 **"Sports are sometimes another activity that almost-men engage in to prolong childhood and avoid becoming men":** Kimmel, *Guyland*.

78 **"Guyland rests on a bed of middle-class entitlement, a privileged sense that you are special, that the world is there for you to take":** Kimmel, *Guyland*.

78   **Conflicts regarding viewing habits are usually easily resolved:** Walter Gantz, Lawrence A. Wenner, Christina Carrico, and Matthew Knorr, "Televised Sports and Marital Relationships," *Sociology of Sport Journal* 12 (1995): 306–23.

CHAPTER 5: BEER, HERE!

82   **The truth is concessions don't make that much money for the beer makers themselves:** Bryan Spillane, *U.S. Beverage Alcohol Primer*, 2014 edition. Bank of America Merrill Lynch, February 28, 2014, 9.

84   **Coors Light ended up being the number-two light beer brand in the United States:** Spillane, *U.S. Beverage Alcohol Primer*, 9.

84   **This connection with boxing is part of the reason Crown (Corona, Corona Light, Modelo Especial) has clocked a 10 percent growth:** Spillane, *U.S. Beverage Alcohol Primer*, 11.

85   **"Dear Drunk Guy, Thank You 4 All The Love and Support!! Now Take This Ball And Shut The Phuck Up!!":** Nick Schwartz, "Brandon Phillips Writes Message to Heckler: 'Dear Drunk Guy,'" *USA Today*, 21 June 2015, http://ftw.usatoday.com/2014/06/brandon-phillips-reds-heckler-drunk-guy (accessed 27 September 2014).

85   **"Hopefully, they're super-duper drunk":** "Chad Greenway Wants Fans Drunk," *ESPN*, 6 December 2012, http://espn.go.com/chicago/nfl/story/_/id/8720790/chad-greenway-minnesota-vikings-wants-metrodome-fans-super-duper-drunk (accessed 18 October 2014).

85   **"All you have to do is come to the game, drink beer, do whatever you want, party in the parking lot":** "Nick Saban Criticizes Alabama Fans," *ESPN*, 26 October 2013, http://espn.go.com/college-football/story/_/id/9880250/alabama-crimson-tide-punish-students-leaving-early (accessed 18 October 2014).

85   **"We're just trying to have a little bit of a good time here at the ballgame":** Steve Jones, "Louisville Coach Jeff Walz Says

He's Buying the Beer," *Courier-Journal*, 13 November 2013, http://archive.courier-journal.com/usatoday/article/3515059 (accessed 9 October 2014).

86   **After fans rioted at the U.S. Open of Surfing in Southern California, organizers banned alcohol at the venue:** Anthony Clark Carpio, "After Huntington Beach Riot, Music and Alcohol Out for Surfing Contest," *Los Angeles Times*, 4 April 2014 . (18 October 2014).

86   **There's plenty of excessive drinking without consistent street violence at events like Mardi Gras:** Jerry M. Lewis, *Sports Fan Violence in North America* (Lanham, Md.: Rowman & Littlefield, 2007).

87   **Traffic fatalities increased after the game at a rate of more than 40 percent:** Donald A. Redelmeier and Craig L. Stewart, "Driving Fatalities on Super Bowl Sunday," *New England Journal of Medicine* 348, no. 4 (2003): 368–69. http://www. nejm.org/doi/full/10.1056/NEJM200301233480423 (accessed 19 October 2014).

87   **The one good thing about a fan's team losing is that the drive home is safer:** Stacy Wood, Melayne M. McInnes, and David A. Norton, "The Bad Thing about Good Games: The Relationship between Close Sporting Events and Game-Day Traffic Fatalities," *Journal of Consumer Research*, 38, no. 4 (2011): 611–21.

87   **Part of the argument during the appeal was centered on a culture of intoxication at Giants Stadium:** Michael T. Burr, "N.J. Court Tosses 'Culture of Intoxication' Verdict," *Inside Counsel*, 1 April 2007, http://www.insidecounsel.com/2007/04/ 01/nj-court-tosses-culture-of-intoxication-verdict. (accessed 19 October 2014).

87   **The concessionaire settled with the family for $25 million:** Mark Mueller, "Paralyzed Girl and Mom Get $25M Settlement from Beer Vendor," *NJ.com*, 4 December 2008, http://www.nj. com/news/ledger/topstories/index.ssf/2008/12/paralyzed_girl_ and_mom_got_25m.html (accessed 19 October 2014).

88   **"If the coarse behavior was leading to adults not taking kids to the games, because of language and other things, that's not a good sign":** Bob Hertzel, "Luck: Control Key to Beer Proposal," *Times West Virginian*, 13 April 2011, http://www.timeswv.com/sports/article_6f35c640-4411-51ed-ae22-baed2b655004.html?mode=jqm (accessed 18 October 2014).

88   **Many more institutions permit alcohol advertising at athletic events in signage, in programs, or on radio broadcasts:** Mary Kate Murphy, "More Fun for Fans," *Athletic Management*, June/July 2014, http://www.athleticmanagement.com/2013/05/26/more_fun_for_fans/index.php (accessed 18 October 2014).

92   **"Alcohol is clearly the drug with the most evidence to support a direct intoxication–violence relationship":** Peter Hoaken and Sherry H. Stewart, "Drugs of Abuse and the Elicitation of Human Aggressive Behavior," *Addictive Behaviors* 28, no. 9 (2003): 1,533.

94   **Three officers required medical treatment at the scene:** Angela Hill, "Dozens of Brawls Reported at Raiders Game," *Oakland Tribune*, 9 September 2009, http://www.insidebayarea.com/search/ci_10421066 (accessed 18 October 2014).

94   **Incensed fans busted windows, looted stores, and torched cars, an example of Americans pissed off at a loss:** Glen Martin, Nanette Asimov, Wyatt Buchanan, and Jim Zamora, "Raider Rage: Oakland Police No Match for Street Mayhem," *San Francisco Chronicle*, 27 January 2003.

94   **Beer sales were banned for a game in 1990, after a fight sent a Steeler fan to intensive care:** Victor Merina, "Police Arrest 31 Fans at Rowdy Raiders Game," *Los Angeles Times*, 1 October 1990, http://articles.latimes.com/1990-10-01/local/me-1237_1_police-officers (accessed 18 October 2014).

94   **Fans booed their own starting quarterback, Dan Pastorini, when he went down with a broken leg:** Dan Pastorini and John P. Lopez, *Taking Flak: My Life in the Fast Lane* (Bloomington, Ind.: AuthorHouse, 2011).

100   **"Over 1.46 million drivers were arrested in 2006 for driving under the influence of alcohol or narcotics":** Mothers against

Drunk Driving, "Drunk Driving in America," *Madd.org*, www.
mad.org/drunk-driving-in-america (accessed 15 January 2014).

CHAPTER 6: THE VOICE OF THE FAN

103   **She received numerous letters from Steelers fans, lashing out
at her for causing the accident, in which Pittsburgh's
starting signal-caller broke several bones and suffered a
concussion:** Jonathan D. Silver, "Roethlisberger, Car Driver Are
Both Charged," *Pittsburgh Post-Gazette*, 20 June 2006, http://
www.post-gazette.com/sports/steelers/2006/06/20/
Roethlisberger-car-driver-are-both-charged/stories/
200606200107 (accessed 28 September 2014).

105   **Some Ohio State fans incessantly trash talked him:** Matt
Hinton, "Relentless Buckeye Fans Have Driven Kirk Herbstreit
from Ohio," *Yahoo! Sports*, 12 March 2011, http://sports.yahoo.
com/ncaa/football/blog/dr_saturday/post/-Relentless-Buckeye-
fans-have-driven-Kirk-Herbs?urn=ncaaf-wp39 (accessed 18
October 2014).

106   **Facebook ranks as the top social media network for 71
percent of online adults in the United States:** Maeve Duggan
and Aaron Smith, "Social Media Update 2013," *Pew Research
Center*, Internet and American Life Project RSS, 30 December
2013, http://www.pewinternet.org/2013/12/30/social-media-
update-2013 (accessed 26 September 2014).

106   **There were 45 million people worldwide posting,
commenting, and liking content about the games:** "2014
Sochi Winter Olympics on Facebook," *Facebook*, 24 February
2014, http://newsroom.fb.com/news/2014/02/2014-sochi-
winter-olympics-on-facebook (accessed 19 October 2014).

106   **For the Super Bowl XLVII matchup between the Seahawks
and Broncos, 50 million people joined in the conversation:**
"Super Bowl XLVIII on Facebook," *Facebook*, 2 February
2014, http://newsroom.fb.com/news/2014/02/super-bowl-xlviii-
on-facebook (accessed 18 October 2014).

106   Twitter, with 18 percent of the adult online population, says
       Super Bowl XLVIII generated almost 25 million tweets:
       Duggan and Smith, "Social Media Update 2013."

108   Science was too polarizing for the masses to engage in
       reasonable conversation: Suzanne LaBarre, "Why We're
       Shutting Off Our Comments," *Popular Science*, 24 September
       2013, http://www.popsci.com/science/article/2013-09/why-
       were-shutting-our-comments (accessed 28 September 2014).

108   Brandon Jacobs suffered death threats for failing a fantasy
       football fan: Nina Mandell, "Brandon Jacobs Received a Death
       Threat from a Fantasy Football Owner," *USA Today*, 22 October
       2013, http://ftw.usatoday.com/2013/10/brandon-jacobs-
       received-a-death-threat-from-a-fantasy-football-owner (accessed
       18 October 2014).

108   When the 49ers' Kyle Williams fumbled two punt returns in
       the 2012 NFC Championship game, he immediately took a
       beating on social media: Katie Dowd, "Kyle Williams
       Receiving Death Threats after NFC Championship," *San
       Francisco Chronicle*, 23 January 2012, http://blog.sfgate.com/
       49ers/2012/01/23/kyle-williams-receiving-death-threats-after-
       nfc-championship (accessed 18 October 2014).

108   After a difficult loss, the Montreal Impact's Davy Arnaud
       received the message, "I hope your family dies in a fire":
       Canadian Press, "Impact's Davy Arnaud Receives Twitter
       Threats," *CBC*, 10 July 2013, http://www.cbc.ca/sports/soccer/
       impact-s-davy-arnaud-receives-twitter-threats-1.1344575
       (accessed 18 October 2014).

108   Scott Cousins faced threats after a home plate collision with
       Giants star catcher Buster Posey: Associated Press, "Scott
       Cousins Receiving Death Threats after Home Plate Collision
       with Giants' Buster Posey," *New York Daily News*, 4 June 2011,
       http://www.nydailynews.com/sports/baseball/scott-cousins-
       receiving-death-threats-home-plate-collision-giants-buster-
       posey-article-1.125066 (accessed 18 October 2014).

108   The son of Lakers coach Mike Brown, Elijah, a high school
       student at the time, got nasty messages when the Lakers

started out poorly in 2012: Chris Chase, "Mike Brown's Son Receiving Threats on Twitter," *USA Today*, 9 November 2012, http://www.usatoday.com/story/gameon/2012/11/09/mike-browns-son-receiving-threats-on-twitter/169440 (accessed 18 October 2014).

108   **Kristen Blake told reporters that she had to block more than 500 followers:** Dave McMenamin, "Steve Blake, Wife Get Hate Tweets," *ESPN*, 18 May 2012, http://espn.go.com/los-angeles/nba/story/_/id/7943732/steve-blake-los-angeles-lakers-wife-receive-threats-twitter (accessed 18 October 2014).

109   **Mark Cuban, the outspoken owner of the Dallas Mavericks, calls this phenomenon "Twitter courage":** Tim MacMahon, "Mark Cuban Talks Lakers Fans," *ESPN*, 25 November 2012, http://espn.go.com/dallas/nba/story/_/id/8672046/mark-cuban-owner-dallas-mavericks-snipes-los-angeles-lakers-fans (accessed 18 October 2014).

111   **One in five Americans have been affected by cyberstalking, harassing e-mails, and other undesired contact online:** *National Online Safety Study Fact Sheet*, Report, National Cyber Security Alliance/McAfee, 21 September 2012.

111   **"There's no denying people do weird things":** Del Harvey, The Strangeness of Scale at Twitter," *TED Talk*, March 2014, https://www.ted.com/talks/del_harvey_the_strangeness_of_scale_at_twitter?language=en (accessed 16 April 2014).

112   **Twitter eventually responded to media criticism and online petitions by rolling out an in-tweet "report abuse" button:** Danielle Keats Citron, *Hate Crimes in Cyberspace* (Cambridge, Mass.: Harvard University Press, 2014). Kindle Edition.

112   **The company has publicly wrestled with complaints from advertisers and community members:** Citron, *Hate Crimes in Cyberspace*.

CHAPTER 7: THE ART OF NOISE

118   **The Princeton Pep Club organized student cheering in the stands:** "History of Cheerleading," *International Cheer Union*, http://cheerunion.org/history/cheerleading (accessed 25 September 2014).

119   **Students at University of Michigan football games sat together and formed a giant "M" with paper cards as a sign of spirit:** Michelle O'Brien, *Historic Photos of University of Michigan Football* (New York: Turner Publishing, 2008). Kindle Edition.

119   **Oklahoma State claims to have had one of the first student sections:** "Athletic Facilities: Gallagher-Iba Arena," *Oklahoma State Athletics*, http://www.okstate.com/facilities/gallagher-iba. html (accessed 28 September 2014).

119   **Leaders of the University of San Francisco's "rooting section" wore letterman cardigans and guided fellow students in cheers:** University of San Francisco, *The Don 1957 Yearbook* (San Francisco, Calif.: University of San Francisco, 1957), 122. http://digitalcollections.usfca.edu/cdm/ compoundobject/collection/p15129coll4/id/2527/rec/45 (accessed 19 October 2014).

119   **The Show unveiled its debut Michael Jackson big head with the hopes of psyching out opposing players:** George Dohrmann, "How Big Heads Became a Part of College Basketball Culture," *SI.com*, 27 February 2013, http://www.si. com/college-basketball/2013/02/27/big-heads (accessed 19 October 2014).

120   **The Crazies elevated the personal taunt to an art form:** "Cameron Crazies," *Duke University Athletics*, http://www. goduke.com/ViewArticle.dbml?ATCLID=1391403 (accessed 18 October 2014).

121   **The one-off tomfoolery of the student in the Speedo lives on in infamy:** "Speedo Man," *ESPN*, 3 March 2012, http://espn.go. com/video/clip?id=7641271 (accessed 18 October 2014).

129   **Bibby told reporters at the time they were the "rudest fans"**
        he had ever seen: Dan Raley, "Pac-10 Men: Ducks Ruffle
        Bibby's Feathers," *Seattle Post-Intelligencer*, 6 February 2002,
        http://www.seattlepi.com/sports/article/Pac-10-Men-Ducks-
        ruffle-Bibby-s-feathers-1079540.php (accessed 18 October
        2014).

130   **In 1988, students from Arizona State University chanted**
        "PLO, PLO" to distract guard Steve Kerr: Tracy Dobbs,
        "Arizona St. Apologizes to Kerr: Arizona Guard Was Target of
        Taunts by Fans before Game," *Los Angeles Times*, 1 March
        1988, http://articles.latimes.com/1988-03-01/sports/sp-257_1_
        arizona-state (accessed 26 January 2014).

132   **The Bears' definitive win over the Trojans gave them a total**
        of 12 conference wins and brought them one step closer to
        success: Associated Press, "California 71, USC 60," *ESPN*, 4
        March 2006, http://scores.espn.go.com/ncb/recap?gameId=
        260630025 (accessed 18 October 2014).

133   **Redick had to trade in his cell number:** Mark Schlabach,
        "Duke's Redick Is Fans' Object of Disaffection," *Washington
        Post*, 12 February 2005, http://www.washingtonpost.com/wp-
        dyn/articles/A17550-2005Feb11.html (accessed 19 October
        2014).

133   **"I'm able to internalize all the hateful things that are said to**
        me, and it gets my competitive juices going": Schlabach,
        "Duke's Redick Is Fans' Object of Disaffection."

133   **Carlos Boozer was hit in the head by a water bottle thrown**
        by a student and required medical attention: Sam Borden,
        "UM Officials Take Steps to Control Fans at Cole," *Baltimore
        Sun*, 1 February 2001, http://articles.baltimoresun.com/2001-02-
        01/sports/0102010886_1_fans-cole-field-house-duke (accessed
        19 October 2014).

133   **To that end, Maryland's president consulted with the state**
        attorney general's office:
        Howard Wasserman, "Free Speech on Public College
        Campuses. Fan Profanity," *The First Amendment Center*, 10

September 2004, http://www.firstamendmentcenter.org/fan-profanity (accessed 15 February 2014).

134 **"One man's vulgarity is another's lyric":** *Cohen v. California*, 403 U.S. 15 (1971), http://www.law.cornell.edu/supremecourt/text/403/15 (accessed 19 October 2014).

134 **Students instituted a T-shirt exchange, during which one could trade in an X-rated shirt for something PG-13:** Kevin Van Valkenburg, "Terps Fans Retain Spirit, Lose Vulgarity," *Baltimore Sun*, 13 February 2005, http://articles.baltimoresun.com/2005-02-13/sports/0502130151_1_comcast-center-crowd-terps (accessed 19 October 2014).

134 **When Redick and Duke rolled onto campus for the next year's game, complaints about profanity declined:** David Ginsburg, "Maryland Outlasts Duke in OT, 99–92," *Umterps.com*, 12 February 2005, http://www.umterps.com/ViewArticle.dbml?SPID=120728&DB_OEM_ID=29700&ATCLID=207294375 (accessed 19 October 2014).

136 **The University of Illinois avoids the issue by banning signs and banners:** "State Farm Center Basketball Fan Guide," *University of Illinois*, 2013–2014, http://grfx.cstv.com/photos/schools/ill/sports/m-baskbl/auto_pdf/2013-14/misc_non_event/statefarmcenter-fanguide-2013.pdf (accessed 18 October 2014).

137 **The athletic director and head football coach sent an e-mail to students at the University of Wisconsin asking them to tone down their vulgarity:** Deborah Ziff, "Alvarez, Bielema Send Message to Badger Ticket Holders: Keep It Classy," *Wisconsin State Journal*, 14 October 2011, http://host.madison.com/sports/college/football/alvarez-bielema-send-message-to-badger-ticket-holders-keep-it/article_8e5eb11a-f5e7-11e0-bd6b-001cc4c002e0.html (accessed 28 September 2014).

CHAPTER 8: THE AGE OF ENTITLEMENT: HOW WE ARE SHAPING A NEW GENERATION OF SPORTS FANS

140   **They simply raised ticket prices to such a degree that working-class people can't afford a ticket:** David Conn, "The Premier League Has Priced Out Fans, Young and Old," *Guardian*, 16 August 2011, http://www.theguardian.com/sport/david-conn-inside-sport-blog/2011/aug/16/premier-league-football-ticket-prices (accessed 18 October 2014); Owen Gibson, "Atmosphere and Fans' Role in Premier League Games Becomes a Concern," *Observer*, 16 November 2013, http://www.theguardian.com/football/2013/nov/16/premier-league-fans-atmosphere-concern (accessed 18 October 2014).

141   **The best seat in the house to watch the Dallas Cowboys play at their new stadium, opened in 2009, required a fee of $150,000:** "Cowboys Release Ticket Prices for New Stadium, Cheapest Seat $59," *Sports Business Daily*, 16 May 2008, http://www.sportsbusinessdaily.com/Daily/Issues/2008/05/Issue-165/Facilities-Venues/Cowboys-Release-Ticket-Prices-For-New-Stadium-Cheapest-Seat-$59.aspx (accessed 18 October 2014).

141   **PSL fees are required for two-thirds of the seats and range from $4,000 to $30,000:** Mike Florio, "Woody Johnson: Jets Won't Lower Personal Seat License Prices," *NBC Sports*, 13 May 2010, http://profootballtalk.nbcsports.com/2010/05/13/woody-johnson-jets-wont-lower-personal-seat-license-prices (accessed 18 October 2014).

142   **Fans have also been documented tossing urine bombs from hillsides during the Tour de France and the stands at Penn State's Beaver Stadium:** Matt Slater, "Tour de France: Mark Cavendish Has Urine Thrown at Him," *BBC*, 10 July 2013, http://www.bbc.com/sport/0/cycling/23251598 (accessed 18 October 2014); Bill Livingston, "Penn State's Happy Valley a Hostile Environment for Ohio State and Especially for Terrelle Pryor," *Cleveland.com*, 6 November 2009, http://www.cleveland.com/livingston/index.ssf/2009/11/happy_valley_hostile_environme.html (accessed 18 October 2014).

142   **A Pittsburgh Pirates security guard lost his finger when it got caught in a fence during a scuffle:** Sadie Gurman, "PNC Park Guard Loses Finger, Pittsburgh Cop Injures Shoulder in Struggle with Belligerent Fan," *Pittsburgh Post-Gazette*, 16 May 2012, http://www.post-gazette.com/sports/pirates/2012/05/16/PNC-Park-guard-loses-finger-Pittsburgh-cop-injures-shoulder-in-struggle-with-belligerent-fan/stories/201205160146 (accessed 18 October 2014).

142   **Polls show that the majority of Americans believe popular culture has gotten cruder:** "Two-Thirds of Public Believe American Society Is Uncivil," *Powell Tate DC*, 22 June 2010, http://www.powelltate.com/press-room/two-thirds_of_public_believe_american_society_is_uncivil (accessed 18 October 2014).

142   **She cursed after forgetting to bring her glasses onstage:** "Streep's Golden Globes Post 50 Moment: 'Oh S**t My Glasses!'" *Huffington Post*, 16 January 2012, http://www.huffingtonpost.com/2012/01/16/golden-globe-boomer-moment_n_1208459.html (accessed 18 October 2014).

142   **Lady Gaga used profanity on Saturday Night Live:** Molly O. Fitzpatrick, "No Real Need to Shelter from the F-Bomb," *Harvard Crimson*, 16 October 2009, http://www.thecrimson.com/article/2009/10/16/fbomb-comedy-live-saturday (accessed 18 October 2014).

143   **"It's something much deeper and more existentially disruptive":** Christopher Hayes, *Twilight of the Elites: America after Meritocracy* (New York: Crown, 2012). Kindle Edition.

143   **"While people feel like they *know* an actor, they feel like they *own* a sports star":** Luke Cyphers, "Fan Fright Going to the Ol' Ballgame Has Never Been Scarier," *New York Daily News*, 25 August 1996, http://www.nydailynews.com/archives/sports/fan-fright-ol-ballgame-scarier-article-1.748475 (accessed 18 October 2014).

144   **"An institution that rewards the reckless will act as a spawning ground for recklessness":** Hayes, *Twilight of the Elites*.

145   **California even created a self-esteem task force:** For more on
       the self-esteem movement, see Jean M. Twenge, *Generation
       Me: Why Today's Young Americans Are More Confident,
       Assertive, Entitled—and More Miserable Than Ever Before*
       (New York: Simon & Schuster, 2006). Kindle Edition.

146   **"People whose self-esteem is high but lack a firm basis in
       genuine accomplishment are especially prone to be violent":**
       Roy Baumeister, *Evil: Inside Human Violence and Cruelty* (New
       York: Holt Paperbacks, 1999), 25.

146   **"America has overdosed on self-admiration":** Jean M.
       Twenge and Keith W. Campbell, *The Narcissism Epidemic:
       Living in the Age of Entitlement* (New York: Simon & Schuster,
       2009). Kindle Edition.

146   **"We found so many examples of narcissism in American
       culture that we had to stop collecting them":** Twenge and
       Campbell, *The Narcissism Epidemic.*

147   **"Americans are obsessed with people who are obsessed with
       themselves":** Twenge and Campbell, *The Narcissism Epidemic.*

147   **"I just did it my way. I'm not a martyr, and I'm not a do-
       gooder. I just want to go out and rock. And man, I rocked
       here":** Twenge and Campbell, *The Narcissism Epidemic.*

147   **"I love me some me":** Katie Thomas, "Sports Stars Seek Profit
       in Catchphrases," *New York Times*, 9 December 2010, http://
       www.nytimes.com/2010/12/10/sports/10trademark.html?_r=0
       (accessed 18 October 2014).

148   **Another bodyguard, a state trooper, stood in front of the
       bathroom that the two had entered and ignored a friend who
       was trying to intervene:** "Accuser: Roethlisberger Exposed
       Self," *ESPN*, 16 April 2010, http://sports.espn.go.com/nfl/news/
       story?id=5094224 (accessed 18 October 2014).

148   **Rodriguez posed in a *Details* magazine photo shoot that
       showed him kissing his own reflection in a mirror:** Jason
       Gay, "Confessions of a Damned Yankee," *Details*, May 2009,
       http://www.details.com/culture-trends/cover-stars/200903/
       yankee-alex-rodriguez-talks-steroids-and-madonna (accessed 18
       October 2014).

148 **"There is a symbiotic relationship":** Mike Wise, "A Call for Civility," *Washington Post*, 3 July 2011, http://www. washingtonpost.com/sports/2011/07/02/AG1flwwH_story.html (accessed 11 October 2014).

148 **He was eventually violently tackled and arrested:** Bernie Augustine and Daniel O'Leary, "Fan Runs Out on Citi Field during MLB All-Star Game after Getting 1,000 Retweets He Asked for on Twitter," *New York Daily News*, 17 July 2013, http://www.nydailynews.com/sports/baseball/twitter-dare-results-fan-running-field-all-star-game-article-1.1400666 (accessed 19 October 2014).

149 **A judge ruled that the proceeds from the ball should be split between the two litigants:** *Popov v. Hayashi* WL 31833731 (2002), http://www.hofstra.edu/PDF/law_property_glazer_assign1_sp07.pdf -page=1&zoom=auto,-74,497 (accessed 19 October 2014).

149 **"You'd have more money than your parents":** Bill Shaikin, "Downing Comes to Bonds' Defense," *Los Angeles Times*, 2 August 2007, http://articles.latimes.com/2007/aug/02/sports/sp-bonds2 (accessed 18 October. 2014).

150 **Brandon Jacobs received a death threat from a disgruntled fantasy owner:** Ebenezer Samuel, "NY Giants RB Brandon Jacobs Slams Fantasy Football after Getting Death Threat on Twitter," *New York Daily News*, 24 October 2013, http://www. nydailynews.com/sports/football/giants/jacobs-rips-fantasy-football-owners-death-threats-article-1.1494661 (accessed 18 October 2014).

150 **Jones-Drew realized the conflict and apologized to other fantasy owners:** Chris Chase, "Maurice Jones-Drew Takes a Knee, Apologizes to Fantasy Owners," *Yahoo! Sports*, 15 November 2009, http://sports.yahoo.com/nfl/blog/shutdown_corner/post/Maurice-Jones-Drew-takes-a-knee-apologizes-to-f?urn=nfl,202651 (accessed 18 October 2014).

151 **"If the narcissism epidemic continues, there will be more entitlement":** Twenge and Campbell, *The Narcissism Epidemic*.

CONCLUSION: MOVING THE CHAINS

155   **No arrests were made using this tool:** Vickie Chachere,
        "Biometrics Used to Detect Criminals at Super Bowl," *ABC
        News*, 13 February 2001, http://abcnews.go.com/Technology/
        story?id=98871 (accessed 18 October 2014).

156   **Alameda County sheriff Greg Ahern expressed interest in
        IBIS2 and met with Kephart and his company several times:**
        Ali Winston, "Sheriff Sought Controversial Surveillance
        Software," *East Bay Express*, 6 March 2013, http://www.
        eastbayexpress.com/oakland/sheriff-sought-controversial-
        surveillance-software/Content?oid=3480918 (accessed 18
        October 2014).

156   **During early Olympic Games, *mastigophoroi* and
        rabdouchoi , Greek for "whip-bearers" and "truncheon-
        bearers," respectively, roamed the fields:** Guttmann, *Sports
        Spectators*.

157   **Police arrested approximately 50 people:** Lornet Turnbull,
        Debbie Gebolys, and Alice Thomas, "Reconstructing the Riot:
        What Happened . . . and What Didn't," *Columbus Dispatch*, 8
        December 2002, p. 1A. Home Final Edition.

159   **It required stadiums to post emergency numbers for fans to
        text in case of problems:** John Egan, "New California Law
        Represents 'Small Step' in Fighting Fan Violence,"
        Examiner.com, 1 January 2013, http://www.examiner.com/
        article/new-california-law-represents-small-step-fighting-fan-
        violence (accessed 31 October 2014).

159   **The school's president and athletic director ended up
        sending apologies in response to e-mail complaints from
        Texas fans for their rough treatment in the stands:** "Ohio
        State Officials Apologize to Texas Fans," *ESPN*, 15 September
        2005, http://sports.espn.go.com/ncf/news/story?id=2161919
        (accessed 18 October 2014).

160   **Approximately 40 people were arrested, and dozens of fires
        burned:** Associated Press, "Police Arrest 40 after OSU Win, but
        Columbus Relatively Calm," *USA Today*, 19 November 2006,

http://usatoday30.usatoday.com/sports/college/football/2006-11-19-ohio-michigan-arrests_x.htm (accessed 18 October 2014).

160 **A one-punch homicide can fall between accepted legal definitions of murder and manslaughter:** Anna Patty, "Proposed Laws Will Give 20 Years for 'One-Punch' Killings," *Sydney Morning Herald*, 13 November 2013, http://www.smh.com.au/nsw/proposed-laws-will-give-20-years-for-onepunch-killings-20131112-2xenc.html (accessed 18 October 2014).

161 **"People attending events where alcohol is typically present do not have to drink to experience, or be subject to, the aggression-enhancing effects of alcohol":** "Alcohol Primes and Aggressions," *University of Kent News Centre*, 9 June 2014, http://www.kent.ac.uk/newsarchive/news/stories/alcohol-related_agression/20 14.html (accessed 25 October 2014).

BIBLIOGRAPHY

BOOKS

Allt, Nicholas. *The Boys from Mersey*. London: Milo Books, 2011. Kindle Edition.

Allt, Nicky, ed. *Here We Go Gathering Cups in May: Liverpool in Europe, the Fans Story*. Edinburgh, U.K.: Canongate Books, 2009. Kindle Edition.

Annussek, Greg A. *Hitler's Raid to Save Mussolini: The Most Infamous Commando Operation of World War II*. Cambridge, Mass.: Da Capo, 2005. Google Books download.

Baumeister, Roy. *Evil: Inside Human Violence and Cruelty*. New York: Holt Paperbacks, 1999.

Blythe, Will. *To Hate Like This Is to Be Happy Forever*. New York: Harper, 2007.

Bognon, Pierre. *The Anatomy of Sports Fans: Reflections on Fans and Fanatics*. New Canaan, Conn.: Editions Bognon, 2008.

Brimson, Dougie. *Kicking Off: Why Hooliganism and Racism Are Killing Football*. United Kingdom: Category C Publishing, 2011. Kindle Edition.

Bronson, Po, and Ashley Merryman. *NurtureShock: New Thinking about Children*. New York: Twelve, 2009.

Buford, Bill. *Among the Thugs*. New York: Vintage, 1993.

Campomar, Andreas. *Golazo! The Beautiful Game from the Aztecs to the World Cup: The Complete History of How Soccer Shaped Latin America*. New York: Riverhead, 2014. Kindle Edition.

Citron, Danielle Keats. *Hate Crimes in Cyberspace*. Cambridge, Mass.: Harvard University Press, 2014. Kindle Edition.

Comeron, Manuel. *The Prevention of Violence in Sport*. Strasbourg, France: Council of European Publishing, 2002. Google Books download.

Cook, William A. *Diamond Madness: Classic Episodes of Rowdyism, Racism, and Violence in Major League Baseball*. Mechanicsburg, Pa.: Sunbury Press, 2013. Kindle Edition.

Dunning, Eric, Patrick Murphy, Ivan Waddington, and Antonios Astrinkakis, eds. *Fighting Fans: Football Hooliganism as a World Phenomenon*. Dublin: University College Dublin Press, 2002.

Earnheardt, Adam C., Paul M. Haridakis, and Barbara S. Hugenberg. *Sports Fans, Identity, and Socialization: Exploring the Fandemonium*. Lanham, Md.: Lexington, 2012.

Faludi, Susan. *Stiffed: The Betrayal of the American Man*. New York: HarperCollins E-books, 2011. Kindle Edition.

Foot, John. *Winning at All Costs: A Scandalous History of Italian Football*. New York: Nation Books, 2006. Kindle Edition.

Frosdick, Steve, and Peter Marsh. *Football Hooliganism*. Portland, Ore.: Willan, 2005. Kindle Edition.

Gager, John G. *Curse Tablets and Binding Spells from the Ancient World*. New York: Oxford University Press, 1992. Kindle Edition.

Gall, Caroline. *Service Crew: The Inside Story of Leeds United's Hooligan Gangs*. London: Milo Books, 2011. Kindle Edition.

Gerrard, Michael, and Richard Giulianotti. "Cruel Britannia? Glasgow Rangers, Scotland, and 'Hot' Football Rivalries." In *Fear and Loathing in World Football*, ed. Gary Armstrong and Richard Giulianotti, 23–43. New York: Berg, 2001.

Glare, P. G. W., ed. *Oxford Latin Dictionary*. New York: Oxford University Press, 1982.

Guttmann, Allen. *Sports Spectators*. New York: Columbia University Press, 1986. Kindle Edition.

Hayes, Christopher. *Twilight of the Elites: America after Meritocracy*. New York: Crown, 2012. Kindle Edition.

Hess, Jeanne. *Sportuality: Finding Joy in the Games*. Bloomington, Ind.: Balboa Press, 2012. Kindle Edition.

Hopkins, Keith, and Mary Bear. *The Colosseum*. London: Profile Books, 2005.

Hornby, Nick. *Fever Pitch*. New York: Riverhead Books, 1992. Kindle Edition.

Hyman, Mark. *Until It Hurts: America's Obsession with Youth Sports and How It Harms Our Kids*. Boston: Beacon Press, 2009. Kindle Edition.

Kahle, Lynn, and Angeline Close, eds. *Consumer Behavior Knowledge for Effective Sports and Event Marketing*. East Sussex, U.K.: Taylor and Francis, 2011. Kindle Edition.

Kimmel, Michael. *Guyland: The Perilous World Where Boys Become Men*. New York: Harper-Collins E-books, 2009. Kindle Edition.

Le Bon, Gustave. *The Crowd: A Study of the Popular Mind*. Mineola, N.Y.: Dover Books, 1895. Kindle Edition.

Lewis, Jerry M. *Sports Fan Violence in North America*. Lanham, Md.: Rowman & Littlefield, 2007.

Markovits, Andrei S., and Emily W. Albertson. *Sportista: Female Fandom in the United States*. Philadelphia, Pa.: Temple University Press, 2012. Kindle Edition.

Markovits, Andrei S., and Lars Rensmann. *Gaming the World: How Sports Are Reshaping Global Politics and Culture*. Princeton, N.J.: Princeton University Press, 2010. Kindle Edition.

McPhail, Clark. *The Myth of the Madding Crowd*. New York: Walter de Gruyter, 1991. Google Books download.

Morris, Desmond. *The Soccer Tribe*. London: Jonathan Cape, 1981.

Morris, Desmond, and Peter Marsh. *Tribes*. Salt Lake City, Utah: Peregrine Smith, 1988.

Murad, Mauricio. *A violência no futebol*. São Paulo, Brazil: Saraiva, 2012.

Nash, Bruce. *The Baseball Hall of Shame: The Best of Blooperstown*. Guilford, Conn.: Lyons Press, 2012. Kindle Edition.

O'Brien, Michelle. *Historic Photos of University of Michigan Football*. New York: Turner Publishing, 2008. Kindle Edition.

Paoletti, Mario, and Pilar Bravo. *Borges Verbal*. Buenos Aires, Argentina: Emecé, 1999.

Parks, Tim. *A Season with Verona: A Soccer Fan Follows His Team around Italy in Search of Dreams, National Character, and . . . Goals!* New York: Arcade Publishing, 2012. Kindle Edition.

Pastorini, Dan, and John P. Lopez. *Taking Flak: My Life in the Fast Lane*. Bloomington, Ind.: AuthorHouse, 2011.

Pennant, Cass, and Andy Nicholls. *England's Hooligan Army*. UK: Endeavour Press, 2012. Kindle Edition.

Pinker, Steven. *The Better Angels of Our Nature: Why Violence Has Declined*. New York: Penguin, 2011. Kindle Edition.

Rea, Stephen. *Finn McCool's Football Club: The Birth, Death, and Resurrection of a Pub Soccer Team in the City of the Dead*. Gretna, La.: Pelican, 2009. Kindle Edition.

Reicher, Scott, and Cliff Stott. *Mad Mobs and Englishmen? Myths and Realities of the 2011 Riots*. London: Constable and Robinson, 2011. Google Books Edition.

Riess, Steve. *Sport in Industrial America, 1850–1920*. Oxford, UK: John Wiley and Sons, 2013. Google Books download.

Rozenblit, Bruce. *Us against Them: How Tribalism Affects the Way We Think*. Kansas City, Kan.: Transcendent Publications, 2008. Kindle Edition.

Simons, Eric. *The Secret Lives of Sports Fans: The Science of Sports Obsession*. New York: Overlook Duckworth, 2013.

Sperber, Murray. *Beer and Circus: How Big-Time College Sports Are Crippling Undergraduate Education*. New York: Henry Holt and Company, 2000.

Spillane, Bryan. *U.S. Beverage Alcohol Primer*, 2014 edition. Bank of America Merrill Lynch, February 28, 2014.

St. John, Warren. *ESPN Guide to Psycho Fan Behavior*. New York: ESPN Books, 2007.

Sternberg, Robert, ed. *The Psychology of Hate*. Washington, D.C.: American Psychological Association, 2005.

Tacitus. *The Annals*. Oxford, U.K.: Acheron Press, 2012. Kindle Edition.

Tiger, Lionel. *The Decline of Males*. New York: Golden Books, 1999.

———. *Men in Groups*. New Brunswick, N.J.: Transaction, 2005. Google Books download.

Toner, Jerry. *Popular Culture in Ancient Rome*. Cambridge, U.K.: Polity Press, 2013. Kindle Edition.

Twenge, Jean M. *Generation Me: Why Today's Young Americans Are More Confident, Assertive, Entitled—and More Miserable Than Ever Before*. New York: Simon & Schuster, 2006. Kindle Edition.

Twenge, Jean M., and Keith W. Campbell. *The Narcissism Epidemic: Living in the Age of Entitlement*. New York: Simon & Schuster, 2009. Kindle Edition.

University of San Francisco. *The Don 1957 Yearbook* (San Francisco, Calif.: University of San Francisco, 1957). http://digitalcollections.usfca.edu/cdm/compoundobject/collection/p15129coll4/id/2527/rec/45 (accessed 19 October 2014).

Vialli, Gianluca, and Gabrielle Marcotti. *The Italian Job: A Journey to the Heart of Two Great Footballing Cultures*. London: Bantam, 2006.

Wann, Daniel L., Merrill J. Melnick, Gordon W. Russell, and Dale G. Pease. *Sports Fans: The Psychology and Social Impact of Spectators*. New York: Routledge, 1993.

Zimbardo, Philip. *The Lucifer Effect: Understanding How Good People Turn Evil*. New York: Random House, 2007.

JOURNAL ARTICLES

Bandura, Albert. "Moral Disengagement in the Perpetration of Inhumanities." *Personality and Social Psychology Review* 3 (1999): 193–209.

Bartholow, Bruce D., and Adrienne Heinz. "Alcohol and Aggression without Consumption Alcohol Cues, Aggressive Thoughts, and Hostile Perception Bias." *Psychological Science* 17, no. 1 (2006): 30–37.

Berkowitz, Leonard. "The Effects of Observing Violence." *Scientific American* 210, no. 2 (1964): 35–41.

Bernhardt, P. C., J. M. Dabbs, J. A. Fielden, and C. D. Lutter. "Testosterone Changes during Vicarious Experiences of Winning and Losing among Fans at Sporting Events." *Physiology and Behavior* 65, no. 1 (1998): 59–62.

Bizer, George Y., and Richard E. Petty. "Exploring the Valence-Framing Effect: Negative Framing Enhances Attitude Strength." *Political Psychology* 32 (2011): 59–80.

Brentin, Dario. "'A Lofty Battle for the Nation': The Social Roles of Sport in Tudjman's Croatia." *Sport in Society: Cultures, Commerce, Media, Politics* 16, no. 8 (2013): 993–1,008.

Brill, A. A. "The Why of the Fan." *North American Review* 228 (1929): 429–34.

Card, David, and Gordon B. Dahl. "Family Violence and Football: The Effect of Unexpected Emotional Cues on Violent Behavior." *Quarterly Journal of Economics* 126, no. 1 (2011): 103–43.

Cialdini, Robert. B., Richard J. Borden, Avril Thorne, Marcus Randall Walker, Stephen Freeman, and Lloyd Reynolds Sloan. "Basking in Reflected Glory: Three (Football) Field Studies." *Journal of Personality and Social Psychology* 34, no. 3 (1976): 366–75.

Ditter, Susan M., Randy W. Elder, Ruth A. Shults, David A. Sleet, Richard Compton, and James L. Nichols. "Effectiveness of Designated Driver Programs for Reducing Alcohol-Impaired Driving." *American Journal of Preventive Medicine* 28, no. 5 (2005): 280–87.

Erickson, Darin J., Traci L. Toomey, Kathleen M. Lenk, Gunna R. Kilian, and Lindsey E. A. Fabian. "Can We Assess Blood Alcohol Levels of Attendees Leaving Professional Sporting Events?" *Alcoholism: Clinical and Experimental Research* 35, no. 4 (2011): 689–94.

Gantz, Walter, Lawrence A. Wenner, Christina Carrico, and Matthew Knorr. "Televised Sports and Marital Relationships." *Sociology of Sport Journal* 12 (1995): 306–23.

Gorman, Bob, and David Weeks. "Foul Play: Fan Fatalities in Twentieth-Century Organized Baseball." *Nine* 12, no. 1 (2003): 115–32.

Greatrex, Geoffrey. "The Nika Riot: A Reappraisal." *Journal of Hellenic Studies* 117 (1997): 60–86.

Hoaken, Peter, and Sherry H. Stewart. "Drugs of Abuse and the Elicitation of Human Aggressive Behavior." *Addictive Behaviors* 28, no. 9 (2003): 1,533–54.

Lenk, Kathleen M., Traci L. Toomey, and Darin J. Erickson. "Alcohol-Related Problems and Enforcement at Professional Sports Stadiums." *Drugs: Education, Prevention, and Policy* 16, no. 5 (2009): 451–62.

Lenk, Kathleen M., Traci L. Toomey, Darin J. Erickson, Gunna R. Kilian, Toben F. Nelson, and Lindsey E. A. Fabian. "Alcohol Policies and Practices at Professional Sports Stadiums." *Public Health Reports* 125, no. 5 (2010): 665–73.

McPhail, Clark. "Presidential Address: The Dark Side of Purpose: Individual and Collective Violence in Riots." *Sociological Quarterly* 35, no. 1 (1994): 1–32.

Munsey, Christopher. "Frisky, but More Risky." *American Psychological Association* 30, no. 7 (July/August 2006): 40.

Pedersen, William C., Eduardo A. Vasquez, Bruce D. Bartholow, Marianne Grosvenor, and Ana Truong. "Are You Insulting Me? Exposure to Alcohol Primes Increases Aggression Following Ambiguous Provocation." *Personality and Social Psychology Bulletin* 40, no. 8 (11 July 2014): 1–13.

Toomey, Traci L., Darin J. Erickson, Kathleen M. Lenk, and Gunna R. Kilian. "Likelihood of Illegal Alcohol Sales at Professional Sport Stadiums." *Alcoholism: Clinical and Experimental Research* 32, no. 11 (2008): 1,859–64.

Toomey, Traci L., Darin J. Erickson, Kathleen M. Lenk, Gunna R. Kilian, Cheryl L. Perry, and Alexander C. Wagenaar. "A Randomized Trial to Evaluate a Management Training Program to Prevent Illegal Alcohol Sales." *Addiction* 103, no. 3 (2008): 405–13.

Vamplew, Wray. "Sports Crowd Disorder in Britain, 1870–1914: Causes and Controls." *Journal of Sport History* 7, no. 1 (Spring 1980): 5–20.

Wakefield, Kirk, and Daniel. L. Wann. "An Examination of Dysfunctional Sport Fans: Method of Classification and Relationships with Problem Behaviors." *Journal of Leisure Research* 38 (2006): 168–86.

Wann, Daniel L., Gaye Haynes, Bryan McLean, and Paul Pullen. "Sport Team Identification and Willingness to Consider Anonymous Acts of Hostile Aggression." *Aggressive Behavior* 29, no. 5 (2003): 406–13.

Wood, Stacy, Melayne M. McInnes, and David A. Norton. "The Bad Thing about Good Games: The Relationship between Close Sporting Events and Game-Day Traffic Fatalities." *Journal of Consumer Research* 38, no 4 (2011): 611–21.

NEWSPAPER AND WEBSITE ARTICLES

"110 Kicked Out of Candlestick Park during NFC Championship Game." *Los Angeles Times*, 24 January 2010, http://latimesblogs.latimes.com/lanow/2012/01/nfc-championship-candlestick-park-arrests.html (accessed 12 October 2014).

"2014 Sochi Winter Olympics on Facebook." *Facebook*, 24 February 2014, http://newsroom.fb.com/news/2014/02/2014-sochi-winter-olympics-on-facebook (accessed 19 October 2014).

Abrams, Jonathan. "The Malice at the Palace." *Grantland*, 20 March 2012, http://grantland.com/features/an-oral-history-malice-palace (accessed 18 October 2014).

"Accuser: Roethlisberger Exposed Self." *ESPN*, 16 April 2010, http://sports.espn.go.com/nfl/news/story?id=5094224 (accessed 18 October 2014).

"Alcohol Primes and Aggressions." *University of Kent News Centre*, 9 June 2014, http://www.kent.ac.uk/newsarchive/news/stories/alcohol-related_agression/20 14.html (accessed 25 October 2014).

Arudou, Debito. "J. League and Media Mush Show Red Card to Racism." *Japan Times*, 12 March 2014, http://www.japantimes.co.jp/community/2014/03/12/issues/j-league-and-media-must-show-red-card-to-racism/#.VCH3PvaB_rY (accessed 18 October 2014).

Associated Press. "Brazilian Fan Killed by Thrown Toilet Bowl." *ESPN*, 3 May 2014, http://www.espnfc.com/futebol-brasileiro/story/1807916/brazilian-fan-killed-by-thrown-toilet-bowl-in-recife (accessed 18 October 2014).

———. "California 71, USC 60." *ESPN*, 4 March 2006, http://scores.espn.go.com/ncb/recap?gameId=260630025 (accessed 18 October 2014).

———. "German Club Sells Out 'Ghost Game.'" *ESPN*, 11 March 2012, http://espn.go.com/sports/soccer/story/_/id/7672386/german-club-dynamo-dresden-sells-stadium-ban (accessed 11 October 2014).

———. "Greece Suspends All Team Sports after Volleyball Fan Killed." *USA Today*, 30 March 2007, http://usatoday30.usatoday.com/sports/2007-03-30-greece-ban_N.htm (accessed 11 October 2014).

———. "Man Unapologetic for Spreading Ashes at Linc." *ESPN*, 30 November 2005, http://sports.espn.go.com/nfl/news/story?id=2241909 (accessed 18 October 2014).

———. "Man Who Threw Chair during Pacers–Pistons Brawl Gets Probation." *USA Today*, 3 May 2005, http://usatoday30.usatoday.com/sports/basketball/nba/2005-05-03-fan-probation_x.htm (accessed 18 October 2014).

———. "Massachusetts YMCA Bans Parents from Youth Basketball Games." *MassLive.com*, 25 February 2010, http://www.masslive.com/news/index.ssf/2010/02/massachusetts_ymca_bans_parent.html (accessed 18 October 2014).

———. "Police: PSU Rioters Caused $190K in Damages." *WDEL*, 21 December 2011, http://www.wdel.com/story.php?id=39677 (accessed 9 January 2015).

———. "Police Arrest 40 after OSU Win, but Columbus Relatively Calm." *USA Today*, 19 November 2006, http://usatoday30.usatoday.com/sports/college/football/2006-11-19-ohio-michigan-arrests_x.htm (accessed 18 October 2014).

———. "Romanian Soccer Fan Charged in Attack on Player." *ESPN*, 31 October 2011, http://sports.espn.go.com/espn/wire?section=soccer&id=7173201 (accessed 11 October 2014).

———. "Scott Cousins Receiving Death Threats after Home Plate Collision with Giants' Buster Posey." *New York Daily News*, 4 June 2011, http://www.nydailynews.com/sports/baseball/scott-cousins-receiving-death-threats-home-plate-collision-giants-buster-posey-article-1.125066 (accessed 18 October 2014).

———. "Two Admit Guilt in Bryan Stow Attack." *ESPN*, 20 February 2014, http://espn.go.com/los-angeles/mlb/story/_/id/10489372/two-men-admit-guilt-dodger-stadium-attack-bryan-stow (accessed 18 October 2014).

———. "UEFA Investigates Italian Soccer Head over Racism." *USA Today*, 20 August 2014, http://www.usatoday.com/story/sports/soccer/2014/08/20/uefa-investigates-italian-soccer-head-over-racism/1432617 (accessed 18 October 2014).

"Athletic Facilities: Gallagher-Iba Arena." *Oklahoma State Athletics*, http://www.okstate.com/facilities/gallagher-iba.html (accessed 28 September 2014).

Augustine, Bernie, and Daniel O'Leary. "Fan Runs Out on Citi Field during MLB All-Star Game after Getting 1,000 Retweets He Asked for on Twitter." *New York Daily News*, 17 July 2013, http://www.nydailynews.com/sports/baseball/twitter-dare-results-fan-running-field-all-star-game-article-1.1400666 (accessed 19 October 2014).

Belluck, Pam, and Katie Zezima. "Death of Red Sox Fan Leads to Stricter Rules," *New York Times*, 23 October 2004, http://www.nytimes.com/2004/10/23/sports/baseball/23boston. html?_r=0.Assessed (accessed 11 October 2014).

Bennett, Bridget. "Officials Warn 'Zero Tolerance' after Rowdy Dinkytown Crowd." *Minnesota Daily*, 11 April 2014, http://www.mndaily.com/news/campus/2014/04/11/hundreds-swarm-dinkytown (accessed 12 October 2014).

"Bonds's Gift to Stow's Children: College Education." *ESPN.com*, 26 May 2011, http://sports. espn.go.com/mlb/news/story?id=6590118 (accessed 22 October 2014).

Borden, Sam. "UM Officials Take Steps to Control Fans at Cole." *Baltimore Sun*, 1 February 2001, http://articles.baltimoresun.com/2001-02-01/sports/0102010886_1_fans-cole-field-house-duke (accessed 19 October 2014).

"Brazil Referee Decapitated after Stabbing Player." *BBC*, 7 July 2013, http://www.bbc.com/news/world-latin-america-23215676 (accessed 18 October 2014).

Broadley, Lise. "Comox Valley Man Apologizes for Role in Vancouver Riot." *Comox Valley Echo*, 4 October 2012, http://www.comoxvalleyecho.com/news/local/comox-valley-man-apologizes-for-role-in-vancouver-riot-1.970666 (accessed 11 October 2014).

Burke, Timothy. "Two Hours of the Lexington Police Scanner after UK Wins, Set to Music." *Deadspin*, 6 April 2014, http://deadspin.com/5898759/heres-what-kentuckys-championship-celebration-sounded-like-over-the-lexington-police-scanner (accessed 10 April 2014).

Burr, Michael T. "N.J. Court Tosses 'Culture of Intoxication' Verdict." *Inside Counsel*, 1 April 2007, http://www.insidecounsel.com/2007/04/01/nj-court-tosses-culture-of-intoxication-verdict (accessed 19 October 2014).

Butterfield, Fox. "Man Convicted in Fatal Beating in Dispute at Son's Hockey Game." *New York Times*, 12 January 2002, http://www.nytimes.com/2002/01/12/us/man-convicted-in-fatal-beating-in-dispute-at-son-s-hockey-game.html (accessed 18 October 2014).

"Cameron Crazies." *Duke University Athletics*, http://www.goduke.com/ViewArticle.dbml? ATCLID=1391403 (accessed 18 October 2014).

"Canada 2012 Crime and Safety Report: Vancouver." *Bureau of Diplomatic Security*, 3 April 2012, https://www.osac.gov/pages/contentreportdetails.aspx?cid=12304 2013 (accessed 12 October 2014).

Canadian Press. "Impact's Davy Arnaud Receives Twitter Threats." *CBC*, 10 July 2013, http:// www.cbc.ca/sports/soccer/impact-s-davy-arnaud-receives-twitter-threats-1.1344575 (accessed 18 October 2014).

Canova, Brian. "Riot Police Disperse 1,500 Students at UMass-Amherst Following Super Bowl." *MassLive.com*, 5 February 2012, http://www.masslive.com/news/index.ssf/2012/02/ riot_erupts_at_umass_amherst_f_1.html (11 October 2014).

Carpio, Anthony Clark. "After Huntington Beach Riot, Music and Alcohol Out for Surfing Contest." *Los Angeles Times*, 4 April 2014, http://www.latimes.com/local/lanow/la-me-ln-in-huntington-beach-riots-20140404-story.html (accessed 11 October 2014).

Carter, Jon. "Rewind: The Heysel Aftermath." *ESPN*, 2 June 2011, http://www.espnfc.com/ story/925085/rewind-the-heysel-aftermath-in-1985 (accessed 18 October 2014).

Chachere, Vickie. "Biometrics Used to Detect Criminals at Super Bowl." *ABC News*, 13 February 2001, http://abcnews.go.com/Technology/story?id=98871 (accessed 18 October 2014).

"Chad Greenway Wants Fans Drunk." *ESPN*, 6 December 2012, http://espn.go.com/chicago/ nfl/story/_/id/8720790/chad-greenway-minnesota-vikings-wants-metrodome-fans-super-duper-drunk (accessed 18 October 2014).

Chadiha, Jeffri. "Trash Talk: All about Finding an Edge." *ESPN.com*, 29 January 2014, http:// espn.go.com/nfl/playoffs/2013/story/_/id/10360951/the-art trash-talking (accessed 12 September 2014).

Chase, Chris. "Maurice Jones-Drew Takes a Knee, Apologizes to Fantasy Owners." *Yahoo! Sports*, 15 November 2009, http://sports.yahoo.com/nfl/blog/shutdown_corner/post/

Maurice-Jones-Drew-takes-a-knee-apologizes-to-f?urn=nfl,202651 (accessed 18 October 2014).

———. "Mike Brown's Son Receiving Threats on Twitter." *USA Today*, 9 November 2012, http://www.usatoday.com/story/gameon/2012/11/09/mike-browns-son-receiving-threats-on-twitter/169440 (accessed 18 October 2014).

Coleman, Sheila, Ann Jemphrey, Phil Scraton, and Paula Skidmore. "The Liverpool Experience." *Hillsborough Independent Panel*, April 1990, http://hillsborough.independent.gov.uk/repository/SYP000119160001.html (accessed 18 October 2014).

"Commissioner's Directive on Postgame Activity." *Kentucky High School Athletic Association*, 8 October 2013, http://khsaa.org/10082013-commissioners-directive-on-postgame-activity (accessed 18 October 2014).

Conn, David. "The Premier League Has Priced Out Fans, Young and Old." *Guardian*, 16 August 2011, http://www.theguardian.com/sport/david-conn-inside-sport-blog/2011/aug/16/premier-league-football-ticket-prices (accessed 18 October 2014).

Coslett, Paul. "Heysel Disaster." *BBC*, 4 December 2008, http://www.bbc.co.uk/liverpool/content/articles/2006/12/04/local_history_heysel_feature.shtml (accessed 18 October 2014).

Coté, Joe, and Jaxon Van Derbeken. "Crackdown at Candlestick: Raider Rivalry on Hold." *San Francisco Chronicle*, 22 August 2011, http://www.sfgate.com/49ers/article/Crackdown-at-Candlestick-Raider-rivalry-on-hold-2334044.php (accessed 18 October 2014).

"Court Docs Detail Bryan Stow's Beating." *ESPN*, 2 August 2011, http://espn.go.com/los-angeles/mlb/story/_/id/6824307/court-docs-detail-beating-san-francisco-giants-fan-bryan-stow (accessed 18 October 2014).

"Cowboys Release Ticket Prices for New Stadium, Cheapest Seat $59." *Sports Business Daily*, 16 May 2008, http://www.sportsbusinessdaily.com/Daily/Issues/2008/05/Issue-165/Facilities-Venues/Cowboys-Release-Ticket-Prices-For-New-Stadium-Cheapest-Seat-$59.aspx (accessed 18 October 2014).

Cullen, Kevin. "Asking for Trouble." *Boston Globe*, 21 July 2008, http://www.boston.com/news/local/articles/2008/07/21/asking_for_trouble/ (accessed 11 October 2014).

Cyphers, Luke. "Fan Fright Going to the Ol' Ballgame Has Never Been Scarier." *New York Daily News*, 25 August 1996, http://www.nydailynews.com/archives/sports/fan-fright-ol-ballgame-scarier-article-1.748475 (accessed 18 October 2014).

"David Beckham's Big Night Is Ruined as PSG Ligue 1 Trophy Celebrations Descend into Chaos and Rioting." *Independent*, 14 May 2013, http://www.independent.co.uk/sport/football/european/david-beckhams-big-night-is-ruined-as-psg-ligue-1-trophy-celebrations-descend-into-chaos-and-rioting-8614731.html (accessed 10 October 2014).

Dhillon, Sunny. "Young Man Sentenced to 17 Months in First Stanley Cup Riot Conviction." *Globe and Mail*, 16 February 2012, http://www.theglobeandmail.com/news/british-columbia/young-man-sentenced-to-17-months-in-first-stanley-cup-riot-conviction/article546842 (accessed 10 October 2014).

Dobbs, Tracy. "Arizona St. Apologizes to Kerr: Arizona Guard Was Target of Taunts by Fans before Game." *Los Angeles Times*, 1 March 1988, http://articles.latimes.com/1988-03-01/sports/sp-257_1_arizona-state (accessed 26 January 2014).

Dohrmann, George. "How Big Heads Became a Part of College Basketball Culture." *SI.com*, 27 February 2013, http://www.si.com/college-basketball/2013/02/27/big-heads (accessed 19 October 2014).

Dowd, Katie. "Kyle Williams Receiving Death Threats after NFC Championship." *San Francisco Chronicle*, 23 January 2012, http://blog.sfgate.com/49ers/2012/01/23/kyle-williams-receiving-death-threats-after-nfc-championship (accessed 18 October 2014).

Duggan, Maeve, and Aaron Smith. "Social Media Update 2013." *Pew Research Center*, Internet and American Life Project RSS, 30 December 2013, http://www.pewinternet.org/2013/12/30/social-media-update-2013 (accessed 26 September 2014).

Dwyer, Kelly. "Kobe Bryant Goes on a Facebook Rant, Vowing to Return While Still Casting Doubts about Rehab." *Yahoo! Sports*, 13 April 2013, http://sports.yahoo.com/blogs/nba-ball-dont-lie/kobe-bryant-goes-facebook-vent-vowing-return-while-151947306--nba.html (accessed 9 October 2014).

Egan, John. "New California Law Represents 'Small Step' in Fighting Fan Violence." *Examiner.com*, 1 January 2013, http://www.examiner.com/article/new-california-law-represents-small-step-fighting-fan-violence (accessed 31 October 2014).

Estes, Andrea. "The Mother of Postgame Victim Rips City Officials." *Boston Globe*, 9 February 2004, http://www.boston.com/news/local/massachusetts/articles/2004/02/09/riot_victims_mother_rips_menino_and_hussey (accessed 11 October 2014).

"Fan Ordered to Compensate Spartak Moscow for Swastika Display." *RiaNovosti*, 25 February 2014, http://en.ria.ru/russia/20140225/187881368/Fan-Ordered-to-Compensate-Spartak-Moscow-for-Swastika-Display.html (accessed 18 October 2014).

"Fans Celebrate across France as Algeria Makes World Cup History." *France 24*, 27 June 2014, http://www.france24.com/en/20140627-algeria-world-cup-france-celebration-history (accessed 12 October 2014).

Fitzpatrick, Molly O. "No Real Need to Shelter from the F-Bomb." *Harvard Crimson*, 16 October 2009, http://www.thecrimson.com/article/2009/10/16/fbomb-comedy-live-saturday (accessed 18 October 2014).

Florio, Mike. "Woody Johnson: Jets Won't Lower Personal Seat License Prices." *NBC Sports*, 13 May 2010, http://profootballtalk.nbcsports.com/2010/05/13/woody-johnson-jets-wont-lower-personal-seat-license-prices (accessed 18 October 2014).

"Football Policing." *British Transport Police*, http://www.btp.police.uk/advice_and_info/how_we_tackle_crime/football_policing.aspx (accessed 11 October 2014).

"Fred critica as organizadas e teme por tragédia após jogo contra o Horizonte." *Globo Esporte*, 4 August 2014, http://globoesporte.globo.com/futebol/times/fluminense/noticia/2014/04/fred-ataca-torcidas-organizadas.html (accessed 18 October 2014).

Fredrix, Emily. "Anheuser-Busch to Keep Sports Marketing Strong." *USA Today*, 17 July 2008, http://usatoday30.usatoday.com/money/economy/2008-07-17-3650253233_x.htm (accessed 1 October 2014).

Gay, Jason. "Confessions of a Damned Yankee." *Details*, May 2009, http://www.details.com/culture-trends/cover-stars/200903/yankee-alex-rodriguez-talks-steroids-and-madonna (accessed 18 October 2014).

Gelzinis, Peter. "Like Angry Father, Like Angry Son." *Boston Herald*, 9 February 2011, http://www.bostonherald.com/news_opinion/columnists/2011/02/angry_father_angry_son (accessed 9 October 2014).

Gibson, Owen. "Atmosphere and Fans' Role in Premier League Games Becomes a Concern." *Observer*, 16 November 2013, http://www.theguardian.com/football/2013/nov/16/premier-league-fans-atmosphere-concern (accessed 18 October 2014).

Ginsburg, David. "Maryland Outlasts Duke in OT, 99–92." *Umterps.com*, 12 February 2005, http://www.umterps.com/ViewArticle.dbml?SPID=120728&DB_OEM_ID=29700&ATCLID=207294375 (accessed 19 October 2014).

Gurman, Sadie. "PNC Park Guard Loses Finger, Pittsburgh Cop Injures Shoulder in Struggle with Belligerent Fan." *Pittsburgh Post-Gazette*, 16 May 2012, http://www.post-gazette.com/sports/pirates/2012/05/16/PNC-Park-guard-loses-finger-Pittsburgh-cop-injures-shoulder-in-struggle-with-belligerent-fan/stories/201205160146 (accessed 18 October 2014).

Hertzel, Bob. "Luck: Control Key to Beer Proposal." *Times West Virginian*, 13 April 2011, http://www.timeswv.com/sports/article_6f35c640-4411-51ed-ae22-baed2b655004.html?mode=jqm (accessed 18 October 2014).

Hill, Angela. "Dozens of Brawls Reported at Raiders Game." *Oakland Tribune*, 9 September 2009, http://www.insidebayarea.com/search/ci_10421066 (accessed 18 October 2014).

Hinton, Matt. "Relentless Buckeye Fans Have Driven Kirk Herbstreit from Ohio." *Yahoo! Sports*, 12 March 2011, http://sports.yahoo.com/ncaa/football/blog/dr_saturday/post/-Relentless-Buckeye-fans-have-driven-Kirk-Herbs?urn=ncaaf-wp39 (accessed 18 October 2014).

"History of Cheerleading." *International Cheer Union*, http://cheerunion.org/history/cheerleading (accessed 25 September 2014).

Ho, Vivian, and Kevin Fagan. "Fan Says He Was Attacked by 3 Men at 49ers Game." *San Francisco Chronicle*, 23 December 2011, http://www.sfgate.com/bayarea/article/Fan-says-he-was-attacked-by-3-men-at-49ers-game-2423742.php (accessed 18 October 2014).

Hughes, Ian. "Albert Ebosse: Player's Death Leads to League Suspension." *BBC*, 25 August 2014, http://www.bbc.com/sport/0/football/28902441 (accessed 18 October 2014).

"Hundreds Dead in Stampede at Football Match." *Guardian*, 26 May 1964, http://www.theguardian.com/football/2014/may/26/stadium-disaster-lima-peru-1964-archive (accessed 11 October 2014).

Jones, Steve. "Louisville Coach Jeff Walz Says He's Buying the Beer." *Courier-Journal*, 13 November 2013, http://archive.courier-journal.com/usatoday/article/3515059 (accessed 9 October 2014).

"Justinian Didn't Understand Fans." *Wichita Eagle*, 2 November 2008, p. 2(D).

Karp, Hannah. "Brazil's Biggest Fear: Argentina Fans." *Wall Street Journal*, 15 June 2014, http://blogs.wsj.com/dailyfix/2014/06/15/argentinafans (accessed 25 July 2014).

Kenning, Chris, and Mike Wynn. "Lexington Arrests, Fires Follow Victory." *Courier-Journal* (Louisville), 3 April 2012, p. A6.

Kilpatrick, David D. "Egyptian Soccer Riot Kills More Than 70." *New York Times*, 1 February 2012, http://www.nytimes.com/2012/02/02/world/middleeast/scores-killed-in-egyptian-soccer-mayhem.html (accessed 11 October 2014).

Klingaman, Mike. "Detroit Fans Have History of Combustible Behavior." *Baltimore Sun*, 25 November 2004, http://articles.baltimoresun.com/2004-11-25/sports/0411250093_1_pistons-detroit-tigers (accessed 11 October 2014).

Kovac, Adam, and Matt Holsapple. "Purdue Students Stir Pandemonium." *USA Today*, 2 April 2001, http://usatoday30.usatoday.com/sports/basketba/marchmania/2001womens/championship/2001-04-01-aftermath.htm (accessed 11 October 2014).

L.A. Times News Service. "High School League Rescinds Postgame Handshake Ban." *Wilmington Star-News*, 21 April 1994, http://news.google.com/newspapers?nid=1454&dat=19940421&id=i2NSAAAAIBAJ&sjid=AxUEAAAAIBAJ&pg=3664,2296843 (accessed 18 October 2014).

LaBarre, Suzanne. "Why We're Shutting Off Our Comments." *Popular Science*, 24 September 2013, http://www.popsci.com/science/article/2013-09/why-were-shutting-our-comments (accessed 28 September 2014).

"Levante's Papakouli Diop Dances to Defy Racist Supporters." *Guardian*, 4 May 2014, http://www.theguardian.com/football/2014/may/04/papakouli-diop-racism-atletico-levante (accessed 18 October 2014).

Lindblom, Mike. "136.6 decibels! Hawks Fans Break Guinness Mark for Loudest Stadium." *Seattle Times*, 16 September 2013, http://seattletimes.com/html/seahawks/2021833455_seahawksscene16xml.html (accessed 18 October 2014).

"List of Victims." *Salvemos Al Futbol*, http://salvemosalfutbol.org/lista-de-victimas-de-incidentes-de-violencia-en-el-futbol (accessed 25 October 2014).

Livingston, Bill. "Penn State's Happy Valley a Hostile Environment for Ohio State and Especially for Terrelle Pryor." *Cleveland.com*, 6 November 2009, http://www.cleveland.com/livingston/index.ssf/2009/11/happy_valley_hostile_environme.html (accessed 18 October 2014).

Lyons, Richard D. "Baudouin I, King of Belgium, Dies at 62." *New York Times*, 1 August 1993, http://www.nytimes.com/1993/08/01/obituaries/baudouin-i-king-of-belgium-dies-at-62.html (accessed 18 October 2014).

MacMahon, Tim. "Mark Cuban Talks Lakers Fans." *ESPN*, 25 November 2012, http://espn.go.com/dallas/nba/story/_/id/8672046/mark-cuban-owner-dallas-mavericks-snipes-los-angeles-lakers-fans (accessed 18 October 2014).

Mandell, Nina. "Brandon Jacobs Received a Death Threat from a Fantasy Football Owner." *USA Today*, 22 October 2013, http://ftw.usatoday.com/2013/10/brandon-jacobs-received-a-death-threat-from-a-fantasy-football-owner (accessed 18 October 2014).

———. "Derek Jeter Announces on Facebook 2014 Will Be His Final Season." *For the Win*, 12 February 2014, http://ftw.usatoday.com/2014/02/derek-jeter-announces-on-facebook-2014-will-be-his-final-season (accessed 9 October 2014).

Martin, Glen, Nanette Asimov, Wyatt Buchanan, and Jim Zamora. "Raider Rage: Oakland Police No Match for Street Mayhem." *San Francisco Chronicle*, 27 January 2003.

McCallum, Jack. "Sir Charles Speaks—as Usual." *SportsIllustrated.CNN.com*, 5 March 2002, http://sportsillustrated.cnn.com/inside_game/jack_mccallum/news/2002/03/05/nba_insider (accessed 27 January 2015).

McKirdy, Andrew. "Players Push for More Action against Racism Scourge." *Japan Times*, 24 March 2014, http://www.japantimes.co.jp/sports/2014/03/24/soccer/j-league/players-push-for-more-action-against-racism-scourge/#.VCH1-_aB_rY (accessed 18 October 2014).

McMenamin, Dave. "Steve Blake, Wife Get Hate Tweets." *ESPN*, 18 May 2012, http://espn.go.com/los-angeles/nba/story/_/id/7943732/steve-blake-los-angeles-lakers-wife-receive-threats-twitter (accessed 18 October 2014).

McShane, Larry. "Jets Fan Fireman Ed Cleared of Assault as Giants Fan Christopher Black Drops Charges." 28 October 2010, http://www.nydailynews.com/news/crime/jets-fan-fireman-ed-cleared-assault-giants-fan-christopher-black-drops-charges-article-1.192581. (accessed 18 October 2014).

Medina, Regina. "After Phils Rally, Fire Volunteer Finds Himself in Hot Seat." *Philadelphia Daily News*, 11 November 2008, p. 12.

Merina, Victor. "Police Arrest 31 Fans at Rowdy Raiders Game." *Los Angeles Times*, 1 October 1990, http://articles.latimes.com/1990-10-01/local/me-1237_1_police-officers (accessed 18 October 2014).

Moses, Don. "Letters to the Editor." *San Francisco Chronicle*, 17 January 2012.

Mothers against Drunk Driving. "Drunk Driving in America." *Madd.org*, www.mad.org/drunk-driving-in-america (accessed 15 January 2014).

Mueller, Mark. "Paralyzed Girl and Mom Get $25M Settlement from Beer Vendor." *NJ.com*, 4 December 2008, http://www.nj.com/news/ledger/topstories/index.ssf/2008/12/paralyzed_girl_and_mom_got_25m.html (accessed 19 October 2014).

Murphy, Mary Kate. "More Fun for Fans." *Athletic Management*, June/July 2014, http://www.athleticmanagement.com/2013/05/26/more_fun_for_fans/index.php (accessed 18 October 2014).

Myers, Gary, Frank DiGiacomo, and Bill Hutchinson. "Cowboys Fan Uses Taser Gun on Jets Crowd at MetLife Stadium Despite Security on 9/11 Anniversary." *New York Daily News*, 13 September 2011, http://www.nydailynews.com/sports/football/jets/cowboys-fan-taser-gun-jets-crowd-metlife-stadium-security-9-11-anniversary-article-1.957926 (accessed 18 October 2014).

Neumann, Thomas. "Vancouver Evokes Infamous Sports Riots." *ESPN.com*, June 24, 2012, http://m.espn.go.com/wireless/story?storyPage=neumann-110617_vancouver_canucks_riot&wjb (accessed 22 November 2014).

"NFL Teams Implement Fan Code of Conduct." *NFL.com*, 5 August 2008, http://www.nfl.com/news/story/09000d5d809c28f9/printable/nfl-teams-implement-fan-code-of-conduct (accessed 13 October 2014).

"Nick Saban Criticizes Alabama Fans." *ESPN*, 26 October 2013, http://espn.go.com/college-football/story/_/id/9880250/alabama-crimson-tide-punish-students-leaving-early (accessed 18 October 2014).

Norwood, Robyn. "Savage Attack on Giants Fan Stirs Emotions, Debate in L.A." *USA Today*, 10 April 2011, http://usatoday30.usatoday.com/sports/baseball/2011-04-10-giants-fan-attack-stow-dodgers_N.htm (accessed 9 October 2014).

"Ohio State Officials Apologize to Texas Fans." *ESPN*, 15 September 2005, http://sports.espn.go.com/ncf/news/story?id=2161919 (accessed 18 October 2014).

Otis, Sam. "Wake Up Cleveland! Let's Have No More Pop Bottle Throwing or Other Forms of Unsportsmanlike Outbursts." *Cleveland Plain Dealer*, 13 May 1929.

Patty, Anna. "Proposed Laws Will Give 20 Years for 'One-Punch' Killings." *Sydney Morning Herald*, 13 November 2013, http://www.smh.com.au/nsw/proposed-laws-will-give-20-years-for-onepunch-killings-20131112-2xenc.html (accessed 18 October 2014).

Peters, Jerrad. "El Superclásico: The Immigrant Story of River and Boca." *Sportsnet*, 4 October 2013, http://www.sportsnet.ca/soccer/el-superclasico-the-immigrant-story-of-river-and-boca (accessed 18 October 2014).

"Preparing for the Final Whistle." *Der Spiegel*, 17 September 2007, http://www.spiegel.de/international/zeitgeist/preparing-for-the-final-whistle-german-soccer-club-builds-cemetery-for-its-fans-a-506164.html (accessed 14 October 2014).

Press Association. "Roma Fined €50,000 over Racial Abuse Aimed at Milan Players." *Guardian*, 13 May 2013, http://www.theguardian.com/football/2013/may/13/roma-fined-racial-abuse-milan (accessed 24 August 2014).

Public Religion Research Institute. "January Religion and Politics Tracking Survey, 2014." *Public Religion Research Institute*, 16 January 2014, http://publicreligion.org/research/2014/01/jan-2014-sports-poll (accessed 11 October 2014).

Pugmire, Jerome, Associated Press. "PSG Riot: Paris Saint-Germain Title Celebrations Marred by Fan Violence." *Huffington Post*, 13 May 2013, http://www.huffingtonpost.com/2013/05/13/psgs-fan-violence-paris-parade_n_3268973.html (accessed 9 January 2015).

Raley, Dan. "Pac-10 Men: Ducks Ruffle Bibby's Feathers." *Seattle Post-Intelligencer*, 6 February 2002, http://www.seattlepi.com/sports/article/Pac-10-Men-Ducks-ruffle-Bibby-s-feathers-1079540.php (accessed 18 October 2014).

"The Real Numbers behind Those 'Racist Tweets' from Bruins Fans.'" *Boston.com*, http://www.boston.com/sports/blogs/obnoxiousbostonfan/2014/05/exclusive_the_real_numbers_beh.html (accessed 1 September 2014).

"Recent Soccer Stadium Disasters." *USA Today*, 19 June 2001, http://usatoday30.usatoday.com/news/world/2001-05-10-soccer-side.htm (accessed 18 October 2014).

Redelmeier, Donald A., and Craig L. Stewart. "Driving Fatalities on Super Bowl Sunday." *New England Journal of Medicine* 348, no. 4 (2003): 368–69. http://www.nejm.org/doi/full/10.1056/NEJM200301233480423 (accessed 19 October 2014).

Richardson, Franci. "Tragedy at Fenway: At Funeral Mass, Grief, Faith, and Outrage at Riot." *Boston Herald*, 27 October 2004, p. 6.

Ringle, Ken. "Debunking the 'Day of Dread' for Women; Data Lacking for Claim of Domestic Violence Surge after Super Bowl." *Washington Post*, 31 January 1993.

"Riot Ends India's Cricket Dream." *South China Morning Post*, 14 March 1996, http://www.scmp.com/article/152791/riot-ends-indias-cricket-dream> (accessed 11 October 2014).

Rogers, Marc. "La Puerta 12: Interview with Pablo Tesoriere." *Argentina Independent*, 27 June 2008, http://www.argentinaindependent.com/socialissues/humanrights/la-puerta-12-interview-with-pablo-tesoriere (accessed 18 October 2014).

"Rugby Fan Can't Explain Self-Mutilation." *Sydney Morning Herald*, 16 November 2005, http://www.smh.com.au/articles/2005/11/16/1132016820398.html (accessed 11 October 2014).

Rumsby, Ben. "Bayern Munich Facing £50,000 Fine for Fans' Homophobic 'Gay Gunners' Banner during Clash against Arsenal." *Telegraph*, 12 March 2014, http://www.telegraph.co.uk/sport/football/teams/arsenal/10692228/Bayern-Munich-facing-50000-fine-for-fans-homophobic-Gay-Gunners-banner-during-clash-against-Arsenal.html (accessed 18 October 2014).

Sakyi-Addo, Kwaku. "At Least 12 Die in Ghana Football Stadium Stampede." *Guardian*, 10 May 2001, http://www.theguardian.com/world/2001/may/11/football (accessed 11 October 2014).

Sampson, Zachary T. "Winthrop Man Charged with Disturbing the Peace for Pointing Laser at Players during High School Hockey Game." *Boston Globe*, 7 March 2012, http://www.bostonglobe.com/metro/2012/03/07/winthrop-man-charged-with-disturbing-peace-for-pointing-laser-players-during-high-school-hockey-game/5qc2VLdywUNQidekomrGvM/story.html (accessed 18 October 2014).

Samuel, Ebenezer. "NY Giants RB Brandon Jacobs Slams Fantasy Football after Getting Death Threat on Twitter." *New York Daily News*, 24 October 2013, http://www.nydailynews.com/sports/football/giants/jacobs-rips-fantasy-football-owners-death-threats-article-1.1494661 (accessed 18 October 2014).

"SBD/SBJ Reader Survey: Thoughts on Teams, Leagues, Motorsports, and Colleges." *Sports Business Journal*, 29 November 2012, http://www.sportsbusinessdaily.com/Daily/Issues/

2012/11/29/Reader-Survey/Reader-Survey.aspx?hl=
nfl%20games%20comfortable%20children&sc=0 (accessed 26 January 2015).

Schlabach, Mark. "Duke's Redick Is Fans' Object of Disaffection." *Washington Post*, 12 February 2005, http://www.washingtonpost.com/wp-dyn/articles/A17550-2005Feb11.html (accessed 19 October 2014).

Schwartz, Nick. "Barcelona's Dani Alves Eats Banana That Was Thrown at Him by a Fan." *USA Today*, 27 April 2014, http://ftw.usatoday.com/2014/04/barcelona-dani-alves-banana (accessed 18 October 2014).

———. "Brandon Phillips Writes Message to Heckler: 'Dear Drunk Guy.'" *USA Today*, 21 June 2015, http://ftw.usatoday.com/2014/06/brandon-phillips-reds-heckler-drunk-guy (accessed 27 September 2014).

Shaikin, Bill. "Downing Comes to Bonds' Defense." *Los Angeles Times*, 2 August 2007, http://articles.latimes.com/2007/aug/02/sports/sp-bonds2 (accessed 18 October 2014).

Shelburne, Ramona. "Bryan Stow Lawyer Approached MLB." *ESPN*, 3 November 2011, http://espn.go.com/los-angeles/mlb/story/_/id/7187358/bryan-stow-lawyer-eyes-reasonable-deal-mlb (accessed 18 October 2014).

Silver, Jonathan D. "Roethlisberger, Car Driver Are Both Charged." *Pittsburgh Post-Gazette*, 20 June 2006, http://www.post-gazette.com/sports/steelers/2006/06/20/Roethlisberger-car-driver-are-both-charged/stories/200606200107 (accessed 28 September 2014).

"Six Arrested, Police Officer among Injured during Giants Celebrations in San Francisco." *San Jose Mercury News*, 2 November 2010, http://www.mercurynews.com/giants/ci_16500838?source=rss (accessed 11 October 2014).

Slater, Matt. "Tour de France: Mark Cavendish Has Urine Thrown at Him." *BBC*, 10 July 2013, http://www.bbc.com/sport/0/cycling/23251598 (accessed 18 October 2014).

Snel, Alan. "Police Disperse Rowdy Fans, Cars Overturned in LoDo Revelry." *Denver Post*, 26 January 1998, p. A1.

Snow, Taylor C. "UMass Crime Log: Super Bowl Edition."

Sparre, Kirsten. "FIFA Takes Action against Croatian Fans Forming Human Swastika." *Play the Game*, 24 August 2006, http://www.playthegame.org/news/news-articles/2006/fifa-takes-action-against-croatian-fans-forming-human-swastika (accessed 18 October 2014).

"Speedo Man." *ESPN*, 3 March 2012, http://espn.go.com/video/clip?id=7641271 (accessed 18 October 2014).

Squires, Nick. "Decline of Monte dei Paschi di Siena, World's Oldest Bank, Leaves City Paying the Price." *Telegraph*, 8 September 2012, http://www.telegraph.co.uk/news/worldnews/europe/italy/9530852/Decline-of-Monte-dei-Paschi-di-Siena-worlds-oldest-bank-leaves-city-paying-the-price.html (accessed 30 May 2014).

"State Farm Center Basketball Fan Guide." *University of Illinois*, 2013–2014, http://grfx.cstv.com/photos/schools/ill/sports/m-baskbl/auto_pdf/2013-14/misc_non_event/statefarmcenter-fanguide-2013.pdf (accessed 18 October 2014).

"Streep's Golden Globes Post 50 Moment: 'Oh S**t My Glasses!'" *Huffington Post*, 16 January 2012, http://www.huffingtonpost.com/2012/01/16/golden-globe-boomer-moment_n_1208459.html (accessed 18 October 2014).

"Super Bowl XLVIII on Facebook." *Facebook*, 2 February 2014, http://newsroom.fb.com/news/2014/02/super-bowl-xlviii-on-facebook (accessed 18 October 2014).

Theodorou, Angelina. "As FIFA Attempts to Curb Racism at the World Cup, a Look at Hate Speech Laws Worldwide." *Pew Research Center*, 20 June 2014, http://www.pewresearch.org/fact-tank/2014/06/20/as-fifa-attempts-to-curb-racism-at-the-world-cup-a-look-at-hate-speech-laws-worldwide (accessed 1 September 2014).

Thomas, Katie. "Sports Stars Seek Profit in Catchphrases." *New York Times*, 9 December 2010, http://www.nytimes.com/2010/12/10/sports/10trademark.html?_r=0 (accessed 18 October 2014).

Thorman, Joel. "Eric Winston: Fans Cheering Matt Cassel's Injury Are 'Sickening.'" *Arrowhead Pride*, 7 October 2012, http://www.arrowheadpride.com/2012/10/7/3470224/eric-winston-quotes-matt-cassel-injury-fans-cheering (accessed 11 October 2014).

Turnbull, Lornet, Debbie Gebolys, and Alice Thomas. "Reconstructing the Riot: What Happened . . . and What Didn't." *Columbus Dispatch*, 8 December 2002, p. 1A. Home Final Edition.

"Two-Thirds of Public Believe American Society Is Uncivil." *Powell Tate DC*, 22 June 2010, http://www.powelltate.com/press-room/two-thirds_of_public_believe_american_society_is_uncivil (accessed 18 October 2014).

Uechi, Jenny. "Vancouver No Stranger to Grey Cup Riots." *Vancouver Observer*, 27 November 2011, http://www.vancouverobserver.com/sports/2011/11/27/vancouver-no-stranger-grey-cup-riots (accessed 12 October 2014).

Van Valkenburg, Kevin. "Terps Fans Retain Spirit, Lose Vulgarity." *Baltimore Sun*, 13 February 2005, http://articles.baltimoresun.com/2005-02-13/sports/0502130151_1_comcast-center-crowd-terps (accessed 19 October 2014).

Vendel, Christine. "Man Who Died Outside Arrowhead Stadium Was Punched Repeatedly, Authorities Say." *Kansas City Star*, 4 December 2013, http://www.kansascity.com/news/local/article333159/Man-who-died-outside-Arrowhead-Stadium-was-punched-repeatedly-authorities-say.html (accessed 18 October 2014).

Ward, Clifford. "Lisle Man Accused of Death, Rape Threats over Volleyball Game Substitution." *Chicago Tribune*, 30 October 2012, http://articles.chicagotribune.com/2012-10-30/news/chi-lisle-father-volleyball-arrest-20121030_1_kasik-lisle-man-berlin (accessed 18 October 2014).

Watts, Jonathan. "Angry Brazilian Fans Break into World Cup Centre and Attack Players and Staff." *Guardian*, 2 February 2014, http://www.theguardian.com/football/2014/feb/03/brazilian-football-fans-assault-team-players (accessed 18 October 2014).

Weir, Tom. "Kiffin Haters Riot, but Haiti Might Benefit." *USA Today*, 14 January 2010, http://content.usatoday.com/communities/gameon/post/2010/01/620006197/1 (accessed 11 October 2014).

White, Duncan. "Anniversary Monument Honours Heysel Dead." *Telegraph*, 30 May 2005, http://www.telegraph.co.uk/sport/football/2360360/Anniversary-monument-honours-Heysel-dead.html (accessed 18 October 2014).

Winston, Ali. "Sheriff Sought Controversial Surveillance Software." *East Bay Express*, 6 March 2013, http://www.eastbayexpress.com/oakland/sheriff-sought-controversial-surveillance-software/Content?oid=3480918 (accessed 18 October 2014).

Wise, Mike. "A Call for Civility." *Washington Post*, 3 July 2011, http://www.washingtonpost.com/sports/2011/07/02/AG1flwwH_story.html (accessed 11 October 2014).

Yarroch, Gustavo. "Berni confirmó que tampoco habrá visitants en el próximo torneo." *Clarin*, 29 July 2014, http://www.clarin.com/deportes/Berni-confirmo-visitantes-proximo-torneo_0_1183681975.html (accessed 18 October 2014).

Young, James. "World Cup 2014: Another Supporter's Death Fuels Brazil Security Concerns." *Independent*, 4 May 2014, http://www.independent.co.uk/sport/football/worldcup/world-cup-2014-another-supporters-death-fuels-brazil-security-fears-9321432.html (accessed 18 October 2014).

"Yugoslavia's Soccer Riot Leaves 138 Injured." *United Press International*, 14 May 1990, International Section.

Ziff, Deborah. "Alvarez, Bielema Send Message to Badger Ticket Holders: Keep It Classy." *Wisconsin State Journal*, 14 October 2011, http://host.madison.com/sports/college/football/alvarez-bielema-send-message-to-badger-ticket-holders-keep-it/article_8e5eb11a-f5e7-11e0-bd6b-001cc4c002e0.html (accessed 28 September 2014).

REPORTS, LETTERS, DOCUMENTS, SPEECHES, WEBSITES, AND TRIAL TRANSCRIPTS

"2003 Survey: Parents Believe Rash of Adult Violence at Youth Sporting Events Requires Nationwide Solution. Sporting Kid Magazine." *Free Library*, 19 March 2003, http://

www.thefreelibrary.com/Survey:%20Parents%20Believe%20Rash%20of%20Adult%20Violence%20at%20Youth%20Sporting...-a098929366 (accessed 16 October 2014).

"2014 Sportsmanship Survey." *Liberty Mutual Insurance Play Positive*, 3 June 2014, https://play-positive.libertymutual.com/2014-sportsmanship-survey?src=cm-dtxt-brd-ssn-rs1406101057&utm_source=ussnow&utm_medium=a&utm_term=june2014&utm_content=sportsmanshipsurvey&utm_campaign=survey (accessed 11 October 2014).

"The Avuncular Letter," January 17, 1984. Terry Sanford Records and Papers. Duke University Archives. Box 145.

Commission Investigating the Death of Victoria Snelgrove. *Stern Report*, 25 May 2005, https://www.cityofboston.gov/Images_Documents/sternreport_tcm3-8954.pdf (accessed 14 October 2014).

Furlong, John, and Douglas J. Keefe. *The Night the City Became a Stadium: Independent Review of the 2011 Vancouver Stanley Cup Playoffs Riot*. Report, August 31, 2011, http://www.ag.gov.bc.ca/public_inquiries/docs/vancouverriotreview/report.pdf (accessed 10 October 2014).

Honorable Lord Justice Taylor. *The Hillsborough Stadium Disaster*. Report. London: Presented to Parliament, August 1989. http://www.southyorks.police.uk/sites/default/files/Taylor%20Interim%20Report.pdf (accessed 14 October 2014).

Message of the Holy Father. *To the Managers, Players, and Supporters of the Roma Sports Association*. Speeches 2000, 30 November 2000, http://www.clerus.org/bibliaclerusonline/en/e3l.htm#bbj (accessed 11 October 2014).

National Online Safety Study Fact Sheet. Report. National Cyber Security Alliance/McAfee, 21 September 2012.

Office of the Vice Chancellor for Student Affairs and Campus Life. *Acceptable Fan Behavior*. http://www.umass.edu/stuaf/responsiblefans (accessed 21 September 2014).

The Ohio State University Task Force on Preventing Celebratory Riots. *Final Report*. Columbus: Ohio State University, 7 April 2003.

"Probability of Competing beyond High School." *National Collegiate Athletic Association*, September 2013. http://www.ncaa.org/about/resources/research/probability-competing-beyond-high-school (accessed 15 October 2014).

"Rock the Stick." Advertisement. *San Francisco Chronicle*, 20 January 2012, p. B3.

"Super Bowl XLVIII Nielsen Twitter TV Ratings." *Nielsen Company*, 3 February 2014, http://www.nielsen.com/us/en/insights/news/2014/super-bowl-xlviii-nielsen-twitter-tv-ratings-post-game-report.html (accessed 24 October 2014).

Thatcher, Margaret. "Margaret Thatcher Press Conference after Heysel Stadium Disaster." London, 30 May 1985. http://www.margaretthatcher.org/document/106060 (accessed 21 September 2014).

Transcript, Pre-Trial Hearing, *People v. Louie Sanchez and Marvin Norwood* (Los Angeles County Superior Court, 22 June 2012): 329, 456.

Transcript, Recorded Jail Cell Conversations between Louie Sanchez and Marvin Norwood, *People v. Louie Sanchez and Marvin Norwood* (Los Angeles County Superior Court, 8 June 2012): 9.

United Nations Office on Sport for Development and Peace. "Sport for Development and Peace." *United Nations*, http://www.un.org/wcm/content/site/sport/home/sport (accessed 14 October 2014).

VIDEOS

"The Art of Noise." *Outside the Lines*. ESPN, 9 March 2014, http://espn.go.com/video/clip?id=10567965 (accessed 16 October 2014).

"Bryan Stow Takes in Game One." *ESPN*, 21 October 2014, http://espn.go.com/video/clip?id=11742807.go.com/mlb/news/story?id=6355357 (accessed 22 October 2014).

Harvey, Del. "The Strangeness of Scale at Twitter." *TED Talk*, March 2014, https://www.ted.com/talks/del_harvey_the_strangeness_of_scale_at_twitter?language=en (accessed 16 April 2014).

"Mean Tweets." *Dallascowboys.com*, 27 June 2014, http://www.dallascowboys.com/video/2014/07/07/cowboys-players-read-mean-tweets-fans (accessed 31 August 2014).

"NFL Fan Violence." *Outside the Lines*. *ESPN*, 18 October 2012.

"Speech by Monica Nizzardo." Play the Game Conference. Cologne, Germany, 4 October 2011. https://www.youtube.com/watch?v=IpIXgrdWHTk (accessed 1 November 2014).

Zimbardo, Philip. "The Psychology of Evil." *TED Talk*, February 2008, https://www.ted.com/talks/philip_zimbardo_on_the_psychology_of_evil (accessed 11 October 2014).

INDEX

ABOUT THE AUTHOR

Justine Gubar is a four-time Emmy Award–winning investigative journalist. For almost two decades, she has worked as a television producer for ESPN, where she has covered major sporting events. These have included NBA, MLB, and NFL playoffs; the Final Four; and the Olympics. She has produced stories, shows, and news coverage for a variety of programs, including *Outside the Lines*, *SportsCenter*, and *College Game-Day*. During her time at ESPN, Gubar has covered a wide range of off-the-field issues, for example, performance-enhancing drug use, domestic violence, and homophobia in sport. Her work has appeared on ESPN television networks throughout the world, in print on ESPN.com, and on ESPN Radio. She has worked on stories in Africa, Asia, Europe, the Middle East, and South America, investigating topics ranging from labor violations in Cambodian apparel factories to Lance Armstrong's drug use in the Tour de France.

In 2011, Gubar was honored with a Women in Cable Television (WICT) Signature Accolade for *Herstory: Ten Times Over*, a documentary about basketball camps for girls in Nigeria. This project also received a NAMIC (National Association of Multi-Ethnicity in Communications) Vision Award. That same year, Gubar also won a Hoover Media Fellowship from Stanford's Hoover Institute.

Gubar was awarded a John S. Knight Journalism Fellowship and spent 2006–2007 in residence at Stanford University. She has spoken to various organizations, including the National Association of High School Athletic Associations, the Association of Women in Sports Media, and the Commonwealth Club.

Prior to working at ESPN, Gubar worked for Court TV and ABC News.

A graduate of Wesleyan University, she is a native New Yorker now living in San Francisco. She realizes there is a whole country in between and has traveled to all 50 states, many while reporting for ESPN.